Great Pianists
on Piano Playing

Godowsky, Hofmann, Lhévinne, Paderewski
and 24 Other Legendary Performers

James Francis Cooke

DOVER PUBLICATIONS, INC.
Mineola, New York

Bibliographical Note

This Dover edition, first published in 1999, is an unabridged, lightly corrected and reorganized reprint of the work originally published by Theodore Presser Co., Philadelphia, 1917, under the title: *Great Pianists on Piano Playing / Study Talks with Foremost Virtuosos by James Francis Cooke*, subtitled "A series of personal educational conferences with renowned masters of the keyboard, presenting the most modern ideas upon the subjects of technic, interpretation, style and expression."

The original contents page has been lightly edited and newly set, with the original roman chapter numbers in the text replaced to match that listing. The author's semi-alphabetical chapter sequence has been retained as it appeared in the 1917 edition.

With one exception, pianists' photographs—now grouped between pages 120 and 121—prefaced each chapter in the original. The photograph of Ferruccio Busoni originally appeared in *The New Grove Dictionary of Music and Musicians*, Vol. 3, p. 509; © Macmillan Publishers Limited 1980. There was none in Cooke's original edition. Expanded photograph captions are newly added.

Library of Congress Cataloging-in-Publication Data

Great pianists on piano playing : Godowsky, Hofmann, Lhévinne, Paderewski, and 24 other legendary performers / [compiled by] James Francis Cooke.
    p.   cm.
    Originally published: Philadelphia : T. Presser, 1917.
    ISBN 0-486-40845-0 (pbk.)
    1. Piano—Instruction and study. 2. Pianists. 3. Piano—Performance. I. Cooke, James Francis, 1875–1960.
786.2'143—dc21   99-38221
                                                   CIP

Manufactured in the United States of America
Dover Publications, Inc., 31 East 2nd Street, Mineola, N.Y. 11501

CONTENTS

28 photographic portraits appear between pages 120–121

1

THE ARTIST'S LIFE

The Virtuoso's Career as It Really Is

The father of a young woman who was preparing to become a virtuoso once applied to a famous musical educator for advice regarding the future career of his daughter. "I want her to become one of the greatest pianists America has ever produced," he said. "She has talent, good health, unlimited ambition, a good general education, and she is industrious." The educator thought for awhile, and then said, "It is very likely that your daughter will be successful in her chosen field, but the amount of grinding study she will be obliged to undergo to meet the towering standards of modern pianism is awful to contemplate. In the end she will have the flattery of the multitude, and, let us hope, some of their dollars as well. In return, she may have to sacrifice many of the comforts and pleasures which women covet. The more successful she is, the more of a nomad she must become. She will know but few days for years when she will not be compelled to practice for hours. She becomes a kind of chattel of the musical public. She will be harassed by ignorant critics and perhaps annoyed by unreliable managers. In return she has money and fame, but, in fact, far less of the great joy and purpose of life than if she followed the customary domestic career with some splendid man as her husband. When I was younger I used to preach quite an opposite sermon, but the more I see of the hardships of the artist's life the less I think of the dollars and the fame it brings. It is hard enough for a man, but it is twice as hard for a woman."

GOLDEN BAIT

Some cynic has contended that the much-despised "Almighty Dollar" has been the greatest incentive to the struggling virtuoso in European music centers. Although this may be true in a number of cases, it is certainly unjust in others. Many of the virtuosos find travel in America so distasteful that notwithstanding the huge golden bait, the managers have the greatest difficulty in inducing the pianists to come back. Indeed, there are many artists of great renown whom the managers would be glad to coax to our country but who have withheld tempting offers for years. One of these is Moritz Moszkowski, probably the most popular of modern pianoforte composers of high-class music. Grieg, when he finally consented to make the voyage to America, placed his price at two thousand five hundred dollars for every concert—a sum which any manager would regard prohibitive, except in the case of one world-famous pianist. Grieg's intent was obvious.

The inconveniences of travel in America have been ridiculously exaggerated in Europe, and many virtuosos dread the thought of an American trip, with the great ocean yawning between the two continents, and red-skinned savages just beyond New York or certainly not far from Chicago. De Pachmann detests the ocean, and when he comes over in his favorite month of June he does not dare return until the following June. Others who have never visited America must get their idea of American travel from some such account as that of Charles Dickens in his unforgivable *American Notes* (1842), in which he said, in describing one of our railroads:

"There is a great deal of jolting, a great deal of noise, a great deal of wall, not much window, a locomotive engine, a shriek and a bell. The cars are like shabby omnibuses holding thirty, forty, fifty people. In the centre of the carriage there is usually a stove, fed with charcoal or anthracite coal, which is for the most part red hot. It is insufferably close, and you see the hot air fluttering between yourself and any other object you may happen to look at."

There could have been but little improvement in our railroads in 1872 when Rubinstein came to America, for although he accepted $40,000 for 215 concerts during his first trip, he refused an offer of $125,000 for only 50 concerts when a manager tried to persuade him to return.

American railroads now present the acme of comfort, convenience, and even luxury in travel, yet the European artist has difficulty in adjusting himself to journeys of thousands of miles crowded in a short winter season when he has been accustomed to little trips of a few hundred kilometers. He comes to dread the trains as we might a prison van. Paderewski resorts to a private car, but even this luxurious mode of travel may be very monotonous and exhausting.

The great distances must certainly account for some of the evidences of strain which deform the faces and exhaust the minds of so many virtuosos. The traveling salesman seems to thrive upon miles of railroad travel as do the crews of the trains, but the virtuoso, dragged from concert to concert by his showman, grows tired—oh, so tired, pale, wan, listless and indifferent! At the beginning of the season he is quite another person. The magnetism that has done so much to win him fame shines in his eyes and seems to emanate from his finger-tips, but the difference in his physical being at the end of the season is sickening. Like a bedraggled, worn-out circus coming in from the wear and tear of a hard season, he crawls wearily back to New York with a cinematographic recollection of countless telegraph poles flying past the windows, audience after audience, sleeping cars, budding geniuses, the inevitable receptions with their equally inevitable chicken salad or lukewarm oysters, and the "sweet young things," who, like Heine's mythical tribe of *Asra*, must love or perish. Some virtuosos have the physical strength to endure all this, even enjoy it, but many have confessed to me that their American tours have been literal nightmares.

One of the greatest pianists was obliged to stay in New York for a while before attempting the voyage homeward. At the time he was so weak from the rigors of the tour that he could scarcely write his name. His haggard face suggested the tortures of a Torquamada rather than Buffalo, Kansas City, Denver and Pittsburgh. His voice was tired and faltering, and his chief interest was that of the invalid—getting home as soon as possible. To have talked with him upon music at that time would have been an injustice. Accordingly, I led him away from the subject and dwelt upon the woes of his native Poland, and, much to his surprise, left him without the educational material of which I had been in quest. He asked the reason, and I told him that a musical conference at that time could serve no purpose.

As men and women, aside from the attainments which have made them illustrious, virtuosos are for the most part very much like ordinary mortals who have to content themselves at the foot of Parnassus. It has been my privilege to know thirty or more of the most eminent artists, and some have become good personal friends. It is interesting to observe how several very different types of individuals may succeed in winning public favor as virtuosos. Indeed, except for the long-haired caricature which the public accepts as the conventional virtuoso there is no "virtuoso type." Here is a business man, here an artist, here an engineer, here a jurist, here an actor, here a poet and here a freak, all of them distinguished performers. Perhaps the enthusiastic music-lover will resent the idea of a freak becoming famous as a pianist, but I have known no less than three men who could not possibly be otherwise described, but who have nevertheless made both fame and fortune as virtuosos.

FREAK PIANISTS

The anthropologist who chooses to conduct special investigations of freaks can find no more entertaining field than that of the remarkable freaks of the brain, shown in the cases of some astonishing performers whose intelligence and mental capacity in other ways has been negligible. The classic case of Blind Tom, for instance, was that of a freak not so very far removed in kind from the Siamese Twins, or General Tom Thumb. Born a slave in Georgia, and wholly without what teachers would term a musical education, Blind Tom amazed many of the most conservative musicians of his time. It was possible for him to repeat difficult compositions after hearing them played only once. I conversed with him a number of years ago in New York, only to find that intellectually and physically he was allied to the *cretin*.

Blind Tom's peculiar ability has led many hasty commentators to conclude that music is a wholly separate mental faculty to be found particularly in a more or less shiftless and irresponsible class of gifted but intellectually limited human beings. The few cases of men and women whose musical talent seems to eclipse their minds so that they remain in utter darkness to everything else in life, should not be taken as a basis for judging other artists of real genius and undisputed mental breadth. I have in mind, however, the case of one pianist who is very widely known and highly lauded, but who is very slightly removed from the class of Blind Tom. A trained alienist, one acquainted with the difference between the eccentricities which frequently accompany greatness and the unconscious physical and psychical evidences of idiocy which so clearly agree with the antics of the chimpanzee or the droll Capuchin monkeys, might find in the performer to whom I refer a subject for some very interesting, not to say startling reflections. Few have ever been successful in inducing this pianist to talk upon any other subject than music for more than a few minutes at a time. Another pianist, who was distinguished as a Liszt pupil, and who toured America repeatedly, seemed to have a hatred for the piano that amounted to an obsession. "Look," he exclaimed, "I am its slave. It has sent me round and round the world, night after night, year after year. It has cursed me like a wandering Jew. No rest, no home, no liberty. Do you wonder that I drink to forget it?"

A Pathetic Example

And drink he did in Bacchanalian measure! One time he gave an unconscious exhibition of his technical ability that, while regrettable, would have been of immense interest to psychologists who are seeking to prove that music depends upon a separate operation of a special "faculty." During his American tours I called frequently upon this virtuoso for the purpose of investigating his method of playing. He was rarely free from the influence of alcohol for more than a few hours at a time. One morning it was necessary for me to see him professionally, and when I found him at his hotel he was in a truly disgraceful condition. I remember that he was unable to stand, from the fact that he fell upon me while I was sitting in a Morris chair. He was barely able to talk, and just prior to my leaving he insisted upon scrawling upon his visiting card, "Zur freundlichen Errinerung, auf einen sehr späten Abend." (Friendly remembrances of a very late evening.) Since it was still very early in the morning, it may be realized that he had lost all idea of his whereabouts. Nevertheless, he sat at the piano keyboard and played tremendously difficult compositions by Liszt and Brahms—compositions which compelled his hands to leap from one part of the keyboard to the other as in the case of the Liszt *Campanella*. He never missed a note until he lost his balance upon the piano stool and fell to the floor. Disgusting and pathetic as the exhibition was, I could not help feeling that I was witnessing a marvelous instance of automatism, that wonderful power of the mind working through the body to reproduce, apparently without effort or thought, operations which have been repeated so many times that they have become "second nature." More than this, it indicated clearly that while the better part of the man's body was "dead to the world," the faculty he had cultivated to the highest extent still remained alive. Some years later this man succumbed to alcoholism.

THE PIANIST OF TO-DAY

Contrasted with a type of this kind may be mentioned such men as Sauer, Rachmaninov, d'Albert, Paderewski, Godowsky, Bachaus, Rosenthal, Pauer, Joseffy, Stojowski, Scharwenka, Gabrilowitsch, Hofmann, Bauer, Lhevinne, to say nothing of the ladies, Bloomfield-Zeisler, Carreño, Goodson, *et al.*, many of whom are intellectual giants. Most all are exceedingly regular in their habits, and at least two are strong temperance advocates. Intellectually, pianists of this class represent a very remarkable kind of mentality. One is impressed with the surprising quickness with which their brains operate even in ordinary conversation. Speaking in alien languages, they find comparatively little difficulty in expressing themselves with rapidity and fluency. Very few great singers ever acquire a similar ease. These pianists are wonderfully well read, many being acquainted with the literature of three or more tongues in the original. Indeed, it is not unusual to find them skipping through several languages during ordinary conversation without realizing that they are performing linguistic feats that would put the average college graduate to shame. They are familiar with art, science, politics, manufactures, even in their most recent developments. "What is your favorite type of aëroplane?" asked one some years ago in the kindergarten days of cloud navigation. I told him that I had made no choice, since I had never seen a flying machine, despite the fact that I was a native of the country that gave it birth. He then vouchsafed his opinions and entered into a physical and mechanical discussion of the matter, indicating that he had spent hours in getting the whole subject straightened out in his mind. This same man, a German, knew whole cantos of the *Inferno* by heart, and could repeat long scenes from *King Lear* with a very creditable English accent.

The average American "tired business man" who is inclined to look upon the touring virtuoso as "only a pianist" would be immensely surprised if he were called upon to compare his store of "universal" information with that of the performer. He would soon see that his long close confinement behind the bars of the dollar sign had made him the intellectual inferior of the musician he almost ignores. But it is hardly fair to compare these famous interpreters with the average "tired business man." They are the Cecil Rhodes, the Thomas Edisons, the Maurice Maeterlincks of their fields. It is easy enough to find musicians of smaller life opportunities basking in their ignorance and conceit.

While the virtuoso may be described as intellectual in the broader sense of the term, he usually has a great fear of becoming academic. He aspires to be artistic rather than scholarly. He strives to elevate rather than to teach—in the strictly pedagogical sense. Some of the greatest performers have been notoriously weak as teachers. They do not seek the

walls of the college, neither do they long for the cheap
Bohemianism that so many of the French feuilletonists
delight in describing. (Why should the immorality
of the artist's life be laid at the doors of fair Bohemia?)
The artist's life is wrapped up in making his readings
of master works more significant, more eloquent,
more beautiful. He is interested in everything that
contributes to his artistry, whether it be literature,
science, history, art or the technic of his own interpretative development. He penetrates the various
mystic problems which surround piano playing by the
infallible process of persistent study and reflection.
The psychical phase of his work interests him immensely, particularly the phenomena of personal attraction—often called magnetism.

THE MAGIC OF MAGNETISM

Magnetism is surely one of the most enviable pos-
sessions of the successful pianist. Just what magnetism is and how it comes to be, few psychologists
attempt to relate. We all have our theories, just
why one pianist who often blunders as readily as a
Rubinstein, or who displays his many shortcomings at
every concert can invariably draw larger audiences
and arouse more applause than his confrère with
weaker vital forces, although he be admittedly a better technician, a more highly educated gentleman
and perhaps a more sensitive musician.

Charles Frohman, keenest of theatrical producers,
attributed the actor's success to "vitality," and in

doing this he merely chose one of the weaker synonyms
of magnetism. Vitality in this sense does not imply
great bodily strength. It is rather soul-strength,
mind-strength, life-strength. Professor John D. Quackenbos, A.M., M.D., formerly of Columbia University, essays the following definition of magnetism
in his excellent *Hypnotic Therapeutics:*

"Magnetism is nothing more than earnestness and sincerity,
coupled with insight, sympathy, patience and tact. These essentials
cannot be bought and cannot be taught. They are 'born by nature,'
they are dyed with 'the red ripe of the heart.' "

But Dr. Quackenbos is a physician and a philosopher. Had he been a lexicographer he would have
found the term magnetism far more inclusive. He
would at least have admitted the phenomenon which
we have witnessed so often when one possessed with
volcanic vitality overwhelms a great audience.

The old idea that magnetism is a kind of invisible
form of intellectual or psychic electricity has gone
down the grotesque phrenological vagaries of Gall as
well as some of the pseudoscientific theories of that
very unusual man, Mesmer. We all possess what is
known as magnetism. Some have it in an unusual
degree, as did Edwin Booth, Franz Liszt, Phillips
Brooks and Bismarck. It was surely neither the
art nor the ability of Daniel Webster that made his
audiences accept some of his fatuous platitudes as
great utterances, nor was it the histrionic talent
alone of Richard Mansfield that enabled him to wring
success from such an obvious theatrical contraption

as *Prince Karl.* Both Webster, with his fathomless eyes and his ponderous voice, and Mansfield, with his compelling personality, were exceptional examples of magnetism.

A NOTABLE EXAMPLE

Among virtuosos Paderewski is peculiarly forceful in the personal spell he casts over his audience. Someone has said that it cost one hundred thousand dollars to exploit his hair before he made his first American tour. But it was by no means curiosity to see his hair which kept on filling auditorium after auditorium. I attended his first concert in New York, and was amazed to see a comparatively small gathering of musical zealots. His command of the audience was at once imperial. The critics, some of whom would have found Paderewski's hirsute crown a delightful rack upon which to hang their ridicule, went into ecstasies instead. His art and his striking personality, entirely apart from his appearance, soon made him the greatest concert attraction in the musical world. Anyone who has conversed with him for more than a few moments realizes what the meaning of the word magnetism is. His entire bearing—his lofty attitude of mind, his personal dignity all contribute to the inexplicable attraction that the arch hypnotist Mesmer first described as animal magnetism.

That magnetism of the pianist must be considered wholly apart from personal beauty and great physical strength is obvious to anyone who has given the subject a moment's thought. Many of the artists already mentioned (in this book) who possess magnetism similar to that of Paderewski could surely never make claim for personal beauty. Neither is magnetism akin to that attraction we all experience when we see a powerful, well-groomed horse, a sleek hound, a handsome tiger—that is, it is not mere admiration for a beautiful animal. Whether it has any similarity to the mysterious charm which makes the doomed bird lose control of its wings upon the approach of a snake is difficult to estimate. Certainly, in the paraphernalia of the modern recital with its lowered lights and its solitary figure playing away at a polished instrument one may find something of the physical apparatus employed by the professional hypnotist to insure concentration—but even this can not account for the pianist's real attractiveness. If Mr. Frohman's "vitality" means the "vital spark," the "life element," it comes very close to a true definition of magnetism, for success without this precious Promethean force is inconceivable. It may be only a smouldering ember in the soul of a dying Chopin, but if it is there it is irresistible until it becomes extinct. Facial beauty and physical prowess all made way for the kind of magnetism that Socrates, George Sand, Julius Cæsar, Henry VIII, Paganini, Emerson, Dean Swift or Richard Wagner possessed.

More wonderful still is the fact that magnetism is by no means confined to those who have finely trained intellects or who have achieved great reputations.

Some vaudeville buffoon or some gypsy fiddler may have more attractive power than the virtuoso who had spent years in developing his mind and his technic. The average virtuoso thinks far more of his "geist," his "talent" (or as Emerson would have it, "the shadow of the soul—the otherwise") than he does of his technic, or his cadenzas. By what mystic means magnetism may be developed, the writer does not pretend to know. Possibly by placing one's deeper self (shall we say "subconscious self") in closer communion with the great throbbing problems of the invisible though perpetually evident forces of nature which surround us we may become more alive, more sensitively vivified. What would it mean to the young virtuoso if he could go to some occult master, some seer of a higher thought, and acquire that lodestone which has drawn fame and fortune to the blessed few? Hundreds have spent fortunes upon charlatans in the attempt.

All artists know the part that the audience itself plays in falling under the magnetic spell of the performer. Its connection with the phenomena of autosuggestion is very clear. Dr. Wundt, the famous German psychologist, showed a class of students how superstitions unconsciously acquired in early life affect sensible adults who have long since passed the stage at which they might put any credence in omens. At a concert given by a famous player, the audience has been well schooled in anticipation. The artist always appears under a halo his reputation has made for him. This very reputation makes his conquest far easier than that of the novice who has to prove his ability before he can win the sympathy of the audience. He is far more likely to find the audience *en rapport* than indifferent. Sometime, at the play in a theater, watch how the audience will unconsciously mirror the facial expressions of the forceful actor. In some similar manner, the virtuoso on the concert platform sensitizes the minds and emotions of the sympathetic audience. If the effect is deep and lasting, the artist is said to possess that Kohinoor of virtuosodom—magnetism.

Some widely read critics have made the very natural error of confounding magnetism with personality. These words have quite different connotations—personality comprehending the more subtle force of magnetism. An artist's individual worth is very closely allied with his personality—that is, his whole extrinsic attitude toward the thought and action of the world about him. How important personality is may be judged by the widely advertised efforts of the manufacturers of piano-playing machines to convince the public that their products, often astonishingly fine, do actually reproduce the individual effects which come from the playing of the living artist. Piano-playing machines have their place, and it is an important one. However, wonderful as they may be, they can never be anything but machines. They bring unquestioned joy to thousands, and they act as missionaries for both music and the music-teacher by taking the art into countless homes where it might otherwise never have penetrated, thus creating the foundation for a strong desire for a thorough study of music. The piano-playing machine may easily boast of a mechanism as wonderful as that of a Liszt, a d'Albert or a Bachaus, but it can no more claim personality than the typewriter upon which this article is being written can claim to reproduce the individuality which characterizes the handwriting of myriads of different persons. Personality, then, is the virtuoso's one great unassailable stronghold. It is personality that makes us want to hear a half dozen different renderings of a single Beethoven sonata by a half dozen different pianists. Each has the charm and flavor of the interpreter.

But personality in its relation to art has been so exquisitely defined by the inimitable British essayist, A. C. Benson, that we can do no better than to quote his words:

"I have lately come to perceive that the one thing which gives value to any piece of art, whether it be book, or picture, or music, is that subtle and evasive thing which is called personality. No amount of labor, of zest, even of accomplishment, can make up for the absence of this quality. It must be an almost instinctive thing, I believe. Of course, the mere presence of personality in a work of art is not sufficient, because the personality revealed may be lacking in charm; and charm, again, is an instinctive thing. No artist can set out to capture charm; he will toil all the night and take nothing; but what every artist can and must aim at is to have a perfectly sincere point of view. He must take his chance as to whether his point of view is an attractive one; but sincerity is the one indispensable thing. It is useless to take opinions on trust, to retail them, to adopt them; they must be formed, created, felt. The work of a sincere artist is almost certain to have some value; the work of an insincere artist is of its very nature worthless."

Mr. Benson's "charm" is what the virtuoso feels as magnetism. It puts something into the artist's playing that he cannot define. For a moment the vital spark flares into a bewildering flame, and all his world is peopled with moths hovering around the "divine fire."

The Greatest Thing of All

If we have dwelt too long upon magnetism, those who know its importance in the artist's life will readily perceive the reason. But do not let us be led away into thinking that magnetism can take the place of hard work. Even the tiny prodigy has a career of work behind him, and the master pianist has often climbed to his position over *Matterhorns* and *Mt. Blancs* of industry. Days of practice, months of study, years of struggle are part of the biography of almost every one who has attained real greatness. What a pity to destroy time-old illusions! Some prefer to think of their artist heroes dreaming their lives away in the hectic cafés of Pesth or buried in the melancholy, absinthe and paresis of some morbid cabaret of Paris. As a matter of fact, the best known pianists live a totally different life—a life of grind, grind, grind—incessant study, endless practice and ceaseless search for means to raise their artistic standing. In some quiet country villa, miles away from the center of unlicensed Bacchanalian revels, the virtuoso may be found working hard upon next season's repertoire.

After all, the greatest thing in the artist's life is W-O-R-K.

2

ARE PIANISTS BORN OR MADE?

SOME years ago the Director of the Leipsic Conservatorium gave the writer a complete record of the number of graduates of the conservatory from the founding to the late nineties. Of the thousands of students who had passed through the institution only a few had gained wide prominence. Hardly one student in one hundred had won his way into the most voluminous of the musical biographical dictionaries. The proportion of distinguished graduates to those who fail to gain renown is very high at Leipsic compared with many other institutions. What becomes of the thousands of students all working frantically with the hope of becoming famous pianists? Surely, so much earnest effort can not be wasted even though all can not win the race? Those who often convince themselves that they have failed go on to perform a more useful service to society than the laurel-crowned virtuoso. Unheralded and unapplauded, they become the teachers, the true missionaries of *Frau Musik* to the people.

What is it then, which promotes a few "fortunate" ones from the armies of students all over America and Europe and makes of them great virtuosos? What must one do to become a virtuoso? How long must one study before one may make a *début?* What does a great virtuoso receive for his performances? How long does the virtuoso practice each day? What exercises does he use? All these and many more similar questions crop up regularly in the offices of music critics and in the studios of teachers. Unfortunately, a definite answer can be given to none, although a great deal may be learned by reviewing some of the experiences of one who became great.

Some virtuosos actually seem to be born with the heavenly gift. Many indeed are sons and daughters of parents who see their own demolished dreams realized in the triumphs of their children. When little Nathan creeps to the piano and quite without the help of his elders picks out the song he has heard his mother sing,—all the neighbors in Odessa know it the next day. "A wonder child perhaps!" Oh happy augury of fame and fortune! Little Nathan shall have the best of instruction. His mother will teach him at first, of course. She will shape his little fingers to the keyboard. She will sing sweet folk melodies in his ear,—songs of labor, struggle, exile. She will count laboriously day after day until he "plays in time." All the while the little mother sees far beyond the Ghetto,—out into the great world,—grand auditoriums, breathless crowds, countless lights, nobles granting trinkets, bravos from a thousand throats, Nathan surrounded by endless wreaths of laurel,—Oh, it is all too much,—"Nathan! Nathan! you are playing far too fast. One, two, three, four,—one, two, three, four,—there, that is the tempo Clementi would have had it. Fine! Some day, Nathan, you will be a great pianist and—" etc., etc.

Nathan next goes to the great teacher. He is already eight years old and fairly leaping out of his mother's arms. Two years with the teacher and Nathan is probably ready for a *début* as a wonder child. The critics are kind. If his parents are very poor Nathan may go from town to town for awhile being exhibited like a trained poodle or a tiny acrobat. The further he gets from home the more severe his critics become, and Nathan and his mother hurry back to the old teachers, who tell them that Nathan must still practice long and hard as well as do something to build up his general education. The world in these days looks askance at the musician who aside from his keyboard accomplishments is a numskull. More sacrifice for Nathan's mother and father,— but what are poverty and deprivation with such a goal in sight? Nathan studies for some years in the schools and in the high schools as well as at the conservatory. In the music school he will doubtless spend six years in all,—two years in the post-graduate or master classes, following the regular four-year course. When sufficiently capable he will take a few pupils at a kopeck or so per lesson to help out with the family expenses.

Nathan graduates from the conservatory with high honors. Will the public now receive him as a great pianist? A concert is planned and Nathan plays. Day and night for years his whole family have been looking forward to that concert. Let us concede that the concert is a triumph. Does he find fame and fortune waiting for him next morning? No indeed,—there are a thousand Nathans all equally accomplished. Again he must work and again he must concertize. Perhaps after years of strife a manager may approach him some day with a contract. Lucky Nathan,—have you not a thousand brothers who may never see a contract? Then,—"Can it be possible Nathan,—is it really America,—America the virtuoso's Golconda!" Nathan makes a glorious *tournée*. Perhaps the little mother goes with him. More likely she stays at home in Odessa waiting with glistening eyes for each incoming mail. Pupils come to Nathan and he charges for each lesson a sum equaling his father's former weekly wage. Away with the Ghetto! Away with poverty! Away with oblivion! Nathan is a real virtuoso,—a veritable *Meister!*

The American Virtuoso of To-day

How does the American aspirant compete with Nathan? Are there not as fine teachers here in America as in Europe? Is it really necessary to go to Europe to "finish" one's musical education? Can one not become a virtuoso in America?—more questions with which editors and teachers are constantly plied. Can one who for years has waged a battle for the American teacher and American musical education answer this question without bias? Can we who trace the roots of our lineage back to barren

Plymouth or stolid New Netherland judge the question fairly and honestly?

One case suffices to show the road which the American virtuoso is likely to travel. She is still a young woman, in her twenties. Among her teachers was one who ranks among the very best in America. Her general education was excellent,—in fact far superior to that of the average young lady of good family in continental Europe. While in her early teens she became the leading feature at conservatory concerts. Her teacher won many a profitable pupil through her brilliant playing. She studies, as do so many American pupils, without making a regular business of it. Compared with the six year all day, week in and week out course which Nathan pursued in Odessa our little compatriot was at a decided disadvantage. But who ever heard of a music student making a regular business of learning the profession as would a doctor or a lawyer? Have not students contented themselves with two lessons a week since time immemorial? Need we go further to discover one of the flaws in our own educational system,—a flaw that is not due to the teacher or to the methods of instruction, but rather to our time-old custom. Two lessons a week are adequate for the student who does not aspire to become a professional, but altogether insufficient for the student who must accomplish a vast amount of work in a comparatively small number of years. She requires constant advice, regular daily instruction and careful attention under experienced instructors. Teachers are not to be blamed if she does not receive this kind of attention, as there are abundant opportunities now in America to receive systematic training under teachers as thorough, as able and as inspiring as may be found in Europe. The excuse that the expense is greater in America falls when we learn the very high prices charged by leading teachers in Germany, Austria and France.

To go back to our particular case, the young lady is informed at the end of a course of two or three lessons a week during two or three years, that she is a full-fledged virtuoso and may now enter the concert field to compete with Carreño, Bloomfield-Zeisler or Goodson. Her playing is obviously superior to that of her contemporary students. Some one insists upon a short course of study abroad,—not because it is necessary, but because it might add to her reputation and make her first flights in the American concert field more spectacular. Accordingly she goes to Europe, only to find that she is literally surrounded by budding virtuosos,—an army of Nathans, any one of whom might easily eclipse her. Against her personal charm, her new-world vigor, her Yankee smartness, Nathan places his years of systematic training, his soul saturated in the music and art of past centuries of European endeavor and perhaps his youth of poverty which makes success imperative. The young lady's European teacher frankly tells her that while her playing is delightful for the salon or parlor she will never do for the great concert hall.

She must learn to play with more power, more virility, more character.   Accordingly he sets her at work along special muscle-building, tone-cultivating, speed-making lines of technic in order to make up for the lack of the training which the young lady might easily have had at home had her parents been schooled to systematic daily study as a necessity.   Her first technical exercises with the new teacher are so simple that the young woman is on the verge of despair until she realizes that her playing is really taking on a new and more mature character.   She has been lifting fifty pound weights occasionally.   Her teacher is training her to lift one hundred pound weights every day.   She has been sketching in pastels,—her teacher is now teaching her how to make Velasquez-like strokes in oils.   Her gain is not a mere matter of loudness.   She could play quite as loud before she went to Europe.   There is something mature in this new style of playing, something that resembles the playing of the other virtuosos she has heard.   Who is the great European master who is working such great wonders for her?   None other than a celebrated teacher who taught for years in America,—a master no better than dozens of others in America right now.   Can the teachers in America be blamed if the parents and the pupils fail to make as serious and continued an effort here?   Atmosphere,—bosh!   Work, long, hard and unrelenting,—that is the salvation of the student who would become a virtuoso.   With our increasing wealth and advancing culture American parents are beginning to discover that given the same work and the same amount of instruction musical education in America differs very slightly from musical education abroad. But we are deserting our young virtuoso most ungallantly. In Berlin she hears so many concerts and recitals, so many different styles of playing, that she begins to think for herself and her sense of artistic discrimination—interpretation, if you will—becomes more and more acute. Provided with funds for attending concerts, she does regularly, whereas in America she neglected opportunities equally good. She never realized before that there could be so much to a Brahms *Intermezzo* or a Chopin *Ballade*. At the end of her first year her American common-sense tells her that a plunge into the concert field is still dangerous. Accordingly she remains two, or possibly three, more years and at the end if she has worked hard she is convinced that with proper management she may stand some chance of winning that fickle treasure, public favor.

"But," persists the reader, "it would have been possible for her to have accomplished the same work at home in America." Most certainly, if she had had any one of the hundred or more virtuoso teachers now resident in the United States all of whom are capable of bringing a highly talented pupil to virtuoso heights,—and if in their teaching they had exerted sufficient will-power to demand from the pupil and the pupil's parents the same conditions which would

govern the work of the same pupil studying in Europe.
Through long tradition and by means of endless
experiences the conditions have been established in
Europe. The student who aspires to become a professional is given a distinctively professional course.
In America the need for such a training is but scantily
appreciated. Only a very few of us are able to ap-
praise the real importance of music in the advancement of human civilization, nor is this unusual, since
most of us have but to go back but a very few generations to encounter our blessed Puritan and Quaker
ancestors to whom all music, barring the lugubrious
Psalm singing, was the inspiration of the devil. The
teachers, as has been said before, are fully ready and
more than anxious to give the kind of training required. Very frequently parents are themselves to
blame for the slender *dilettante* style of playing which
their well-instructed children present. They measure
the needs of the concert hall by the dimensions of the
parlor. The teacher of the would-be professional
pupil aspires to produce a quantity of tone that will
fill an auditorium seating at least one thousand people.
The pupil at home is enjoined not to "bang" or
"pound." The result is a feeble, characterless tone
which rarely fills an auditorium as it should. The
actor can not forever rehearse in whispers if he is to
fill a huge theater, and the concert pianist must have a
strong, sure, resilient touch in order to bring about
climaxes and make the range of his dynamic power
all-comprehensive. Indeed, the separation from home

ties, or shall we call them home interferences, is often more responsible for the results achieved abroad than superior instruction.

Unfortunately, the number of virtuosos who have been taught exclusively in America is really very small. It is not a question of ability upon the part of the teacher or talent upon the part of the pupil. It is entirely a matter of the attitudes of the teacher, the pupil and the pupil's home advisers. Success demands strong-willed discipline and the most lofty standards imaginable. Teachers who have taught for years in America have returned to Europe, doubled and quadrupled their fees, and, under old-world surroundings and with more rigid standards of artistic work, have produced results they declare would have been impossible in America. The author contends that these results would have been readily forthcoming if we in America assumed the same earnest, persistent attitude toward the work itself. If these words do no more than reach the eyes of some of those who are advising students wrongly in this matter they will not have been written in vain. The European concert triumphs of Mrs. H. H. A. Beach, whose training was received wholly in the United States, is an indication of what may be achieved in America if the right course is pursued. Conditions are changing rapidly in our country, particularly in the wonderful West and Middle-West. It seems likely that many pianists without foreign instruction of any kind will have as great success in our concert

field as have many of our best opera singers who have
never had a lesson "on the other side."

Our little pianist has again been playing truant
from our manuscript. Let us see what happens to
her when she finished her work with the famous
teacher abroad. Surely the making of a virtuoso is
an expensive matter. Let us take the estimate of
the young pianist's father, who practically mortgaged
his financial existence to give his daughter the right
musical training.

Lessons with first teacher at $1.00 a lesson. Eighty lessons a year for four years	$240.00
Lessons with second American teacher for two years at $2.00 a lesson	320.00
Lessons with third American teacher at $4.00 a lesson for one year and six months	480.00
Music, books, etc.	160.00
Piano	750.00
Maintenance for eight years at $200.00 a year (minimum estimate)	1600.00
Four years in Europe, travel, board, instruction, advertising, etc.	6000.00
TOTAL	$9550.00

But the expense has only begun, if you please.
The harvest is still a long way off. According to the
fine traditions established by the late P. T. Barnum,
there must be a European furore to precede the
American advent of the musical star. The journalistic astronomers must point their telescopes long and
steadily at the European firmament and proclaim
their discovery in the columns of their papers. Again,
furores are expensive. One must hire an auditorium,
hire an orchestra, and, according to some very frank

and disgusted young virtuosos who have failed to succeed, hire a critic or so like the amusing Trotter in *Fanny's First Play.* What with three and four concerts a night why should not the critics have a *pourboire* for extra critical attention? Fortunately the best papers hold their criticisms above price. Bought criticisms are very rare, and if the young pianist or any representative approaches certain critics with any such suggestion, she may count upon faring very badly in cold type on the following day.

If Miss Virtuoso makes a success, her press notices are sent to her American concert managers, who purchase space in some American musical newspapers and reprint these notices. Publicity of this kind is legitimate, as the American public knows that in most cases these press notices are reprinted solely as advertising. It is simply the commercial process of "acquainting the trade" and if done right may prove one of the most fortunate investments for the young artist. Do not imagine, however, that the pianist's American manager speculates in the problematical success of the coming virtuoso. On the contrary, his fee for putting the artist on his "list" and promoting her interests may range from five hundred dollars to two thousand dollars in advance. After that the manager usually requires a commission on all engagements "booked." Graft? Spoils? Plunder? Not a bit of it. If the manager is a good one—that is, if he is an upright business man well schooled in his work—the investment should prove a good one.

Exploiting a new artist is a matter demanding brains, energy, ingenuity and experience. A manufacturing firm attempting to put some new product upon an already crowded market would spend not $2000.00 a year in advertising, but $100,000.00. The manager must maintain an organization, he must travel, he must advertise and he too must live. If he succeeds in marketing the services of the young virtuoso at one or two hundred dollars a concert, the returns soon begin to overtake the incessant expenses. However, only the most persistent and talented artists survive to reap these rewards. The late Henry Wolfsohn, one of the greatest managers America has ever produced, told the writer frequently that the task of introducing a new artist was one of the most thankless and uncertain undertakings imaginable.

Does the work, the time, the expense frighten you, little miss at the keyboard? Do you fear the grind, the grueling disappoints, the unceasing sacrifices? Then abandon your great career and join the army of useful music workers who are teaching the young people of the land to love music as it should be loved,— not in hysterical outbursts in the concert hall but in the home circle. If you have the unextinguishable fire within your soul, if you have the talent from on high, if you have health, energy, system, vitality, nothing can stop you from becoming great. Advice, interferences, obstacles will be nothing to you. You will work day and night to reach your goal. What better guide could you possibly have than the words of the great pianists themselves? While the ensuing pages were compiled with the view of helping the amateur performer quite as much as the student who would become a professional pianist, you will nevertheless find in the expressions of the really great virtuosos a wealth of information and practical advice.

Most of the following chapters are the results of many different conferences with the greatest living pianists. All have had the revision of the artists in person before publication was undertaken. In order to indicate how carefully and willingly this was done by the pianists it is interesting to note the case of the great Russian composer-virtuoso Rachmaninoff. The original conference was conducted in German and in French. The material was arranged in manuscript form in English. M. Rachmaninoff then requested a second conference. In the mean time he had had the better part of the manuscript translated into his native Russian. However, in order to insure accuracy in the use of words, the writer translated the entire matter back into German in the pianist's presence. M. Rachmaninoff did not speak English and the writer did not speak Russian.

The chapter relating to Harold Bauer is the result of a conference conducted in English. Mr. Bauer's use of his native tongue is as fluent and eloquent as a poet or an orator. In order that his ideas might have the best possible expression the entire chapter was

written several times in manuscript and carefully
rearranged and rephrased by Mr. Bauer in person.
Some of the conferences lasted well on through the
night. The writer's twenty years' experience in
teaching was constantly needed to grasp different
shadings of meaning that some pianists found difficult
to phrase. Many indeed have felt their weakness in
the art of verbal expression and have rejoiced to have
their ideas clothed with fitting words. Complete
frankness and sincerity were encouraged in every
case. The results of the conference with Wilhelm
Bachaus, conceded by many other pianists to be the
foremost "technicalist" of the day, are, it will be
observed, altogether different in the statement of
teaching principles from those of Harold Bauer.
Each is a sincere expression of individual opinion and
the thoughtful student by weighing the ideas of both
may reach conclusions immensely to his personal
advantage.

No wider range of views upon the subject of
pianoforte playing could possibly come between the
covers of a book. The student, the teacher, and the
music lover who acquaints himself with the opinions
of the different masters of the keyboard can not fail
to have a very clear insight into the best contemporary
ideas upon technic, interpretation, style and expression.
The author—or shall he call himself a collector?—
believes that the use of the questions following each
chapter will be found practical and useful in the work
of both clubs and classes. Practice, however, is still

more important than precept. The student might easily learn this book "by heart" and yet be unable to play a perfect scale. Let him remember the words of Locke:

"Men of much reading are greatly learned: but may be little knowing."

After all, the virtuoso is great because he really knows and W-O-R-K-S.

PEPITO ARRIOLA

BIOGRAPHICAL

Pepito Arriola was born on the 14th of December, 1897. A careful investigation of his ancestry reveals that no less than twelve of his forefathers and relations have been pronouncedly musical. His father was a physician, but his mother was a musician. His early musical training was given to him exclusively by his mother. The following was prepared when he was twelve years old and at that time he was apparently a perfectly healthy child, with the normal activity of a boy of his age and with a little more general education in addition to his music than the average child at fifteen or sixteen possesses. He spoke French, German (fluently) and Spanish, but little English. Despite the fact that he had received numerous honors from European monarchs and famous musicians, he was exceptionally modest. In his playing he seemed never to miss a note in even very complicated compositions and his musical maturity and point of view were truly astonishing. The following is particularly valuable from an educational standpoint, because of the absolute unaffectedness of the child's narrative of his own training.

(The following conference was conducted in German and French.)

3

THE STORY OF A WONDER CHILD

PEPITO ARRIOLA

My Earliest Recollections

So much that was of interest to me was continually occurring while I was a child that it all seems like a kind of haze to me. I cannot remember when I first commenced to play, for my mother tells me that I wanted to reach out for the keyboard before I was out of her arms. I have also learned that when I was about two and one-half years of age, I could quite readily play after my mother anything that the size of my hand would permit me to play.

I loved music so dearly, and it was such fun to run over the keyboard and make the pretty sounds, that the piano was really my first and best toy. I loved to hear my mother play, and continually begged her to play for me so that I could play the same pieces after her. I knew nothing of musical notation and played entirely by ear, which seemed to me the most natural way to play. At that time, word was sent to the King of Spain that I showed talent, and he became interested in me, and I played before him.

My Friendship with Arthur Nikisch

A short time afterward, Herr Arthur Nikisch, conductor of the *Gewandhaus* Orchestra at Leipsic, and at one time conductor of the Boston Symphony Orchestra in America, came to Madrid to conduct the Philharmonic Orchestra for a special concert. Some one told him about my playing and I was permitted to play for him. He became so interested that he insisted upon my being taken to Leipsic for further study. I was then four years of age, and although musical advantages in Spain are continually increasing, my mother thought it best at the time that she should follow the great musician's advice and that I should be taken to the German city.

I want to say that in my earliest work, my mother made no effort to push me or urge me to go ahead. I loved to play for the sake of playing, and needed no coaxing to spend time at the keyboard. In my very early years I was permitted to play in public very little, although there were constant demands made to engage me. I was looked upon as a kind of curiosity and my mother wanted me to study in the regular way with good masters, and also to acquire more strength before I played in public very much.

I did, however, play at the great Albert Hall, in London. The big building holds 8000 people, but that was so long ago that I have almost forgotten all about it, except that they all seemed pleased to see a little boy of four playing in so very big a place. I also played for royal personages, including the Kaiser of Germany, who was very good to me and gave me a beautiful pin. I like the Kaiser very much. He seems like a fine man.

MY FIRST REGULAR INSTRUCTION

My first teacher, aside from my mother, was a Herr Dreckendorf, of Leipsic. He was very kind to me and took the greatest pains, but the idea of learning the notes was very distasteful to me. I was terribly bored with the technical exercises he gave me, but have since learned that one can save much time by practicing scales and exercises. Although I do not like them, I practice them every day now, for a little while, so as to get my fingers in good working order.

In about six weeks I knew all that was expected of me in the way of scales in octaves, sixths, thirds, double thirds, etc., and my teacher commenced to turn his attention to studies and pieces. For the first time I found musical notation interesting, for then I realized that it was not necessary for me to wait until some one else played a piece before I could begin to explore its beauties. Ah! it was wonderful, those first days with the pieces. I was in a new country and could hardly wait to master one at a time, so eager was I to reach the next one and see just what it was like.

Herr Dreckendorf gave me some studies by Dussek, Cramer, the *Inventions* of Bach, etc., but before long the fascination of playing beautiful pieces was so great that he found it hard to keep me away from them.

EARLY REPERTORY

So hungry was I to find new musical works that when I was eight and a half years old I could play from memory such pieces as the B flat minor Scherzo, the A flat major Polonaise, and most of the Valses and Études of Chopin. I also played the Sixth Rhapsody of Liszt and the C minor Concerto of Beethoven.

In the mean time we moved to Berlin and this has been our home ever since, so you see I have seen far more of Germany than of my native country, Spain. In fact, it seems more natural for me to speak German than Spanish. At the age of seven it was my good fortune to come under the instruction of Alberto Jonas, the Spanish virtuoso, who for many years was at the head of a large music school in America. I can never be grateful enough to him, for he has taught me without remuneration and not even a father could be kinder to me. When I left Berlin for my present tour, tears came to our eyes, because I knew I was leaving my best friend. Most of my present repertory has been acquired under Jonas and he has been so, so exacting.

He also saw to it that my training was broad, and not confined to those composers whose works appealed most to me. The result is that I now appreciate the works of all the composers for the piano. Beethoven I found very absorbing. I learned the *Appassionata Sonata* in one week's time, and longed for more. My teacher, however, insisted upon my going slowly, and mastering all the little details.

I have also developed a great fondness for Bach, because I like to find how he winds his melodies in and out, and makes such beautiful things of them. I play a great deal of Bach, including the G minor organ Fugue, which Liszt played the devil with in arranging it for the piano. Goodness knows, it was difficult enough for the organ in its original form! I don't see why Liszt wanted to make it more difficult.

Liszt is, of course, considered a great master for the piano, and I play his works with great delight, especially the *Campanella* with its beautiful bell effect, but I cannot look upon Liszt as a pianistic composer in the same way that one thinks of Chopin as a pianistic composer. The piano was Chopin's natural tongue. Liszt's tongue, like that of Beethoven, was the orchestra. He knew no difficulties, according to the manner in which he wrote his own works. Consequently one must think of the orchestra in playing Liszt's works, while the works of Chopin suggest only the piano.

My Daily Practice

During most of my life my practice has never exceeded two hours a day. In this country, while on tour, I never practice more than one and one-half hours. This is not necessary, because of the concerts themselves, which keep up my technical work. I never worry about my fingers. If I can think the pieces right, my fingers will always play the notes. My mother insists upon my being out in the open air all the time I am not studying and practicing, and I am out the better part of the day.

At my practice periods, I devote at least fifteen or twenty minutes to technical exercises, and strive to play all the scales, in the different forms, in all the keys, once each day. I then play some of my concert numbers, continually trying to note if there is any place that requires attention. If there is, I at once spend a little time trying to improve the passage.

It is very largely a matter of thinking the musical thought right, and then saying it in the right way. If you think it right, and your aim at the keyboard is good, you are not likely to hit the wrong notes, even in skips such as one finds in the Rubinstein Valse in E flat. I do not ever remember of hitting the upper note wrong. It all seems so easy to me that I am sure that if other children in America would look upon other examples in the same way, they could not find their work so very difficult. I love to practice Chopin. One cannot be so intimate with Bach; he is a little cold and unfriendly until one knows him very well.

GENERAL EDUCATION

I have said that we play as we think. The mind must be continually improved or the fingers will grow dull. In order to see the beauties in music we must see the beauties in other studies. I have a private teacher who comes to me in Berlin and teaches me different studies. I have studied some Latin, French, and the regular school studies. Electricity interests me more than I can tell you and I like to learn about it, but my greatest interest is in the study of astronomy. Surely nothing could be finer than to look at the stars. I have friends among the astronomers of Berlin who let me look through their telescopes and tell me all about the different constellations and the worlds that look like moons when you see them enlarged. It is all so wonderful that it makes one never cease thinking.

I also like to go to factories and learn how different things are made. I think that there are so many things that one can learn outside of a school-room. For instance, I went to a wire factory recently, and I am sure that I found out a great many things I might never have found out in books. One also learns by traveling, and when I am on my tours I feel that I learn more of the different people and the way they live than I ever could from geographies. Don't you think I am a lucky boy? One must study geography, however, to learn about maps and the way in which countries are formed. I have toured in Germany, Russia, and England, and now in America. America interests me wonderfully. Everything seems so much alive and I like the climate very much.

THEORETICAL STUDIES

Musical theory bores me now, almost as much as my first technical studies did. Richard Strauss, the great German composer, has very kindly offered to teach me. I like him very much and he is so kind, but his thundering musical effects sometimes seems very noisy to me. I know many of the rules of harmony, but they are very uncomfortable and disagreeable to me.

I would far rather write my music as it comes to me. Herr Nikisch says that when I do it that way, I make very few blunders, but I know I can never be a composer until I have mastered all the branches of musical theory. I am now writing a symphony. I played some parts for Herr Nikisch and he has agreed to produce it. Of course, the orchestral parts will have to be written for me, but I know what instruments I want to express certain ideas.

Putting down the notes upon paper is so tiresome. Why can't one think the musical thoughts and have them preserved without the tedious work of writing them out! Sometimes before I can get them on paper they are gone—no one knows where, and the worst of all is that they never come back. It is far greater fun to play the piano, or play football, or go rowing.

READING AND STUDY

I love to read, and my favorite of all books is *The Three Musketeers*. I have also read something of

Shakespeare, Goethe, Schiller, and many other writers. I like parts of the great Spanish novel *Don Quixote*, but I find it hard to read as a whole. I think that music students ought to read a great deal. It makes them think, and it gives them poetical thoughts.

Music is, after all, only another kind of poetry, and if we get poetical ideas from books we become more poetical, and our music becomes more beautiful. The student who thinks only of hammering down keys at the piano cannot play in a manner in which people will take pleasure. Piano playing is so much more than merely pressing down keys. One has to tell people things that cannot be told in words—that is what music is.

At the Concert

I do not know what it is to be nervous at concerts. I have played so much and I am always so sure of what I am going to play that nervousness is out of the question. Of course, I am anxious about the way in which audiences will receive my playing. I want to please them so much and don't want them to applaud me because I am a boy, but would rather have them come as real music-lovers to enjoy the music itself. If I cannot bring pleasure to them in that way I do not deserve to be before the public.

My concerts are usually about one hour in length, although I sometimes play encores for some time after the concert. I make it a practice not to eat for a few hours before the concert, as doctors have told my mother that my mind will be in better shape. I want to thank the many friends I have made among the students who have come to my concerts, and I hope that I may have told them some things which will help them in their work.

QUESTIONS IN STYLE, INTERPRETATION, EXPRESSION AND TECHNIC OF PIANOFORTE PLAYING

SERIES I

PEPITO ARRIOLA

1. Should the talented child be urged or pushed ahead?

2. In what period of time should a very talented child master the elementary outlines of technic?

3. Can Liszt be regarded as a pianistic composer in the same sense as that in which Chopin is considered pianistic?

4. How should a very talented child's practice time be divided?

5. What part does right thinking play in execution?

6. How should the child's general education be conducted?

7. Should the education be confined to the classroom?

8. Should the musical child be encouraged to read fiction?

9. Does music resemble poetry?

10. Should one be careful about the body before concerts?

WILHELM BACHAUS

BIOGRAPHICAL

Wilhelm Bachaus was born at Leipsic, March 24, 1884, two years before the death of Franz Liszt. Nine years younger than Josef Hofmann and a trifle more than one-half the age of Paderewski he represents a different decade from that of other pianists included in this work. Bachaus studied for nine years with Alois Reckendorf, a Moravian teacher who was connected with the Leipsic Conservatory for more than thirty years. Reckendorf had been a student of science and philosophy at the Vienna and the Heidelberg Universities and was an earnest musician and teacher with theories of his own. He took an especial interest in Bachaus and was his only teacher with the exception of one year spent with d'Albert and "three lessons with Siloti." Although Bachaus commenced playing when he was eight years old he feels that his professional *début* was made in London in June, 1901, when he played the tremendously difficult Brahms-Paganini Variations. In 1905, when Bachaus was only twenty-one, he won the famous Rubinstein Prize at Paris. This consists of 5000 francs offered every five years to young men between the ages of twenty and twenty-six.

(The following conference was conducted in English and German.)

4

THE PIANIST OF TO-MORROW
WILHELM BACHAUS

To-day, Yesterday and To-morrow

"It is somewhat surprising how very little difference exists between the material used in piano teaching to-day and that employed forty or fifty years ago. Of course, there has been a remarkable amount of new technical material, exercises, studies, etc., devised, written and published, and some of this presents the advantage of being an improvement upon the old— an improvement which may be termed an advance— but, taken all in all, the advance has been very slight when compared with the astonishing advances made in other sciences and other phases of human progress in this time.

"It would seem that the science of music (for the processes of studying the art are undoubtedly scientific) left little territory for new explorers and inventors. Despite the great number of études that have been written, imagine for one moment what a desert the technic of music would be without Czerny, Clementi, Tausig, Pischna—to say nothing of the great works of Scarlatti and Bach, which have an effect upon the technic, but are really great works of musical art.

THE WONDERFUL EFFICACY OF SCALES

"Personally, I practice scales in preference to all other forms of technical exercises when I am preparing for a concert. Add to this arpeggios and Bach, and you have the basis upon which my technical work stands. Pianists who have been curious about my technical accomplishments have apparently been amazed when I have told them that scales are my great technical mainstay—that is, scales plus hard work. They evidently have thought that I had some kind of alchemic secret, like the philosopher's stone which was designed to turn the baser metals into gold. I possess no secrets which any earnest student may not acquire if he will work in the laboratory of music long enough. There are certain artistic points which only come with long-continued experiment.

"As the chemist finds the desired result by interminable heart-breaking eliminations, so the artist must weigh and test his means until he finds the one most likely to produce the most beautiful or the most appropriate result. But this seeking for the right effect has little to do with the kind of technic which necessitates one to keep every muscle employed in piano-playing properly exercised, and I may reiterate with all possible emphasis that the source of my technical equipment is scales, scales, scales. I find their continued daily practice not only beneficial, but necessary. I still find it desirable to practice scales for half an hour a day.

BACH MUSICALLY OMNIPOTENT

"It seems almost foolish to repeat what has been said so many times about the wonderful old cantor of Leipsic, Johann Sebastian Bach. However, there may still be some who have not yet become acquainted with the indisputable fact that the practice of Bach is the shortest, quickest road to technical finish. Busoni has enlarged upon Bach, impossible as that may seem; but as a modern bridge is sometimes built upon wonderful old foundations, Busoni has taken the idea of Bach and, with his penetrative and interpretative ability, has been able to make the meaning more clear and more effective. Any young pianist who aspires to have his hands in condition to respond to the subtle suggestions of his brain may acquire a marvelous foundation by the use of scales, Bach and arpeggios.

THE OLD THAT IS EVER NEW

"I have seen many ways and means tried out. Some seem like an attempt to save time at the expense of thoroughness. Furthermore, the means which have produced the great pianists of the past are likely to differ but little from those which will produce the pianists of the future.

"The ultra-modern teacher who is inclined to think scales old-fashioned should go to hear de Pachmann, who practices scales every day. De Pachmann, who has been a virtuoso for a great many years, still finds daily practice necessary, and, in addition to scales, he plays a great deal of Bach. To-day his technic is more powerful and more comprehensive than ever, and he attributes it in a large measure to the simplest of means.

DIFFICULTIES IN NEW PIANOFORTE COMPOSITIONS

"I have often been asked if the future of pianoforte composition seemed destined to alter the technic of the instrument, as did the compositions of Liszt, for instance. This is a difficult question, but it would seem that the borderland of pianistic difficulty had been reached in the compositions and transcriptions of Busoni and Godowsky. The new French school of Debussy, Ravel and others is different in type, but does not make any more severe technical demands.

"However, it is hard for one to imagine anything more complicated or more difficult than the Godowsky arrangements of the Chopin studies. I fail to see how pianoforte technic can go much beyond these, unless one gets more fingers or more hands. Godowsky's treatment of these studies is marvelous not only from a technical standpoint, but from a musical standpoint as well. He has added a new flavor to the individual masterpieces of Chopin. He has made them wonderfully clever and really very interesting studies in harmony and counterpoint, so that one forgets their technical intricacies in the beauty of the compositions. One cannot say that their original beauty has been enhanced, but he has made them wonderfully fascinating compositions despite their aggravating complications for the student.

MERE DIFFICULTY NO LONGER ASTOUNDS

"The day when the show of startling technical skill was sufficient to make a reputation for a pianist is, fortunately, past. The mechanical playing devices have possibly been responsible for this. The public refuses to admire anything that can be done by a machine, and longs for something finer, more subtle, more closely allied to the soul of the artist. This does not mean, however, that the necessity for a comprehensive technic is depreciated. Quite the contrary is true. The need for an all-comprehensive technic is greater than ever before. But the public demand for the purely musical, the purely artistic, is being continually manifested.

"Modern composers are writing with this in view rather than huge technical combinations. The giant of to-day, to my mind, is indisputably Rachmaninoff. He is writing the greatest original music for piano of any living composer. All of his compositions are pianistic and he does not condescend to pander to a trifling public taste. He is a man with a great mind, and, in addition to this, he has a delightful sense of proportion and a feeling for the beautiful, all of which makes him a composer of the master mould. His compositions will endure as long as music.

MODERN COMPOSITIONS

"For others of the type of Scriabine I care less, although I am sensible to the beauty of many of their compositions. They have not, however, the splendid mould of Rachmaninoff, nor have they his vigorous originality. Doubtless some of these men will produce great original compositions in the future. Compositions that are simply not bad are hardly worth the paper they are written upon, for they will not last as long. The composition that will last is a great, new, original thought, inspired, noble and elemental, but worked out with the distinctive craftsmanship of the great master.

"I am very partial to Debussy. He has an extraordinary atmosphere, and, after one has formed a taste for him, his compositions are alluring, particularly his *Homage à Rameau, Jardins sous la pluie* and *D'un cahier d'esquisses*, which I have been playing upon my American tour.

THE MOST DIFFICULT COMPOSITIONS

"I have continually been asked, 'What is the most difficult composition?' The question always amuses me, but I suppose it is very human and in line with the desire to measure the highest building, the tallest mountain, the longest river or the oldest castle. Why is such a premium put upon mere difficulty? Strange to say, no one ever seems to think it necessary to inquire, 'What is the most beautiful piece?'

"Difficulty in music should by no means be estimated by technical complications. To play a Mozart concerto well is a colossally difficult undertaking. The pianist who has worked for hours to get such a composition as near as possible to his conception of perfection is never given the credit for his work, except by a few connoisseurs, many of whom have been through a similarly exacting experience. Months may be spent upon comparatively simple compositions, such as the Haydn Sonatas or the Mozart Sonatas, and the musical public is blind to the additional finish or polish so evident to the virtuoso.

Praise that Irritates

"The opposite of this is also true. A little show of bravura, possibly in a passage which has not cost the pianist more than ten minutes of frivolous practice, will turn many of the unthinking auditors into a roaring mob. This is, of course, very distressing to the sincere artist who strives to establish himself by his real worth.

"Of course, there are some compositions which present difficulties which few work hard enough to surmount. Among these might be mentioned the Godowsky-Chopin *études* (particularly the *étude* in A flat, Opus 25, No. 1, which is always especially exasperating for the student sufficiently advanced to approach it); the *Don Juan Fantasie* of Liszt; the Brahms-Paganini *variations* and the Beethoven, Opus 106, which, when properly played, demands enormous technical skill. One certainly saves a lot of bother when one discards it from one's repertoire. If these four pieces are not the most difficult pieces, they are certainly among the most difficult.

WHY NOT SEEK THE BEAUTIFUL?

"But why seek difficulty when there is so much that is quite as beautiful and yet not difficult? Why try to make a bouquet of oak trees when the ground is covered with exquisite flowers? The piano is a solo instrument and has its limitations. Some piano music is said to sound orchestral. As a matter of fact, a great deal of it would sound better with the orchestra.

"Real piano music is rare. The piano appears to be too small for some of our modern Titans among the composers. When they write for the piano they seem to be exhibiting a concealed longing for the one hundred or more men of the modern orchestra. One of the reasons why the works of Debussy appeal to me is that he manages to put so much color into his piano pieces without suggesting the orchestra. Much of his music is wonderful in this respect, and, moreover, the musicians of the future will appreciate this fact more and more.

EXERCISES THAT GIVE IMMEDIATE HELP

"No one exercise can be depended upon to meet all the varied conditions which arise in the practice of the day, but I have frequently employed a simple exercise which seems to 'coax' the hand into muscular activity in a very short time. It is so simple that I am diffident about suggesting it. However, elemental processes lead to large structures sometimes. The

Egyptian pyramids were built ages before the age of steam and electricity, and scientists are still wondering how those massive stones were ever put in place.

"The exercise I use most, apart from scales, is really based upon a principle which is constantly employed in all scale playing and in all piano playing, that of putting the thumb over and under the fingers. Did you ever stop to think how continually this is employed? One hardly goes one step beyond the elemental grades before one encounters it. It demands a muscular action entirely different from that of pressing down the keys either with the finger, forearm or arm motion.

"Starting with the above-named principle and devising new exercises to meet the very human need for variety, I play something like this:

"The next form would employ another fingering—

"The next form might be—

"These I transpose through several keys, for instance—

"Note that I am not giving an arbitrary exercise, but simply suggesting the plan upon which the student may work. There is a great deal of fun in devising new exercises. It assists in helping the student to concentrate. Of course, these exercises are only attempted after all the standard exercises found in books have been exhausted.

AVOID TOO COMPLICATED EXERCISES

"I often think that teachers make a great mistake by giving too complicated exercises. A complicated exercise leads away from clear thinking and concentration. The simple exercise will never seem dull or dry if the pupil's ambition is right. After all, it is not so much what is done as how it is done. Give less thought to the material and more to the correction of the means with which one plays. There should be unceasing variety in studies. A change at every practice period is advisable, as it gives the pupil new material for thought. There are hundreds of different exercises in the different books, and the student has no reason for suffering for want of variety."

Questions in Style, Interpretation, Expression and Technic of Pianoforte Playing

SERIES II

WILHELM BACHAUS

1. Does the technical material of to-day differ greatly from that of forty or fifty years ago?

2. State something of the efficacy of scales.

3. State three sources of technical material sure to interest the student.

4. Do celebrated virtuosos use scales regularly?

5. State what else besides technical skill is required in these days to gain recognition as a virtuoso pianist.

6. Why does Rachmaninoff excel as a composer for pianoforte?

7. State what may be considered the most difficult of piano compositions.

8. Wherein does the appeal of Debussy lie?

9. Give some simple exercises suitable for daily practice.

10. Why are too complicated exercises undesirable?

HAROLD BAUER

BIOGRAPHICAL

Harold Bauer was born in London, England, April 28, 1875. His father was an accomplished amateur violinist. Through him, the future virtuoso was enabled to gain an excellent idea of the beautiful literature of chamber music. When a boy Mr. Bauer studied privately with the celebrated violin teacher, Politzer. At the age of ten he became so proficient that he made his *début* as a violinist in London. Thereafter in his tours of England he met with great success everywhere.

In the artistic circles of London Mr. Bauer met a musician named Graham Moore, who gave him some idea upon the details of the technic of pianoforte playing, which Mr. Bauer had studied or rather "picked up" by himself, without any thought of ever abandoning his career as a violinist. Mr. Moore had expected to rehearse some orchestral accompaniments on a second piano with Paderewski, who was then preparing some concertos for public performance. Mr. Moore was taken ill and sent his talented musical friend, Mr. Bauer, in his place. Paderewski immediately took an interest in his talented accompanist and advised him to go to Paris to continue his studies with Gorski.

After many privations in Paris Mr. Bauer, unable to secure engagements as a violinist, went on a tour of Russia as an accompanist of a singer. In some of the smaller towns Bauer played an occasional piano solo. Returning to Paris, he found that he was still unable to secure engagements as a violinist. His pianistic opportunity came when a celebrated virtuoso who was to play at a concert was taken ill and Bauer was asked to substitute. He gradually gave more attention to the piano and rose to a very high position in the tone world.

5

ARTISTIC ASPECTS OF PIANO STUDY
HAROLD BAUER

THE IMMEDIATE RELATION OF TECHNIC TO MUSIC

"WHILE it gives me great pleasure to talk to the great number of students studying the piano, I can assure you that it is with no little diffidence that I venture to approach these very subjects about which they are probably most anxious to learn. In the first place, words tell very little, and in the second place, my whole career has been so different from the orthodox methods that I have been constantly compelled to contrive means of my own to meet the myriads of artistic contingencies as they have arisen in my work. It is largely for this reason that I felt compelled recently to refuse a very flattering offer to write a book on piano playing. My whole life experience makes me incapable of perceiving what the normal methods of pianistic study should be. As a result of this I am obliged with my own pupils to invent continually new means and new plans for work with each student.

"Without the conventional technical basis to work upon, this has necessarily resulted in several aspects of pianoforte study which are naturally somewhat different from the commonly accepted ideas of the technicians. In the first place, the only technical study of any kind I have ever done has been that technic which has had an immediate relation to the musical message of the piece I have been studying. In other words, I have never studied technic independently of music. I do not condemn the ordinary technical methods for those who desire to use them and see good in them. I fear, however, that I am unable to discuss them adequately, as they are outside of my personal experience.

THE AIM OF TECHNIC

"When, as a result of circumstances entirely beyond my control, I abandoned the study of the violin in order to become a pianist, I was forced to realize, in view of my very imperfect technical equipment, that in order to take advantage of the opportunities that offered for public performance it would be necessary for me to find some means of making my playing acceptable without spending months and probably years in acquiring mechanical proficiency. The only way of overcoming the difficulty seemed to be to devote myself entirely to the musical essentials of the composition I was interpreting in the hope that the purely technical deficiencies which I had neither time nor knowledge to enable me to correct would pass comparatively unnoticed, provided I was able to give sufficient interest and compel sufficient attention to the emotional values of the work. This kind of study, forced upon me in the first instance through reasons of expediency, became a habit, and gradually grew into a conviction that it was a mistake to practice technic at all unless such practice should conduce to some definite, specific and immediate musical result.

"I do not wish to be misunderstood in making this statement, containing, as it does, an expression of opinion that was formed in early years of study, but which, nevertheless, I have never since felt any reason to change. It is not my intention to imply that technical study is unnecessary, or that purely muscular training is to be neglected. I mean simply to say that in every detail of technical work the germ of musical expression must be discovered and cultivated, and that in muscular training for force and independence the simplest possible forms of physical exercises are all that is necessary.

"The singer and the violinist are always studying *music*, even when they practice a succession of single notes. Not so with the pianist, however, for an isolated note on the piano, whether played by the most accomplished artist or the man in the street, means nothing, absolutely nothing.

SEEKING INDIVIDUAL EXPRESSION

"At the time of which I speak, my greatest difficulty was naturally to give a constant and definite direction to my work and in my efforts to obtain a suitable muscular training which should enable me to produce expressive sounds, while I neglected no opportunity of closely observing the work of pianoforte teachers and students around me. I found that most of the techni-

cal work which was being done with infinite pains and
a vast expenditure of time was not only non-productive
of expressive sounds, but actually harmful and misleading as regards the development of the musical
sense. I could see no object in practicing evenness in
scales, considering that a perfectly even scale is essen-
tially devoid of emotional (musical) significance. I
could see no reason for limiting tone production to a
certain kind of sound that was called 'a good tone,'
since the expression of feeling necessarily demands in
many cases the use of relatively harsh sounds. Moreover, I could see no reason for trying to overcome
what are generally called natural defects, such as the
comparative weakness of the fourth finger for example,
as it seemed to me rather a good thing than otherwise
that each finger should naturally and normally possess
a characteristic motion of its own.

"It is *differences* that count in art, not similarities.
Every individual expression is a form of art; why not,
then, make an artist of each finger by cultivating its
special aptitudes instead of adapting a system of training deliberately calculated to destroy these individual
characteristics in bringing *all* the fingers to a common
level of lifeless machines?

"These and similar reflections, I discovered, were
carrying me continually farther away from the ideals
of most of the pianists, students and teachers with
whom I was in contact, and it was not long before I
definitely abandoned all hope of obtaining, by any
of the means I found in use, the results for which I was

striving. Consequently, from that time to the present my work has necessarily been more or less independent and empirical in its nature, and, while I trust I am neither prejudiced nor intolerant in my attitude towards pianoforte education in its general aspect, I cannot help feeling that a great deal of natural taste is stifled and a great deal of mediocrity created by the persistent and unintelligent study of such things as an 'even scale' or a 'good tone.'

"Lastly, it is quite incomprehensible to me why any one method of technic should be superior to any other, considering that as far as I was able to judge, no teacher or pupil ever claimed more for any technical system than that it gave more technical ability than some other technical system. I have never been able to convince myself, as a matter of fact, that one system does give more ability than another; but even if there were one infinitely superior to all the rest, it would still fail to satisfy me unless its whole aim and object were to facilitate musical expression.

"Naturally, studying in this way required my powers of concentration to be trained to the very highest point. This matter of concentration is far more important than most teachers imagine, and the perusal of some standard work on psychology will reveal things which should help the student greatly. Many pupils make the mistake of thinking that only a certain kind of music demands concentration, whereas it is quite as necessary to concentrate the mind upon the playing of a simple scale as for the study of a Beethoven sonata.

THE RESISTANCE OF THE MEDIUM

"In every form of art the medium that is employed offers a certain resistance to perfect freedom of expression, and the nature of this resistance must be fully understood before it can be overcome. The poet, the painter, the sculptor and the musician each has his own problem to solve, and the pianist in particular is frequently brought to the verge of despair through the fact that the instrument, in requiring the expenditure of physical and nervous energy, absorbs, so to speak, a large proportion of the intensity which the music demands.

"With many students the piano is only a barrier— a wall between them and music. Their thoughts never seem to penetrate farther than the keys. They plod along for years apparently striving to make piano-playing machines of themselves, and in the end result in becoming something rather inferior.

"Conditions are doubtless better now than in former years. Teachers give studies with some musical value, and the months, even years, of keyboard grind without the least suggestion of anything musical or gratifying to the natural sense of the beautiful are very probably a thing of the past. But here again I fear the teachers in many cases make a perverted use of studies and pieces for technical purposes. If we practice a piece of real music with no other idea than that of develop-

ing some technical point it often ceases to become a
piece of music and results in being a kind of technical
machinery. Once a piece is mechanical it is difficult
to make it otherwise. All the cogs, wheels, bolts and
screws which an overzealous ambition to become perfect technically has built up are made so evident that
only the most patient and enduring kind of an audience can tolerate them.

The Perversion of Studies

"People talk about 'using the music of Bach' to
accomplish some technical purpose in a perfectly
heart-breaking manner. They never seem to think
of interpreting Bach, but, rather, make of him a kind
of technical elevator by means of which they hope to
reach some marvelous musical heights. We even hear
of the studies of Chopin being perverted in a similarly
vicious manner, but Bach, the master of masters, is
the greatest sufferer.

"It has become a truism to say that technic is only
a means to an end, but I very much doubt if this
assertion should be accepted without question,
suggesting as it does the advisability of studying something that is not music and which is believed at some
future time to be capable of being marvelously trans-
formed into an artistic expression. Properly understood, *technic is art*, and must be studied as such.
There should be no technic in music which is not music
in itself.

THE UNIT OF MUSICAL EXPRESSION

"The piano is, of all instruments, the least expressive naturally, and it is of the greatest importance that the student should realize the nature of its resistance. The action of a piano is purely a piece of machinery where the individual note has no meaning. When the key is once struck and the note sounded there is a completed action and the note cannot then be modified nor changed in the least. The only thing over which the pianist has any control is the length of the tone, and this again may not last any longer than the natural vibrations of the strings, although it may be shortened by relinquishing the keys. It makes no difference whether the individual note is struck by a child or by Paderewski—it has in itself no expressive value. In the case of the violin, the voice and all other instruments except the organ, the individual note may be modified after it is emitted or struck, and in this modification is contained the possibility of a whole world of emotional expression.

"Our sole means of expression, then, in piano playing lies in the relation of one note to the other notes in a series or in a chord. Herein lies the difficulty, the resistance to perfect freedom of which I have spoken before, the principal subject for intelligence and careful study, and yet so few students appear to understand it. Their great effort seems to be to make all the noise in a given series as much alike as coins from a mint. They come to the piano as their only instrument, and never seek to take a lesson from the voice or from the other instruments which have expressive resources infinitely superior to those possessed by the piano. The principal charm of the piano lies in the command which the player has over many voices singing together. But until the pianist has a regard for the individual voice in its relation to the ensemble he has no means with which to make his work really beautiful.

"There is a great need for more breadth in music study. This, as I know, has been said very often, but it does not hurt to say it again. The more a man knows, the more he has experienced, the wider his mental vision in all branches of human information, the more he will have to say. We need men in music with big minds, wide grasp and definite aims. Musicians are far too prone to become overspecialized. They seem to have an unquenchable thirst to master the jargon and the infinite variety of methods which are thrust upon us in these days rather than a genuine desire to develop their musical aims. Music is acquiring a technology as confusing and as extensive as bacteriology. There seems to be no end to the new kinds of methods in the minds of furtive and fertile inventors. Each new method in turn seems to breed another, and so on *ad nauseam*.

"Among other things I would suggest the advisability for pianists to cultivate some knowledge of the construction of their instrument. Strange as it may seem, it is nevertheless a fact that the average pianist knows practically nothing of a piano, being in many cases entirely unaware of such simple things as how the tone is produced. The function of the pedals is as unknown to them as geology is to the coal heaver. This ignorance leads frequently to the employment of motions and methods that can only be characterized as ridiculous in the extreme.

Music First, the Instrument Afterwards

"From the manner in which many ambitious and earnest students play, it would seem that they had their minds fixed upon something which could not be conveyed to the world in any other form than that of the sounds which come from the piano. Of course, the piano has an idiom peculiarly its own, and some composers have employed this idiom with such natural freedom that their music suffers when transposed for any other instrument. The music of Chopin is peculiarly pianistic, but it is, first of all, music, and any one of the wonderful melodies which came from the fertile brain of the Polish-French genius could be played upon one of many different instruments besides the piano. The duty of the interpreter should surely be to think of the composition as such, and to interpret it primarily as music, irrespective of the instrument. Some students sit down before the keyboard to 'play' the piano precisely as though they were going to play a game of cards. They have learned certain rules governing the game, and they do not dare disobey these rules. They think of rules rather than of the ultimate result—the music itself. The idiom of the Italian language is appropriate here. The Italians do not say 'I play the piano,' but rather 'I sound the piano.' (*Suono il pianoforte.*) If we had a little more 'sounding' of the piano, that is, producing real musical effects, and a little less playing on ivory keys, the playing of our students would be more interesting.

Variety the Spice of Art

"It can hardly be questioned that the genesis of all musical art is to be found in song, the most natural, the most fluent and the most beautiful form of musical expression. How much every instrumentalist can learn from the art of singing!

"It is a physical impossibility for the voice to produce two notes in succession exactly alike. They may sound very similar, but there is a difference quite perceptible to the highly trained ear. When a singer starts a phrase a certain amount of motive power is required to set the vocal apparatus in vibration. After the first note has been attacked with the full force of the breath, there is naturally not so much weight or pressure left for the following notes. It is, however, possible for the second note to be as loud, or even louder, than the first note. But in order to obtain the additional force on the second note, it is necessary to compensate for the lack of force due to the loss of the original weight or pressure by increasing what might be called the nervous energy; that is to say, by expelling the breath with proportionately greater speed.

MUSCULAR AND NERVOUS ENERGY

"The manifestation of nervous energy in this manner is quite different from the manifestation of muscular energy, although both are, of course, intimately connected. Muscular energy begins at its maximum and gradually diminishes to the point of exhaustion, whereas nervous energy rises in an inconceivably short space of time to its climax, and then drops immediately to nothing. Nervous energy may be said to be represented by an increased rapidity of emission. It is what the athlete would call a 'spurt.'

"What I have said about the voice applies equally to all other instruments, the piano and the organ alone excepted. It is obvious that the playing of the wind instruments must be subjected to the limitations of the breath, and in the case of the violin and the other stringed instruments, where the bow supplies the motive power, it is impossible for two notes played in succession to sound absolutely alike. If the first note of a phrase is attacked with the weight of the whole bow behind it, the second note will follow with just so much less weight, and if the violinist desires to intensify any of the succeeding tones, he must do so by the employment of the nervous energy I have mentioned, when a difference in the quality of tone is bound to result. The pianist should closely observe and endeavor to imitate these characteristics, which so vividly convey the idea of organic life in all its infinite variety, and which are inherent in every medium for artistic expression.

Phrasing and Breathing

"It would take a book, and by no means a small one, to go into this matter of phrasing which I am now discussing. Even in such a book there would doubtless be many points which would be open to assaults for sticklers in psychological technology. I am not issuing a propaganda or writing a thesis for the purpose of having something to defend, but merely giving a few offhand facts that have benefited me in my work. However, it is my conviction that it is the duty of the pianist to try to understand the analogy to the physical limitations which surround the more natural mediums of musical expression—the voice and the violin—and to apply the result of his observations to his piano playing.

The Natural Effect of Emotions

"There is another relation between phrasing and breathing which the student may investigate to advantage. The emotions have a direct and immediate effect upon the breath, and as the brain informs the nervous system of new emotional impressions the visible evidences may be first observed in the breathing. It is quite unnecessary to go into the physiology or psychology of this, but a little reflection will immediately indicate what I mean.

"It is impossible to witness a disastrous accident without showing mental agitation and excitement in hurried breathing. Joy, anger, fear, love, tranquillity and grief—all are characterized by different modes of breathing, and a trained actor must study this with great closeness.

"The artist at the piano may be said to breathe his phrases. A phrase that is purely contemplative in character is breathed in a tranquil fashion without any suggestion of nervous agitation. If we go through the scale of expression, starting with contemplative tranquillity, to the climax of dramatic intensity, the breath will be emitted progressively quicker and quicker. Every musical phrase has some kind of expressive message to deliver. If a perfectly tranquil phrase is given out in a succession of short breaths, indicating, as they would, agitation, it would be a contradiction, just as it would be perfectly inhuman to suppose that in expressing dramatic intensity it would be possible to breathe slowly.

"In conclusion, I would urge students to cultivate a very definite mental attitude as to what they really desire to accomplish. Do you wish to make music? If so, *think* music, and nothing but music, all the time, down to the smallest detail even in technic. Is your ambition to play scales, octaves, double notes and trills? Then by all means concentrate your mind on them to the exclusion of everything else, but do not be surprised if, when, later on, you want to communicate a semblance of life to your mechanical motions, you succeed in obtaining no more than the jerky movements of a clock-work puppet."

QUESTIONS IN STYLE, INTERPRETATION, EXPRESSION AND TECHNIC OF PIANOFORTE PLAYING

SERIES III

HAROLD BAUER

1. What is the nature of the technical study done by Harold Bauer?

2. Should immediate musical results be sought in technical study?

3. Upon what principle is expression in art based?

4. Is the utmost concentration necessary in all piano playing?

5. How may the piano become a barrier between the student and musical expression?

6. In what spirit should all studies be played?

7. Is the piano an expressive instrument?

8. Should pianists acquire a knowledge of the main feature in the construction of their instrument?

9. How may variety in piano playing be achieved?

10. How is phrasing related to breathing?

FANNY BLOOMFIELD-ZEISLER

BIOGRAPHICAL

Mrs. Fanny Bloomfield-Zeisler was born at Beilitz, Austrian Silesia, July 16, 1866. Two years later her parents took her to Chicago. Her first teachers in Chicago were Bernhard Ziehn and Carl Wolfsohn. At the age of ten she made a profound impression at a public concert in Chicago. Two years later she had the good fortune to meet Mme. Essipoff, who advised her to go to Vienna to study with Theodore Leschetizky. Accordingly she was taken to the Austrian capital and remained under the instruction of the noted pedagogue for five years. Starting with the year 1883, she commenced a series of annual recitals and concerts in different American cities which made her very famous. In 1893 she toured Europe, attracting even more attention than in the homeland. Since then she made several tours of Europe and America, arousing great enthusiasm wherever she appeared. Her emotional force, her personal magnetism and her keen processes of analysis compelled critics everywhere to rank her with the foremost pianists of the day.

6

APPEARING IN PUBLIC

FANNY BLOOMFIELD-ZEISLER

"THE secret of success in the career of a virtuoso is not easily defined. Many elements have to be considered. Given great talent, success is not by any means assured. Many seemingly extraneous qualities must be cultivated; many mistakes must be avoided.

"Let me start out with a caution. No greater mistake could possibly be made than to assume that frequent public appearances or extended concert touring in early youth is essential to a great career as a virtuoso. On the contrary, I would say that such a course is positively harmful. The 'experience' of frequent playing in public is essential if one would get rid of stage fright or undue nervousness and would gain that repose and self-confidence without which success is impossible. But such experience should be had only after the attainment of physical and mental maturity. A young boy or girl, though ever so much of a prodigy, if taken on an extensive concert tour, not only becomes unduly self-conscious, conceited, vain and easily satisfied with his or her work, but—and this is the all-important point —runs the risk of undermining his or her health. The precious days of youth should be devoted primarily to the storing up of health, without which lasting success is impossible. Nothing is more harmful to sound physical development and mental growth than the strain of extensive tours. It is true that one great virtuoso now before the public played frequently before large audiences as an infant prodigy. But, happily, wise and efficient influences served to check this mad career. The young artist was placed in the hands of a great teacher and given a chance to reach full physical maturity and artistic stature before resuming public appearances. Had it been otherwise, it is a matter of common belief that this great talent would have fizzled out.

"By this I do not mean that the pupil should be prevented from playing at recitals in the home city. Playing of this kind gives the pupil confidence and smooths the way for his work as a mature artist. These performances should be rare, except in the case of performances given in the home of the pupil or at the teacher's home. What I object to is the exploitation on a large scale of the infant prodigy.

THOROUGH PREPARATION NECESSARY

"One of the real secrets of success in public appearance is thorough preparation. In fact there is no talisman, no secret that one can pass over to another and say, 'Here is my secret, go thou and do likewise.' What a valuable secret it would be—the mysterious secret processes of the Krupp Gun Works in Germany would be trifling in comparison. Genuine worth is, after all, the great essential, and thorough preparation leads to genuine worth. For instance, I have long felt that the mental technic that the study of Bach's inventions and fugues afford could not be supplied by any other means. The peculiar polyphonic character of these works trains the mind to recognize the separate themes so ingeniously and beautifully interwoven and at the same time the fingers receive a kind of discipline which hardly any other study can secure.

"The layman can hardly conceive how difficult it is to play at the same time two themes different in character and running in opposite directions. The student fully realizes this difficulty when he finds that it takes years to master it. These separate themes must be individualized; they must be conceived as separate, but their bearing upon the work as a whole must never be overlooked.

"The purity of style to be found in Bach, in connection with his marvelous contrapuntal designs, should be expounded to the student at as early an age as his intellectual development will permit. It may take some time to create a taste for Bach, but the teacher will be rewarded with results so substantial and permanent that all the trouble and time will seem well worth while.

"There is also a refining influence about which I would like to speak. The practice of Bach seems to fairly grind off the rough edges, and instead of a raw, bungling technic the student acquires a kind of finish from the study of the old master of Eisenach that nothing else can give him.

"I do not mean to be understood that the study of Bach, even if it be ever so thorough, suffices in itself to give one a perfect technic. Vastly more is necessary. The student who would fit himself for a concert career must have the advice of a great teacher and must work incessantly and conscientiously under his guidance. I emphasize the study of Bach merely because I find it is not pursued as much as it deserves. That technical finish is of the very essence of success in public appearance, goes without saying. It is not only indispensable for a creditable performance, but the consciousness of possessing it contributes to that confidence of the player without which he cannot hope to make an impression upon his audience.

LESCHETIZKY AND 'METHOD'

"Speaking about teachers reminds me to put forth this caution: Do not pin your faith to a method. There is good and, alas! some bad in most methods. We hear a great deal these days about the Leschetizky method. During the five years I was with Leschetizky, he made it very plain that he had no fixed method in the ordinary sense of the word. Like every good teacher, he studied the individuality of each pupil and taught him according to that individuality. It might almost be said that he had a different method for each pupil, and I have often said that Leschetizky's method is to have no fixed method. Of course, there are certain preparatory exercises which with slight variations he wants all his pupils to go through. But it is not so much the exercises in themselves as the patience and painful persistence in executing them to which they owe their virtue. Of course, Leschetizky has his preference for certain works for their great educational value. He has his convictions as to the true interpretation to be given to the various compositions, but those do not form what may properly be called a method. Personally, I am rather skeptical when anybody announces that he teaches any particular method. Leschetizky, without any particular method, is a great force by virtue of his tremendously interesting personality and his great qualities as an artist. He is himself a never-ending source of inspiration. At eighty he was still a youth, full of vitality and enthusiasm. Some student, diffident but worthy, was always encouraged; another was incited by sarcasm; still another was scolded outright. Practical illustration on the piano, showing 'how not to do it,' telling of pertinent stories to elucidate a point, are among the means which he constantly employed to bring out the best that was in his pupils. A good teacher cannot insure success and Leschetizky has naturally had many pupils who will never become great virtuosos. It was never in the pupils and, no matter how great the teacher, he cannot create talent that does not exist.

"The many books published upon the Leschetizky system by his assistants have merit, but they by no means constitute a Leschetizky system. They simply give some very rational preparatory exercise that the assistants give in preparing pupils for the master. Leschetizky himself laughs when one speaks of his 'method' or 'system.'

"Success in public appearance will never come through any system or method except that which works toward the end of making a mature and genuine artist.

WELL-SELECTED PROGRAMS

"Skill in the arrangement of an artist's programs has much to do with his success. This matter has two distinct aspects. Firstly, the program must *look* attractive, and secondly, it must *sound* well in the rendition. When I say the program must look attractive, I mean that it must contain works which interest concert-goers. It should be neither entirely conventional, nor should it contain novelties exclusively. The classics should be represented, because the large army of students expect to be especially benefited by hearing these performed by a great artist. Novelties must be placed on the program to make it attractive to the maturer habitués of the concert room.

"But more important, to my mind, is the other aspect of program making which I have mentioned. There must be contrasts in the character and tonal nature of the compositions played. They must be so grouped that the interest of the hearers will be not only sustained to the end, but will gradually increase. It goes without saying that each composition should have merit and worth as musical literature. But beyond that, there should be variety in the character of the different compositions: the classic, the romantic, and the modern compositions should all be given representation. To play several slow movements or several vivacious movements in succession would tend to tire the listener. Anti-climaxes should be avoided.

"It may truly be said that program making is in itself a high art. It is difficult to give advice on this subject by any general statement. Generalizations are too often misleading. I would advise the young artist to study carefully the programs of the most successful artists and to attempt to discover the principle underlying their arrangement.

"One thing which should never be forgotten is that the object of a concert is not merely to show off the skill of the performer, but to instruct, entertain and elevate the audience. The bulk of the program should be composed of standard works, but novelties of genuine worth should be given a place on the program.

PERSONALITY

"The player's personality is of inestimable importance in winning the approval of the public. I do not refer particularly to personal beauty, although it cannot be doubted that a pleasing appearance is helpful in conquering an audience. What I mean is sincerity, individuality, temperament. What we vaguely describe as magnetism is often possessed by players who can lay no particular claim to personal beauty. Some players seem fairly to hypnotize their audiences—yes, hypnotize them. This is not done by practicing any species of black art, or by consciously following any psychological formula, but by the sheer intensity of feeling of the artist at the moment of performance.

"The great performer in such moments of passion forgets himself entirely. He is in a sort of artistic trance. Technical mastery of the composition being presupposed, the artist need not and does not give thought to the matter of playing the notes correctly, but, re-creating in himself what he feels to have been the mood of the composer, re-creates the composition itself. It is this kind of playing which establishes an invisible cord, connecting the player's and the hearers' hearts, and, swayed himself by the feelings of the moment, he sways his audience. He makes the music he draws from the instrument supreme in every soul in the audience; his feeling and passion are contagious and carry the audience away. These are the moments, not only of the greatest triumph, but of the greatest exultation for the artist. He who cannot thus sway audiences will never rise above mediocrity.

Do Not Attempt the Impossible

"To those who are still in the preparatory stage of development I am glad to give one word of advice. *Do not play pieces that are away beyond your grasp.* This is the greatest fault in our American musical educational systems of to-day. Pupils are permitted to play works that are technically impossible for them to hope to execute without years of preparation. What a huge blunder this is!

"The pupil comes to the teacher, let us say, with the *Second Hungarian Rhapsody* of Liszt. It takes some fortitude for the conscientious teacher to tell the pupil that she should work with the *C Major Sonata* of Haydn instead. The pupil, with a kind of confidence that is, to say the least, dangerous, imagines that the teacher is trying to keep her back, and often goes to another teacher who will gratify her whim.

"American girls think that they can do everything. Nothing is beyond them. This is a country of great accomplishment, and they do not realize that in music 'Art is long.' The virtuoso comes to a great metropolis and plays a Moszkowski concerto of great difficulty. The next day the music stores exhaust their stocks of this work, and a dozen misses, who might with difficulty play a Mendelssohn *Song With Words*, are buried in the avalanche of technical impossibilities that the alluring concerto provides.

Foreign Débuts

"Unfortunately, a foreign *début* seems to be necessary for the artist who would court the favor of the American public. Foreign pianists get engagements long before their managers in America ever hear them. In the present state of affairs, if an American pianist were to have the ability of three Liszts and three Rubinsteins in one person, he could only hope for meager reward if he did not have a great European reputation behind him.

"The condition is absurd and regrettable, but nevertheless true. We have many splendid teachers in America—as fine as there are in the world.

"We have in our larger cities musical audiences whose judgment is as discriminating as that of the best European audiences. Many an artist with a great European reputation has come to this country, and, failing 'to make good' in the judgment of our critics and audiences, went back with his reputation seriously impaired. Nevertheless, as I have stated, the American artist without a European reputation, has no drawing power and therefore does not interest the managers and the piano manufacturers, who nowadays have largely supplanted the managers. This being so, I can only advise the American artist to do as others had to do. Go to Europe; give a few concerts in Berlin, London, Vienna or Paris. Let the concert director who arranges your concerts paper the house, but be sure you get a few critics in

the audience. Have your criticisms translated, and
get them republished in American papers. Then, if
you have real merit, you may get a chance.

"The interest in music in the United States at the
present time is phenomenal. European peoples
have no conception of it. Nowhere in the world can
such interest be found. Audiences in different parts
of the country do not differ very greatly from the
standpoint of intelligent appreciation. When we
consider the great uncultured masses of peasants in
Europe and the conditions of our own farmers,
especially in the West, there is no basis of comparison.
America is already a musical country, a very musical
country. It is only in its failure to properly support
native musicians that we are subject to criticism.

Practical Suggestions

"To the young man or woman who would learn
'The Secret of Public Appearance' I would say:

"1. Look deeply into your natural qualifications.
Use every morsel of judgment you possess to endeavor to determine whether you are talented or
simply 'clever' at music. Court the advice of un-
biased professional musicians and meditate upon the
difficulties leading to a successful career, and do not
decide to add one more musician to the world until
you are confident of your suitability for the work.
Remember that this moment of decision is a very
important time and that you may be upon the thresh-
old of a dangerous mistake. Remember that there

are thousands of successful and happy teachers for one successful virtuoso.

"2. After you have determined to undertake the career of the concert performer let nothing stand in the way of study, except the consideration of your health. Success with a broken-down body and a shattered mind is a worthless conquest. Remember that if you wish a permanent position you must be thoroughly trained in all branches of your art.

"3. Avoid charlatanism and the kind of advertisement that will bring you notoriety at the sacrifice of your self-respect and the respect of your best friends. Remember that real worth is, after all, the thing that brings enduring fame.

"4. Study the public. Seek to find out what pleases it, but never lower the standards of your art. Read the best literature. Study pictures. Travel. Broaden your mind. Acquire general culture.

"5. Be careful of your stage deportment. Endeavor to do nothing at the keyboard that will emphasize any personal eccentricity. Always be sincere and true to your own nature, but within these limits try to make a pleasing impression.

"6. Always be your own severest critic. Be not easily satisfied with yourself. Hitch your wagon to a star. Let your standard of perfection be the very highest. Always strive to reach that standard. Never play in public a piece that you have not thoroughly mastered. There is nothing more valuable than public confidence.   Once secured, it is the greatest asset an artist can possess.

"I have repeatedly been asked to give ten rules for practice.

"It is not possible to formulate ten all-comprehensive rules that could be applied in every case, but the following suggestions will be found valuable to many students:

"1.   Concentrate during every second of your practice.   To concentrate means to bring all your thinking powers to bear upon one central point with the greatest possible intensity.   Without such concentration nothing can be accomplished during the practice period.   One hour of concentrated thinking is worth weeks of thoughtless practice.   It is safe to say that years are being wasted by students in this country who fail to get the most out of their practice because they do not know how to concentrate.   A famous thinker has said: 'The evidence of superior genius is the power of intellectual concentration.'

"2.   Divide your practice time into periods of not more than two hours.   You will find it impossible to concentrate properly if you attempt to practice more than two hours at a time.   Do not have an arbitrary program of practice work, for this course is liable to make your work monotonous.   For one who practices four hours (and that is enough for almost any student), one hour for purely technical work, one hour for Bach, and two hours for pieces is to be recommended.

"3.   In commencing your practice, play over your

piece once or twice before beginning to memorize.
Then, after working through the entire composition,
pick out the more difficult passages for special attention and reiteration.

"4. Always practice slowly at first. This is
simply another way of telling the pupil to concentrate.
Even after you have played your piece at the required speed and with reasonable confidence that it
is correct, never fail to go back now and then and
play it at the speed at which you learned it. This
is a practice which many virtuosos follow. Pieces
that they have played time and time again before
enthusiastic audiences are re-studied by playing them
very slowly. This is the only real way to undo mistakes that are bound to creep into one's performance
when pieces are constantly played in a rapid tempo.

"5. Do not attempt to practice your whole piece
at first. Take a small section or even a phrase. If
you take a longer section than say sixteen bars, you
will find it difficult to avoid mistakes. Of course, when
the piece is mastered you should have all these sections so unified that you can play the entire composition smoothly and without a break.

"6. First memorize *mentally* the section you have
selected for study, and then practice it. If you do
not know it well enough to practice it from memory,
you have not grasped its musical content, but are
playing mechanically.

"7. Occasionally memorize backwards, that is,
take the last few measures and learn them thoroughly,

then take the preceding measures and continue in this way until the whole is mastered. Even after you have played the piece many times, this process often compels a concentration that is beneficial.

"8. When studying, remember that practice is simply a means of cultivating habits. If you play correctly from the start you will form good habits; if you play carelessly and faultily your playing will grow continually worse. Consequently, play so slowly and correctly from the start that you may insure the right fingering, phrasing, tone, touch (staccato, legato, portamento, etc.), pedaling and dynamic effects. If you postpone the attainment of any of these qualities to a later date they are much more difficult to acquire.

"9. Always listen while you are playing. Music is intended to be heard. If you do not listen to your own playing it is very probable that other people will not care to listen to it either.

"10. Never attempt to play anything in public that you have just finished studying. When you are through working upon a piece, put it away to be musically digested, then after some time repeat the same process, and again the third time, when your piece will have become a part of yourself."

QUESTIONS IN STYLE, INTERPRETATION, EXPRESSION AND TECHNIC OF PIANOFORTE PLAYING

SERIES IV

FANNY BLOOMFIELD-ZEISLER

1. How should the public appearances of talented children be controlled?

2. What is the best material for the development of a mental technic?

3. Should one pin one's faith to any one method?

4. What combines to make a program attractive?

5. What should be artist's main object in giving a concert?

6. What part does personality play in the performer's success?

7. What is one of the greatest faults in musical educational work in America?

8. How should practice time be divided?

9. May one memorize "backwards"?

10. Why should one listen while playing?

FERRUCCIO BENVENUTO BUSONI

BIOGRAPHICAL

Ferruccio Benvenuto Busoni was born at Empoli, near Florence, Italy, April 1, 1866. His father was a clarinetist and his mother whose maiden name was Weiss, indicating her German ancestry was an excellent pianist. His first teachers were his parents. So pronounced was his talent that he made his début at the age of eight in Vienna, Austria. He then studied in the Austrian city of Graz with W. A. Remy, whose right name was Dr. Wilhelm Mayer. This able teacher aside from being a learned jurist was also devoted to music and had among his other pupils no less a person than Felix Weingartner.

In 1881 Busoni toured Italy and was made a member of the Reale Accademia Filharmonica at Bologna. In 1886 he went to reside at Leipsic. Two years later he became teacher of pianoforte at the Helsingfors Conservatory in the Finnish capital. In 1890 he captured the famous Rubinstein prizes for both pianoforte and composition. In the same year he became Professor of pianoforte playing at the Moscow Imperial Conservatory. The next year he accepted a similar position in the New England Conservatory at Boston,—returning to Europe for another tour in 1893. After many successful tours he accepted the position of director of the Meister-schule at the Imperial Conservatory in Vienna. His compositions include over one hundred published opus numbers, the most pretentious probably being his *Choral Concerto*. His editions of Bach are masterpieces of technical and artistic erudition.

(The following Conference was conducted in English.)

7

IMPORTANT DETAILS IN PIANO STUDY
FERRUCCIO BENVENUTO BUSONI

THE SIGNIFICANCE OF THE DETAIL

"SOME years ago I met a very famous artist whose celebrity rested upon the wonderful colored glass windows that he had produced. He was considered by most of his contemporaries the greatest of all makers of high-art windows. His fame had extended throughout the artistic circles of all Europe. A little remark he made to me illustrates the importance of detail better than anything of which I can think at present.

"He said, 'If a truly great work of art in the form of a stained glass window should be accidentally shattered to little bits, one should be able to estimate the greatness of the whole window by examining one of the fragments even though all the other pieces were missing.'

"In fine piano playing all of the details are important. I do not mean to say that if one were in another room that one could invariably tell the ability of an artist by hearing him strike one note, but if the note is heard in relation to the other notes in a composition, its proportionate value should be so delicately and artistically estimated by the highly trained performer, that it forms part of the artistic whole.

"For instance, it is quite easy to conceive of compositions demanding a very smooth running performance in which one jarring or harsh note indicating faulty artistic calculation upon the part of the player would ruin the entire interpretation. As examples of this one might cite the Bach *Choral Vorspiel, Nun Freut euch,* of which I have made an arrangement, and such a composition as the Chopin Prelude Opus 28, No. 3, with its running accompaniment in the left hand.

"It is often perfection in little things which distinguishes the performance of the great pianist from that of the novice. The novice usually manages to get the so-called main points, but he does not work for the little niceties of interpretation which are almost invariably the defining characteristic of the interpretations of the real artist—that is, the performer who has formed the habit of stopping at nothing short of his highest ideal of perfection.

LEARNING TO LISTEN

"There is a detail which few students observe which is of such vast importance that one is tempted to say that the main part of successful musical progress depends upon it. This is the detail of learning to listen. Every sound that is produced during the practice period should be heard. That is, it should be heard with ears open to give that sound the intelligent analysis which it deserves.

"Anyone who has observed closely and taught

extensively must have noticed that hours and hours are wasted by students strumming away on keyboards and giving no more attention to the sounds they produce than would the inmates of a deaf and dumb asylum. These students all expect to become fine performers even though they may not aim to become virtuosos. To them the piano keyboard is a kind of gymnasium attached to a musical instrument. They may of course acquire strong fingers, but they will have to learn to listen before they can hope to become even passable performers.

"At my own recitals no one in the audience listens more attentively than I do. I strive to hear every note and while I am playing my attention is so concentrated upon the one purpose of delivering the work in the most artistic manner dictated by the composer's demands and my conception of the piece, that I am little conscious of anything else. I have also learned that I must continually have my mind alert to opportunities for improvement. I am always in quest of new beauties and even while playing in public it is possible to conceive of new details that come like revelations.

"The artist who has reached the period when he fails to be on the outlook for details of this kind and is convinced that in no possible way could his performances be improved, has reached a very dangerous stage of artistic stagnation which will result in the ruin of his career. There is always room for improvement, that is the development of new details, and it is this which gives zest and intellectual interest to the work of the artist. Without it his public efforts would become very tame and unattractive.

Self Development

"In my own development as an artist it has been made evident to me, time and time again, that success comes from the careful observance of details. All students should strive to estimate their own artistic ability very accurately. A wrong estimate always leads to a dangerous condition. If I had failed to attend to certain details many years ago, I would have stopped very far short of anything like success.

"I remember that when I concluded my term as professor of piano at the New England Conservatory of Music I was very conscious of certain deficiencies in my style. Notwithstanding the fact that I had been accepted as a virtuoso in Europe and in America and had toured with great orchestras such as the Boston Symphony Orchestra, I knew better than anyone else that there were certain details in my playing that I could not afford to neglect.

"For instance, I knew that my method of playing the trill could be greatly improved and I also knew that I lacked force and endurance in certain passages. Fortunately, although a comparatively young man, I was not deceived by the flattery of well-meaning, but incapable critics, who were quite willing to convince me that my playing was as perfect as it was possible to make it. Every seeker of artistic truth is more widely awake to his own deficiencies than any of his critics could possibly be.

"In order to rectify the details I have mentioned as well as some I have not mentioned, I have come to the conclusion that I must devise an entirely new technical system. Technical systems are best when they are individual. Speaking theoretically, every individual needs a different technical system. Every hand, every arm, every set of ten fingers, every body and, what is of greatest importance, every intellect is different from every other. I consequently endeavored to get down to the basic laws underlying the subject of technic and make a system of my own.

"After much study, I discovered what I believed to be the technical cause of my defects and then I returned to Europe and for two years I devoted myself almost exclusively to technical study along the individual lines I had devised. To my great delight details that had always defied me, the rebellious trills, the faltering bravura passages, the uneven runs, all came into beautiful submission and with them came a new delight in playing.

Finding Individual Faults

"I trust that my experience will set some ambitious piano students to thinking and that they may be benefited by it. There is always a way of correcting deficiencies if the way can only be found. The first thing, however, is to recognize the detail itself and then to realize that instead of being a detail it is a matter of vast importance until it has been conquered and brought into submission. In playing, always note where your difficulties seem to lie. Then, when advisable, isolate those difficulties and practice them separately. This is the manner in which all good technical exercises are devised.

"Your own difficulty is the difficulty which you should practice most. Why waste time in practicing passages which you can play perfectly well? One player may have difficulty in playing trills, while to another player of equal general musical ability trills may be perfectly easy. In playing arpeggios, however, the difficulties which prove obstacles to the players may be entirely reversed. The one who could play the trill perfectly might not be able, under any circumstance, to play an arpeggio with the requisite smoothness and true legato demanded, while the student who found the trill impossible possesses the ability to run arpeggios and cadenzas with the fluency of a forest rivulet.

"All technical exercises must be given to the pupil with great discretion and judgment just as poisonous medicines must be administered to the patient with great care. The indiscriminate giving of technical exercises may impede progress rather than advance the pupil. Simply because an exercise happens to come in a certain position in a book of technical exercises is no reason why the particular pupil being taught needs that exercise at that particular time.

Some exercises which are not feasible and others which are inexpedient at a certain time, may prove invaluable later in the pupil's progress.

"Take the famous Tausig exercises, for instance. Tausig was a master of technic who had few, if any, equals in his time. His exercises are for the most part very ingenious and useful to advanced players, but when some of them are transposed into other keys as their composer demands they become practically impossible to play with the proper touch, etc. Furthermore, one would be very unlikely to find a passage demanding such a technical feat in the compositions of any of the great masters of the piano. Consequently, such exercises are of no practical value and would only be demanded by a teacher with more respect for tradition than common sense.

Details of Phrasing and Accentuation

"Some students look upon phrasing as a detail that can be postponed until other supposedly more important things are accomplished. The very musical meaning of any composition depends upon the correct understanding and delivery of the phrases which make that composition. To neglect the phrases would be about as sensible as it would be for the great actor to neglect the proper thought division in the interpretation of his lines. The greatest masterpiece of dramatic literature whether it be *Romeo and Juliet*, *Antigone*, *La Malade Imaginaire* or *The Doll's House* becomes nonsense if the thought divisions indicated by the verbal phrases are not carefully determined and expressed.

"Great actors spend hours and hours seeking for the best method of expressing the author's meaning. No pianist of ability would think of giving less careful attention to phrasing. How stupid it would be for the actor to add a word that concluded one sentence to the beginning of the next sentence. How erroneous then is it for the pupil to add the last note of one phrase to the beginning of the next phrase. Phrasing is anything but a detail.

"Fine phrasing depends first upon a knowledge of music which enables one to define the limitations of the phrase and then upon a knowledge of pianoforte playing which enables one to execute it properly. Phrasing is closely allied to the subject of accentuation and both subjects are intimately connected with that of fingering. Without the proper fingers it is often impossible to execute certain phrases correctly. Generally, the accents are considered of importance because they are supposed to fall in certain set parts of given measures, thus indicating the meter.

"In instructing very young pupils it may be necessary to lead them to believe that the time must be marked in a definite manner by such accents, but as the pupil advances he must understand that the measure divisions are inserted principally for the purpose of enabling him to read easily. He should learn to look upon each piece of music as a beautiful tapestry in which the main consideration is

the principal design of the work as a whole and not the invisible marking threads which the manufacturer is obliged to put in the loom in order to have a structure upon which the tapestry may be woven.

BACH, BACH, BACH

"In the study of the subject of accentuation and phrasing it would not be possible for anyone to recommend anything more instructive than the works of Johann Sebastian Bach. The immortal Thüringian composer was the master-weaver of all. His tapestries have never been equalled in refinement, color, breadth and general beauty. Why is Bach so valuable for the student? This is an easy question to answer. It is because his works are so constructed that they compel one to study these details. Even if the student has only mastered the intricacies of the *Two Voice Inventions*, it is safe to say that he has become a better player. More than this, Bach forces the student to think.

"If the student has never thought before during his practice periods, he will soon find that it is quite impossible for him to encompass the difficulties of Bach without the closest mental application. In fact, he may also discover that it is possible for him to work out some of his musical problems while away from the keyboard. Many of the most perplexing musical questions and difficulties that have ever confronted me have been solved mentally while I

have been walking upon the street or lying in bed at night.

"Sometimes the solution of difficult details comes in the twinkling of an eye. I remember that when I was a very young man I was engaged to play a concerto with a large symphony orchestra. One part of the concerto had always troubled me, and I was somewhat apprehensive about it. During one of the pauses, while the orchestra was playing, the correct interpretation came to me like a flash. I waited until the orchestra was playing very loud and made an opportunity to run over the difficult passage. Of course, my playing could not be heard under the *tutti* of the orchestra, and when the time came for the proper delivery of the passage it was vastly better than it would have been otherwise.

"I never neglect an opportunity to improve, no matter how perfect a previous interpretation may have seemed to me. In fact, I often go directly home from the concert and practice for hours upon the very pieces that I have been playing, because during the concert certain new ideas have come to me. These ideas are very precious, and to neglect them or to consider them details to be postponed for future development would be ridiculous in the extreme."

QUESTIONS ON STYLE, INTERPRETATION, EXPRESSION
AND TECHNIC OF PIANO PLAYING

SERIES V

FERRUCCIO BENVENUTO BUSONI

1. What is it which distinguishes the performance of the great pianist from that of the novice?

2. Upon what detail of interpretation does musical performance most depend?

3. Should the student continually estimate his own ability?

4. Which difficulty should you practice most?

5. What was the principle which made the Tausig exercises valuable?

6. Upon what does fine phrasing depend?

7. Why is it that the compositions of Johann Sebastian Bach are so useful in piano study?

8. How may complex musical problems be solved mentally?

9. Is it advisable to isolate difficulties and practice them separately?

10. How should one seize opportunities to improve?

TERESA CARREÑO

Teresa Carreño was born at Caracas, Venezuela, December 22, 1853. She descended from one of the foremost families of Spanish America, which boasted of Simon Bolivar "the Washington of South America" as one of its members. Artists have been known among her ancestors as far back as the fourteenth century when the famous painter Carreño lived in Spain.

Mme. Carreño's first teacher was her father. Later she studied with a German teacher in her native country. At seven she played the *Rondo Capriccio* of Mendelssohn with great *éclat*. A revolution obliged the Carreño family to move to New York. The death of a friend to whom funds had been entrusted placed the party of eighteen refugees in dire straits and a concert was arranged at which the tiny Teresa came to the front and secured sufficient means for their existence.

Gottschalk, then in the height of his fame in New York, became the child's next teacher. She remained with him for two years. Then she went to Paris and became a pupil of Georges Mathias, the famous disciple of Chopin. Her success as a virtuoso pianist in Europe excited the attention of Rubinstein who devoted a great deal of time to giving her invaluable advice and instruction in interpretation. Indeed Rubinstein was so proud of her that he repeatedly introduced her as his daughter in art and would jokingly say "Are not our hands exactly alike?"

Mme. Carreño's brilliance, force, breadth of thought and almost sensuous love for the beautiful made her numerous tours through all of the music-loving countries remarkably successful.

8

DISTINCTIVE PIANO PLAYING
TERESA CARREÑO

EARLY EVIDENCES OF INDIVIDUALITY

IT is difficult for me to discuss the subject of individuality without recollecting one of the most impressive and significant events of my entire career. When I was taken to Europe as a child, for further study, it was my good fortune to meet and play for the immortal Franz Liszt. He seemed deeply interested in my playing, and with the kindliness for which he was always noted he gave me his blessing, a kind of artistic sacrament that has had a tremendous influence upon all my work as an artist. He laid his hand upon my head and among other things said: "Little girl, with time you will be one of us. Don't imitate anyone. Keep yourself true to yourself. Cultivate your individuality and do not follow blindly in the paths of others."

In this one thought Liszt embodied a kind of a pedagogical sermon which should be preached every day in all the schools, conservatories and music studios of the world. Nothing is so pitiful as the evidences of a strong individuality crushed out by an artificial educational system which makes the system itself of paramount importance and the individual of microbic significance.

The signs of individuality may be observed in little folks at a very early age. With some children they are not very pronounced, and the child seems like hundreds of others without any particular inclination, artistic or otherwise. It is then that the teacher's powers of divination should be brought into play. Before any real progress can be made the nature of the child must be studied carefully. In the case of other children, the individuality is very marked at an early age. As a rule, the child with the marked individuality is the one from whom the most may be expected later in life. Sometimes this very individuality is mistaken for precocity. This is particularly the case with musicians. In a few instances the individuality of the master has been developed late in life, as was the case of Richard Wagner, whose early individual tendencies were toward the drama rather than music.

New Problems at Every Step

The teacher in accepting a new pupil should realize that there at once arises new problems at every step. The pupil's hand, mind, body and soul may be in reality different from those of every other pupil the teacher has taught. The individual peculiarities of the hand should be carefully considered. If the hand has long, tapering fingers, with the fingers widely separated, it will need quite different treatment from that of the pupil with a short, compact, muscular hand. If the pupil's mind indicates mental lethargy or a lack of the proper early educational training, this must be carefully considered by the teacher. If the pupil's body is frail and the health uncertain, surely the teacher will not think of prescribing the same work she would prescribe for a robust, energetic pupil who appears never to have had a sick day. One pupil might be able to practice comfortably for four and five hours a day, while another would find her energy and interest exhausted in two hours. In fact, I would consider the study of individuality the principal care or study of the teacher.

The individuality of different virtuoso performers is very marked. Although the virtuoso aspires to encompass all styles—that is, to be what you would call an "all-around" player—it is, nevertheless, the individuality of the player that adds the additional charm to the piano-recital. You hear a great masterpiece executed by one virtuoso, and when you hear the same composition played by another you will detect a difference, not of technical ability or of artistic comprehension, but rather of individuality. Rembrandt, Rubens and Vandyke might have all painted from the same model, but the finished portrait would have been different, and that difference would have been a reflection of the individuality of the artist.

THE TEACHER'S RESPONSIBILITY

Again let me emphasize the necessity for the correct "diagnosis" of the pupil's individuality upon the part of the teacher. Unless the right work is prescribed by the teacher, the pupil will rarely ever survive artistically. It is much the same as with the doctor. If the doctor gives the wrong medicine and the patient dies, surely the doctor is to blame. It makes no difference whether the doctor had good intentions or not. The patient is dead and that is the end of all. I have little patience with these people who have such wonderful intentions, but who have neither the ability, courage nor willingness to carry out these intentions. Many teachers would like to accomplish a very great deal for their pupils, but alas! they are either not able or they neglect those very things which make the teacher's work a mission. One of the teacher's greatest responsibilities lies in determining at first upon a rational educational course by divining the pupil's individuality. Remember that pupils are not all like sheep to be shorn in the same identical fashion with the same identical shears.

EDWARD MACDOWELL'S INDIVIDUALITY

One of the most remarkable cases of a pronounced musical individuality was that of the late Edward MacDowell, who came to me for instruction for a considerable time. He was then quite youthful, and his motives from the very first were of the highest and noblest. His ideals were so lofty that he required little stimulation or urging of any kind. Here it was necessary to study the pupil's nature very carefully, and provide work that would develop his keenly artistic individuality. I remember that he was extremely fond of Grieg, and the marked and original character of the Norwegian tone-poet made a deep impression upon him. He was poetical, and loved to study and read poetry. To have repressed MacDowell in a harsh or didactic manner would have been to have demolished those very characteristics which, in later years, developed in such astonishing fashion that his compositions have a distinctiveness and a style all their own.

It gives me great pleasure to place his compositions upon my programs abroad, and I find that they are keenly appreciated by music lovers in the old world. If MacDowell had not had a strong individuality, and if he had not permitted this individuality to be developed along normal lines, his compositions would not be the treasures to our art that they are.

Developing Individuality Through Poetry

If the teacher discovers a pupil with apparent musical talent, but whose nature has not been developed to appreciate the beautiful and romantic in this wonderful world of ours, he will find it quite impossible to alter the pupil's individuality in this respect by work at the keyboard alone. The mundane, prosaic individual who believes that the sole aim of musical study is the acquisition of technic, or the magic of digital speed, must be brought to realize that this is a fault of individuality which will mar his entire career unless it is intelligently corrected. Years and years spent in practice will not make either a musician or a virtuoso out of one who can conceive of nothing more than how many times he can play a series of notes within the beats of the metronome, beating 208 times a minute.

Speed does not constitute virtuosity, nor does the ability to unravel the somewhat intricate keyboard puzzles of Bach and Brahms make in itself fine piano playing. The mind of the artist must be cultured; in fact, quite as cultured as that of the composer who conceived the music. Culture comes from the observation of many things: Nature, architecture, science, machinery, sculpture, history, men and women, and poetry. I advise aspiring music students to read a great deal of poetry.

I find great inspiration in Shakespeare, inspiration which I know is communicated to my interpretations of musical masterpieces at my concerts. Who can remain unmoved by the mystery and psychology of *Hamlet*, the keen suffering and misery of *King Lear*, the bitter hate and revenge of *Othello*, the sweet devotion of *Romeo and Juliet*, the majesty of *Richard III*, and the fairy beauty of *A Midsummer Night's Dream?* In this wonderful kaleidoscope of all the human passions one can find a world of inspiration. I am also intensely fond of Goethe, Heine, and Alfred de Musset. It gives me pleasure to compare them to the great masters of music. Shakespeare I compare to Brahms, Goethe to Bach and Beethoven, and Heine and Musset to Chopin and Liszt.

Cultivating Vivacity and Brilliancy

Vivacity and brilliancy in playing are largely matters of temperament and a fluent technic. I owe a great deal in this respect to Gottschalk. When he came back to America fresh from the hands of the inimitable Chopin, he took the most minute pains to cultivate this characteristic in my playing. Chopin's own playing was marked by delicacy and an intensity that was apart from the bravura playing of most of the artists of his time. Gottschalk was a keen observer, and he did everything possible to impart this style to me. I have used the studies of Czerny, Liszt, Henselt and Clementi to develop brilliancy with pupils.

It should be remembered that the root of all brilliant playing lies in one thing—accuracy. Without accuracy any attempt at brilliancy must result in "mussiness." It is impossible to explain these things by means of books and theories. Remember what Goethe says: "Alle Theorie is grau, mein Freund" (all theory is foggy or hard to comprehend). One can say fifty times as much in twenty minutes as one can put in a book. Books are necessary, but by no means depend entirely upon books for technical instruction.

Individuals who are careless possess a trait that will seriously mar their individuality as musicians and artists. Carelessness is so often taken for "abandon" in playing. "Abandon" is something

quite different and pertains to that unconsciousness
of technical effort which only comes to the artist
after years of practice. To play with "abandon"
and miss a few notes in this run, play a few false notes
in the next, strike the wrong bass note here and
there, mumble trills and overlook the correct phrasing
entirely, with the idea that you are doing the same
thing you have seen some great virtuoso do, is simply
the superlative degree of carelessness.

To one whose individuality is marred by carelessness let me recommend very slow playing, with the
most minute attention to detail. Technically speaking, Czerny and Bach are of great value in correcting
carelessness. In Czerny the musical structure of
the compositions is so clearly and openly outlined
that any error is easily detected, while in Bach the
structure is so close and compact that it is difficult
to make an error without interrupting the movement
of some other voice that will reveal the error. The
main consideration, however, is personal carefulness,
and it makes little difference what the study is, so
long as the student himself takes great pains to see
that he is right, and exactly right, before he attempts
to go ahead. Most musicians, however, would say
that Bach was the one great stone upon which our
higher technical structure must firmly stand.

Some individuals are so superficial and so "frothy"
that it is difficult to conceive of their doing anything serious or really worth while. It is very hard
for the teacher to work with such a pupil, because

they have not realized themselves as yet. They have not looked into their lives and discerned those things which make life of most importance. Life is not all play, nor is it all sorrow. But sorrow often does much to develop the musician's character, to make him look into himself and discover his more serious purposes. This might also be accomplished by some such means of self-introspection as "Christian Science." Although I am not a "Christian Scientist," I am a great believer in its wonderful principles.

The greatest care must be taken in developing the individualities of the superficial pupils. To give them Bach or Brahms at the outstart would be to irritate them. They must be led to a fondness for music of a deeper or more worthy character by gradual steps in that direction. In my own case I was fortunate in having the advice of mature and famous musicians, and as a child was given music of a serious order only. I have always been grateful for this experience. At one of my first New York concerts I had the honor of having Theodore Thomas as first violinist, and I well remember his natural bent for music of a serious order, which was in a decided contrast to the popular musical taste of the times.

The Importance of Studying Musical History

Every composer has a pronounced individuality. To the experienced musician this individuality becomes so marked that he can often detect the composer's style in a composition which he has never heard. The artist studies the individuality of the composer through the study of his biography, through the study of musical history in general and through the analysis of individual compositions.

Every music student should be familiar with the intensely necessary and extremely valuable subject of musical history. How else can he become familiar with the personal individualities of the great composers? The more I know of Chopin, Beethoven, Scarlatti or Mendelssohn as men, and the more I know of the times in which they lived, the closer I feel to the manner in which they would have wished their compositions interpreted. Consider how markedly different are the individualities of Wagner and Haydn, and how different the interpretations of the works of these masters should be.

Strauss and Debussy are also very different in their methods of composition. Strauss seems to me a tremendous genius who is inventing a new musical language as he goes. Debussy does not appeal to me in the same manner. He always seems to be groping for musical ideas, while with Strauss the greatness of his ideas is always evident and all-compelling.

In closing, let me say that *Time*, *Experience* and *Work* are the moulders of all individuality. Few of us close our days with the same individualities which become evident in our youth. We are either growing better or worse all the time. We rarely stand still. To the musician work is the great sculptor of individuality. As you work and as you think, so will you be. No deed, no thought, no hope is too insignificant to fail to influence your nature. As through work we become better men and women, so through work do we become better musicians. Carlyle has beautifully expressed this thought in "Past and Present" thus: "The latest Gospel in this world is, 'Know thy work and do it.' Blessed is he who has found his work; let him ask no other blessedness. He has a WORK, a life purpose; he has found it and will follow it."

QUESTIONS ON STYLE, INTERPRETATION, EXPRESSION AND TECHNIC OF PIANO PLAYING

SERIES VI

TERESA CARREÑO

1. Why should imitation be avoided?

2. Should individuality in playing be developed at an early age?

3. Should individual physical peculiarities be taken into consideration?

4. In what way was Edward MacDowell's individuality marked?

5. How may individuality be developed through poetry?

6. What studies are particularly useful in the cultivation of brilliant playing?

7. What is the best remedy for careless playing?

8. How must superficial pupils be treated?

9. Why is the study of musical history so important?

10. What may be called the sculptor of individuality in music?

PEPITO ARRIOLA

1897– ? • Spain

WILHELM BACHAUS
[Backhaus]

1884–1969 • Germany

HAROLD BAUER

1873 (1875?)–1951 • England

FANNY BLOOMFIELD-ZEISLER
[Blumenfeld]

1863 (1866?)–1927 • Austria

FERRUCCIO BUSONI

1866–1924 • Italy

TERESA CARREÑO

1853–1917 • Venezuela

OSSIP GABRILOWITSCH

1878–1936 • Russia

RUDOLF GANZ

1877–1972 • Switzerland

LEOPOLD GODOWSKY

1870–1938 • Russia

KATHERINE GOODSON

1872– ? • England

PERCY GRAINGER

1882–1961 • Australia

MARK HAMBOURG

1879–1960 • Russia

JOSEF HOFMANN

1876 (1877?)–1957 • Poland

Ernest Hutcheson

1871–1951 • Australia

ALBERTO JONÁS

1868–1943 • Spain

ALEXANDER LAMBERT
1862 (1863?)–1929 • Poland

JOSEF LHÉVINNE

1874–1944 • Russia

Yolanda Mérö

1887–1963 • Hungary

VLADIMIR DE PACHMANN

1848–1933 • Russia

IGNAZ JAN PADEREWSKI

1860–1941 • Poland

MAX PAUER

1866–1945 • England

SERGEI V. RACHMANINOFF

1873–1943 • Russia

ALFRED REISENAUER

1863–1907 • Germany

OLGA SAMAROFF
[*née* Hickenlooper]

1882–1948 • United States

EMIL [von] SAUER

1862–1942 • Austria

XAVER SCHARWENKA

1850–1924 • Poland

ERNEST SCHELLING

1875 (1876?)–1939 • United States

SIGISMUND [Zygmunt] STOJOWSKI
1869 (1870?)–1946 • Poland

OSSIP GABRILOWITSCH

BIOGRAPHICAL

Ossip Gabrilowitsch was born in St. Petersburg, February 8, 1878. His father was a well-known jurist of the Russian capital. His brothers were musical and his first teacher was one of his brothers. Later, he was taken to Anton Rubinstein who earnestly advocated a career as a virtuoso. Accordingly he entered the classes of Victor Tolstoff at the St. Petersburg Conservatory, then under the supervision of Rubinstein himself. His frequent personal conferences with the latter were of immense value to him. Thereafter he went to Vienna and studied with Leschetizky for two years. He has made many tours of Europe and America as a piano virtuoso and has also appeared as an orchestral conductor with pronounced success. He was a great friend of the late Mark Twain (Samuel L. Clemens) and married one of his daughters.

(The following conference was conducted in English.)

9

ESSENTIALS OF TOUCH

OSSIP GABRILOWITSCH

"Modern pianoforte teachers in many instances seem to make deliberate attempts to complicate the very simple matter of touch. In the final analyses the whole study of touch may be resolved into two means of administering force to the keyboard, *i. e.*, weight and muscular activity. The amount of pressure brought to bear upon the keys depends upon the amount of arm weight and upon the quickness with which the muscles of the hand, forearm, full-arm and back permit the key to be struck. Upon these two means of administering force must depend whatever differentiation in dynamic power and tonal quality the player desires to produce. The various gradations of tone which the virtuoso's hand and arm are trained to execute are so minute that it is impossible for me to conceive of a scientific instrument or scale to measure them. Physiologists have attempted to construct instruments to do this, but little of value has come from such experiments.

A Rigid Arm Undesirable

"Only a comparatively few years ago thousands of teachers were insisting upon having their pupils keep the arms in a still, even rigid, condition during practice. This naturally resulted in the stiffest imaginable kind of a touch, and likewise in a mechanical style of playing that made what has come to be known in later days as 'tone color' impossible.

"At this day the finger touch as it was formerly known has almost gone out of existence. By finger touch I refer to the old custom of holding the hand and forearm almost rigid and depending upon the muscular strength of the fingers for all tonal effects. In fact, I so rarely employ the finger touch, except in combination with the arm touch, that it is almost an insignificant factor as far as my own playing is concerned. By this the reader must not think that the training of the fingers, and particularly the finger tips, is to be neglected. But this training, to my mind, is not so much a matter of acquiring digital strength to produce force as to accustom the fingers to strike the notes with the greatest possible accuracy and speed. This belongs rather to the realm of technic than to that of touch, and behind all technic is the intellect of the player. Technic is a matter of training the finger tips to attack and leave the keys under the absolute discipline of the brain. Touch has a much broader and wider significance. It is touch that reveals the soul of the player.

Touch a Distinguishing Characteristic

"Touch is the distinguishing characteristic which makes one player's music sound different from that of another, for it is touch that dominates the player's means of producing dynamic shading or tone quality. I know that many authorities contend that the quality of tone depends upon the instrument rather than upon the performer. Nevertheless, I am reasonably confident that if I were to hear a number of pianists play in succession upon the same instrument behind a screen and one of these performers were to be my friend, Harold Bauer, I could at once identify his playing by his peculiarly individual touch. In fact, the trained ear can identify different individual characteristics with almost the same accuracy that we identify different voices. One could never forget Leschetizky's touch, or that of many another contemporary pianist.

"No matter how wonderful the pianist's technic—that is, how rapidly and accurately he can play passages of extraordinary difficulty, it is quite worthless unless he possesses that control over his touch which enables him to interpret the composer's work with the right artistic shading. A fine technic without the requisite touch to liberate the performer's artistic intelligence and 'soul' is like a gorgeous chandelier without the lights. Until the lights are ignited all its beauty is obscured in darkness. With an excellent technic and a fine touch, together with a broad musical and general education and artistic temperament, the young player may be said to be equipped to enter the virtuoso field.

Combining Different Touches

"As I have intimated, if the fingers are used exclusively a terribly dry tone must result. The full-arm touch, in which I experience a complete relaxation of the arm from the shoulder to the finger tips, is the condition I employ at most times. But the touches I use are combinations of the different finger, hand and arm touches. These lead to myriads of results, and only the experienced performer can judge where they should be applied to produce desired effects.

"You will observe by placing your hand upon my shoulder that even with the movement of the single finger a muscular activity may be detected at the shoulder. This shows how completely relaxed I keep my entire arm during performance. It is only in this way that I can produce the right kind of singing tone in cantabile passages. Sometimes I use one touch in one voice and an entirely different touch in another voice. The combinations are kaleidoscopic in their multiplicity.

Mechanical Methods Dangerous

"I have never been in favor of the many automatic and mechanical methods of producing touch. They are all dangerous to my mind. There is only one real way of teaching, and that is through the sense of *hearing* of the pupil. The teacher should go to the piano and produce the desired tonal effect, and the pupil should listen and watch the teacher. Then the pupil should be instructed to secure a similar result, and the teacher should persevere until the audible effect is nearly the same. If the pupil, working empirically, does not discover the means leading to this effect, the teacher should call the pupil's attention to some of the physical conditions leading to the result. If the teacher is unable to play well enough to illustrate this, and to secure the right kind of touch from his pupils, he has no business to be a teacher of advanced students. All the theory in the world will never lead to the proper results.

"Rubinstein paid little or no attention to the theory of touch, and, in fact, he frequently stated that he cared little about such things, but who could hear Rubinstein's touch without being benefited? I believe that in teaching touch the teacher should first give his model of the touch required and then proceed from this positive ideal, by means of the so-called Socratic method of inducing the pupil to produce a similar result through repeated questions. In this way the pupil will not be obliged to resign his individuality, as would be the case if he followed strict technical injunctions and rules.

Students Should Hear Virtuosos

"For the same reason it is advisable for the pupil to hear many fine pianists. He should never miss an opportunity to attend the concerts of great virtuosos. I can frankly say that I have learned as much from hearing the concerts of great performers as I have from any other source of educational inspiration. The pupil should listen intelligently and earnestly. When he hears what appeals to him as a particularly fine tonal effect, he should endeavor to note the means the pianist employs to produce this effect.

"He must, however, learn to discriminate between affection or needless movement and the legitimate means to an end. Consequent upon a relaxed full arm is the occasional dropping of the wrist below the level of the keyboard. A few great players practice this at a public recital, and lo! and behold! a veritable cult of 'wrist-droppers' arises and we see students raising and lowering the wrist with exaggerated mechanical stiffness and entirely ignoring the important end in which this wrist dropping was only an incident.

METHODS, AND STILL MORE METHODS

"I am continually amused at the thousand and one different ways of striking the keys that teachers devise and then attach with the label 'method.' These varied contortions are, after all, largely a matter of vision, and have little effect upon the real musical results that the composition demands. Touch, as I have previously said, all comes down to the question of the degree of weight applied to the keyboard and the degree of quickness with which it is applied. In rapid octave and staccato passages the hand touch is largely used. This is the touch most dependent upon local muscular activity. Aside from this the combination of muscular and weight touch almost invariably obtain.

Don't Neglect Ear Training

"I desire to reiterate that if the ideal touch is presented to the pupil's mind, through the medium of the ear, he will be much more successful in attaining the artistic ends required. The pupil must realize clearly *what is good* and *what is bad*, and his *aural sense* must be continually educated in this respect. He should practice slowly and carefully at the keyboard until he is convinced that his arm is at all times relaxed. He cannot make his sense of touch too sensitive. He should even be able to sense the weight or upward pressure which brings the pianoforte key back into position after it has been depressed. The arm should feel as if it were floating, and should never be tense.

"When I am playing I do not think of the arm motion. I am, of course, absorbed in the composition being performed. A relaxed arm has become second nature to me. It comes by itself. Players are rarely able to tell just how they produce their results. There are too many contributing factors. Even with the best-known performers the effects differ at different performances. It is impossible for the performer to give a program repeatedly in identically the same manner. If he did succeed in

doing this, his playing would soon become stereotyped.

"The teacher should, from the very beginning, seek
to avoid stiffness and bad hand positions, such as
crooked fingers or broken-in knuckles. If these details are neglected the pupil is liable to go through
his entire musical career greatly hampered. I would
earnestly advise all teachers to discourage the efforts
of pupils to attain virtuoso heights unless they are
convinced beyond the possibility of a doubt that the
pupil has marvelous talent. The really great performers seem to be endowed with a 'God-given'
insight in the matter of both technic and touch. They
are unquestionably born for it. They possess the
right mental and physical capacity for success. No
amount of training would make a Normandy dray
horse that could compete with a Kentucky thorough-
bred on the race course. It is a pitiful sight to watch
students who could not possibly become virtuosos slave
year after year before an ivory and ebony tread-mill,
when, if they realized their lack of personal qualifications, they could engage in teaching or in some other
professional or mercantile line and take a delight in
their music as an avocation that they would never
find in professional playing.

Artistic Interpretation Paramount

"To some, the matter of touch is of little significance. They are apparently born with an appreciation of tonal values that others might work

years to attain in vain. Those who imagine that touch is entirely a matter of finger tips are greatly mistaken. The ear is quite as important as the organs employed in administering the touch to the keyboard. The pianist should in reality not think of the muscles and nerves in his arm, nor of the ivory and ebony keys, nor of the hammers and strings in the interior of the instrument. He should think first and always of the kind of tone he is eliciting from the instrument, and determine whether it is the most appropriate tonal quality for the proper interpretation of the piece he is playing. He must, of course, spend years of hard thought and study in cultivating this ability to judge and produce the right touch, but the performer who is more concerned about the technical claims of a composition than its musical interpretation can only hope to give an uninteresting, uninspired, stilted performance that should rightly drive all intelligent hearers from his audience hall."

QUESTIONS IN STYLE, INTERPRETATION, EXPRESSION AND TECHNIC OF PIANOFORTE PLAYING

SERIES VII

OSSIP GABRILOWITSCH

1. What are the two means of administering touch?
2. State the effect of a rigid arm upon piano playing.

3. Can a pianist's playing be distinguished by touch?

4. How do the muscles of the shoulder come into action in piano playing?

5. How should the sense of hearing be employed in piano playing?

6. How did Rubinstein regard the theory of touch ?

7. When is the hand touch generally employed?

8. How should the arm feel during the act of touch?

9. Does the virtuoso hamper himself with details of technic during a performance?

10. What should be the pianist's first thought during the moment of performance?

LEOPOLD GODOWSKY

BIOGRAPHICAL

Leopold Godowsky was born at Wilna, Russia (Russian Poland), February 13, 1870. His father was a physician. When Godowsky was nine years old he made his first public appearance as a pianist and met with instantaneous success—success so great that a tour of Germany and Poland was arranged for the child. When thirteen he entered the Royal High School for Music in Berlin as the *protégé* of a rich banker of Königsberg. There he studied under Bargeil and Rudorff. In 1884 he toured America together with Ovide Musin, the violin virtuoso. Two years later he became the pupil of Saint-Saëns in Paris. In 1887 and 1888 he toured France and visited London, where he received a command to appear at the British Court. In 1890 he returned to America and made this country his home for ten years, appearing frequently in concert and engaging in several tours. In 1894–1895 he became head of the piano department of the South Broad Street Conservatory, Philadelphia. He then became director of the Piano Department of the Chicago Conservatory and held this position for five years. In 1900 Godowsky appeared in Berlin and was immediately recognized as one of the great piano masters of his time. In 1909 he became director of the Master School of Piano Playing connected with the Imperial Conservatory of Vienna (a post previously held by Emil Sauer and F. B. Busoni). His success as a teacher has been exceptional. His compositions, particularly his fifty studies upon Chopin Etudes, have won the admiration of the entire musical world.

10

THE REAL SIGNIFICANCE OF TECHNIC
LEOPOLD GODOWSKY

IDEAS UPON TECHNIC OFTEN ERRONEOUS

"IT is quite impossible in a short talk to earnest music students to do more than discuss a few of the more important points in the subject proposed. It may safely be said at the start, however, that the popular conception of technic is quite an erroneous one and one that deserves correction. It is highly necessary that the student should have a correct attitude of mind regarding this matter. First of all, I distinguish between what might be called mere mechanics and technic.

"The art of piano playing as a whole seems to divide itself into three quite distinct channels when it is considered from the educational standpoint. The first channel is that of mechanics. This would naturally include all that pertains to that branch of piano study which has to do with the exercises that develop the hand from the machine standpoint—that is, make it capable of playing with the greatest possible rapidity, the greatest possible power, when power is needed and also provide it with the ability to play those passages which, because of fingering or unusual arrangement of the piano keys, are particularly difficult to perform.

The Brain Side of Piano Study

"In the second channel we would find the study of the technic of the art of playing the instrument. Technic differs from the mechanics of piano playing in that it has properly to do with the intellectual phase of the subject rather than the physical.   It is the brain side of the study not the digital or the manual. To the average student who is short-sighted enough to spend hours hammering away at the keyboard developing the mechanical side of his work, a real conscious knowledge of the great saving he could effect through technic, would be a godsend. Technic properly has to do with Rhythm, Tempo, Accent, Phrasing, Dynamics, Agogics, Touch, etc.

"The excellence of one's technic depends upon the accuracy of one's understanding of these subjects and his skill in applying them to his interpretations at the keyboard. Mechanical skill, minus real technical grasp, places the player upon a lower footing than the piano-playing machines which really do play all the notes, with all the speed and all the power the operator demands. Some of these instruments, indeed, are so constructed that many of the important considerations that we have placed in the realm of technic are reproduced in a surprising manner.

The Emotions in Piano Playing

"However, not until man invents a living soul, can piano playing by machine include the third and vastly important channel through which we communicate the works of the masters to those who would hear them. That channel is the emotional or artistic phase of piano playing. It is the channel which the student must expect to develop largely through his own inborn artistic sense and his cultivated powers of observation of the playing of master pianists. It is the sacred fire communicated from one art generation to the next and modified by the individual emotions of the performer himself.

"Even though the performer may possess the most highly perfected mechanism, technical mastery which enables him to play great masterpieces effectively, if he does not possess the emotional insight, his performances will lack a peculiar subtlety and artistic power that will deprive him of becoming a truly great pianist.

INSPIRING THE STUDENT

"Exercises for the mechanical side of pianoforte playing abound. Czerny alone wrote over one thousand opus numbers. There have also been valuable attempts to provide books to assist the student in his technical work, but it should always be remembered that this depends first of all upon understanding and then upon the ability to translate that understanding to the instrument.

"There can never be any exercises in the emotional side of the student's work other than the entire literature of the instrument. One may as well try to capture the perfume of the flower as define the requirements of the emotional in pianoforte playing. A great deal may be done to inspire the student and suggest ideas which may bring him to the proper artistic appreciation of a passage, but it is this very indefinability which makes the emotional phase one of the most important of all. Attendance at the recitals of artistic pianists is of great help in this connection.

"The student, however, may learn a vast amount about real piano technic and apply his knowledge to his playing through the medium of the proper studies. For instance, in the subject of touch alone, there is a vast store of valuable information which can be gained from a review of the progressive steps through which this significant phase of the subject has passed during the last century. The art of piano playing, considered apart from that of the similar instruments which preceded the piano, is very little over one hundred years old.

Changes in the Mechanism of the Instrument

"During this time many significant changes have been made in the mechanism of the instrument and in the methods of manufacture. These changes in the nature of the instrument have in themselves doubtless had much to do with changes in methods of touch as have the natural evolutions coming through countless experiments made by teachers and performers. Thus we may speak of the subject of touch as being divided into three epochs, the first being that of Czerny (characterized by a stroke touch), the second being that of the famous Stuttgart Conservatory (characterized by a pressure touch), and the third or new epoch which is characterized by weight playing. All my own playing is based upon the last named method, and I had the honor of being one of the first to make application of it when I commenced teaching some twenty years ago.

The Significance of Weight Playing

"In this method of playing, the fingers are virtually 'glued to the keys' in that they leave them the least possible distance in order to accomplish their essential aims. This results in no waste motion of any kind, no loss of power and consequently the greatest possible conservation of energy. In this manner of playing the arm is so relaxed that it would fall to the side if the keyboard were removed from beneath it. Since the hand and the arm are relaxed the back (top) of the hand is almost on a level with the forearm.

"The high angular stroke which characterized the playing of the Czerny epoch and which could hardly fail to cause tired muscles and unbearably stiff playing, is seen very little in these days. By means of it the student was taught to deliver a blow to the keyboard— a blow which permitted very little modification to the requirements of modern technic.

"In my experience as a pianist and as a teacher, I have observed that the weight touch allows the greatest possible opportunity for the proper application of those all-important divisions of technic without which piano playing is not only inartistic, but devoid of all interest. Weight playing permits nothing to interfere with discriminative phrasing, complicated rhythmical problems, the infinitely subtle variation of time for expressive purposes now classed under the head of agogics, all shades of dynamic gradation; in fact everything that falls in the domain of the artist pianist.

Moulding The Fingers To The Keys

"In weight playing the fingers seem to mould the piano keys under them, the hand and arm are relaxed, but never heavy. The maximum of relaxation results in the minimum of fatigue. In legato playing, for instance, the fingers rest upon the fleshy part behind the tip rather than immediately upon the tip as they would in passage work when the player desired to have the effect of a string of pearls. The sensation in legato playing is that of pulling back rather than striking the keys. In passages where force is required the sensation is that of pushing.

"Much might be said of the sensibility of the finger tips as they come in contact with the ivory and ebony keys. Most every artist has a strong consciousness that there is a very manifest relation between his emotional and mental conditions and his tactile sense, that is his highly developed sense of feeling at the finger tips on the keyboard. However, the phenomena may be explained from the psychological standpoint, it is nevertheless true that the feeling of longing, yearning, hope or soulful anticipation, for instance, induces a totally different kind of touch from that of anger, resentment or hate.

"The artist who is incapable of communicating his emotions to the keyboard or who must depend upon artifice to stimulate emotions rarely electrifies his audiences. Every concert is a test of the artist's sincerity, not merely an exhibition of his prowess, or his acrobatic accomplishments on the keyboard. He must have some vital message to convey to his audience or else his entire performance will prove meaningless, soulless, worthless.

"That which is of great importance to him is to have the least possible barrier between his artistic conception of the work he would interpret and the sounds that are conveyed to the ears of his audience. If we obliterate the emotional side and depend upon artifice or what might be called in vulgar parlance "tricks of the trade," pianism will inevitably descend to a vastly lower level. By cultivating a sensibility in touch and employing the technical means which will bring the interpreter's message to the world with the least possible obstruction, we reach the highest in the art. Those who would strain at gnats might contend that with the machinery of the instrument itself, intervening between the touch at the keyboard and the sounding wires, would make the influence of the emotions though the tactile sense (sense of touch) is wholly negligible. To this I can only reply that the experience of the artist and the teacher is always more reliable, more susceptible to finer appreciations of artistic values than that of the pure theorist, who views his problems through material rather than spiritual eyes.   Every observing pianist is familiar with the remarkable influence upon the nerves of the voice-making apparatus that any emotion makes. Is it not reasonable to suppose that the finger tips possess a similar sensibility and that the interpretations of any highly trained artist are duly affected through them?

Individuality, Character and Temperament

"Indeed, Individuality, Character and Temperament are becoming more and more significant in the highly organized art of pianoforte playing.   Remove these and the playing of the artist again becomes little better than that of a piano-playing machine.   No machine can ever achieve the distinguishing charm that this trinity brings to pianoforte playing. Whether the performer is a 'genius' who has carefully developed the performance of a masterpiece until it evidences that distinguishing mark of the authoritative interpretation, or whether he is a 'talent' who improvises as the mood of the moment inspires him and never plays the same composition twice in anything like a similar manner, he need not fear the rivalry of any machine so long as he preserves his individuality, character and temperament.

GENIUS AND WORK

"The fault with many students, however, is the very erroneous idea that genius or talent will take the place of study and work. They minimize the necessity for a careful painstaking consideration of the infinite details of technic. To them, the significance of the developments of Bach, Rameau, and Scarlatti in fingering means nothing. They are content with the superficial. They are incapable of comparing the value of the advances made by Von Bülow, Tausig and other innovators whose lives were given to a large extent to the higher development of the technic of the instrument. They struggle laboriously at the keyboard, imagining that they are dealing with the problem of technic, when in reality they are doing little more than performing a drill in a kind of musical gymnasium—a necessary drill to be sure, but at the same time quite worthless unless directed by a brain trained in the principles of the technic of the art.

QUESTIONS IN STYLE, INTERPRETATION, EXPRESSION AND TECHNIC OF PIANOFORTE PLAYING

SERIES VIII

LEOPOLD GODOWSKY

1. How may the mechanics of playing be distinguished from the larger subject of technic?

2. With what has technic to do?

3. What channel in the study of pianoforte must the pupil develop most thoroughly?

4. Name three epochs into which the subject of touch may be divided.

5. How does weight playing differ from the high angular playing of the Czerny epoch?

6. How should the fingers rest in legato playing?

7. What may be said of the sensitiveness of the finger tips?

8. By what device may pianism descend to a lower level?

9. What qualities must the student preserve above all things?

10. Will genius or talent take the place of study and work?

KATHARINE GOODSON

BIOGRAPHICAL

Miss Katharine Goodson was born at Watford, Herts, England. She commenced the study of music at so very youthful an age that she made several appearances in the English Provinces before she was twelve years of age. Her talent aroused such interest that she was sent to the Royal Academy of Music in London. There she was placed under the artistic guidance of one of the foremost English teachers of pianoforte, Oscar Beringer, with whom she remained for six years. This was followed by four years under Leschetizky in Vienna.

Leschetizky saw splendid opportunities in such talented and regularly trained material and is said to have given particularly careful attention to Miss Goodson. It is not surprising that upon her return to London Miss Goodson made a profound impression upon the musical public and laid the foundation for a splendid reputation. She toured in England, Germany, Austria and America with great success. In the Grove Dictionary, her playing is described in the following manner: "It is marked by an amount of verve and animation that are most rare with the younger English pianists. She has a great command of tone gradation, admirable technical finish, genuine musical taste and considerable individuality of style." In 1903 Miss Goodson married Mr. Arthur Hinton, one of the most brilliant of modern English composers.

11

ANALYZING MASTERPIECES

KATHARINE GOODSON

THE NATURAL TENDENCY TO ANALYZE

"Judging from the mischievous investigations of things in general, which seem so natural for the small boy to make, it would appear that our tendency to analyze things is innate. We also have innumerable opportunities to observe how children, to say nothing of primitive people, struggle to construct—to put this and that together for the purpose of making something new—in other words, to employ the opposite process to analysis, known as synthesis. Moreover, it does not demand much philosophy to perceive that all scientific and artistic progress is based upon these very processes of analysis and synthesis. We pull things apart to find out how they are made and what they are made of. We put them together again to indicate the mastery of our knowledge.

"The measure of musicianship is the ability to do. All the analyzing in the world will not benefit the pupil unless he can give some visible indications of his proficiency. Indeed, important as the process is, it is possible to carry it to extremes and neglect the building process which leads to real accomplishment.

The First Step in Analyzing a New Piece

"A great many of the pupils who have come to me indicate a lamentable neglect in an understanding of the very first things which should have been analyzed by the preparatory teachers. It is an expensive process to study with a public artist unless the preparation has been thoroughly made. Reputation naturally places a higher monetary value upon the services of the virtuoso, and for the student to expect instruction in elementary points in analysis is obviously an extravagance. The virtuoso's time during the lesson period should be spent in the finer study of interpretation—not in those subjects which the elementary teacher should have completed. Often the teacher of an advanced pupil is deceived at the start and assumes that the pupil has a knowledge, which future investigations reveal that he does not possess.

"For instance, the pupil should be able to determine the general structure of a piece he is undertaking and should be so familiar with the structure that it becomes a form of second nature to him. If the piece is a sonata he should be able to identify the main theme and the secondary theme whenever they appear or whenever any part of them appears. Inability to do this indicates the most superficial kind of study.

"The student should know enough of the subject of form in general to recognize the periods into which the piece is divided. Without this knowledge how

could he possibly expect to study with understanding?
Even though he has passed the stage when it is necessary for him to mark off the periods, he should not
study a new piece without observing the outlines—the
architectural plans the composer laid down in constructing the piece. It is one thing for a Sir Chris-
topher Wren to make the plans of a great cathedral
like St. Paul's and quite another thing for him to get
master builders to carry out those plans. By studying the composer's architectural plan carefully the
student will find that he is saving an immense amount
of time. For example, let us consider the Chopin *F
Minor Fantasie.* In this composition the main theme
comes three times, each time in a different key.
Once learned in one key, it should be very familiar
in the next key.

"The student should also know something of the
history of the dance, and he should be familiar with
the characteristics of the different national dances.
Each national dance form has something more than a
rhythm—it has an atmosphere. The word atmosphere may be a little loose in its application here, but
there seems to be no other word to describe what I
mean. The flavor of the Spanish bolero is very different from the Hungarian czardas, and who could
confound the intoxicating swirl of the Italian tarantella with the stately air of cluny lace and silver rapiers
which seems to surround the minuet? The minuet,
by the way, is frequently played too fast. The
minuet from Beethoven's Eighth Symphony is a

notable example. Many conductors have made the error of rushing through it. Dr. Hans Richter conducts it with the proper tempo. This subject in itself takes a tremendous amount of consideration and the student should never postpone this first step in the analysis of the works he is to perform.

THE POETIC IDEA OF THE PIECE

"Despite the popular impression that music is imitative in the sense of being able to reproduce different pictures and different emotions, it is really very far from it. The subject of program music and illustrative music is one of the widest in the art, and at the same time one of the least definite. Except in cases like the Beethoven *Pastoral Symphony*, where the composer has made obvious attempts to suggest rural scenes, composers do not as a rule try to make either aquarelles or cycloramas with their music. They write music for what it is worth as music, not as scenery. Very often the public or some wily publisher applies the title, as in the case of the *Moonlight Sonata* or some of the Mendelssohn *Songs Without Words*. Of course there are some notable exceptions, and many teachers may be right in trying to stimulate the sluggish imaginations of some pupils with fanciful stories. However, when there is a certain design in a piece which lends itself to the suggestion of a certain idea, as does, for instance, the Liszt-Wagner *Spinning Song* from the *Flying Dutchman*, it is interesting to work with a specific picture in view—but never forgetting the real beauty of the piece purely as a beautiful piece of music.

"Some pieces with special titles are notoriously misnamed and carry no possible means of definitely intimating what the composer intended. Even some forms are misleading in their names. The *Scherzos* of Chopin are often very remote from the playful significance of the word—a significance which is beautifully preserved in the *Scherzos* of Mendelssohn.

STUDYING THE RHYTHM

"A third point in analyzing a new piece might be analyzing the rhythm. It is one thing to understand or to comprehend a rhythm and another to preserve it in actual playing. Rhythm depends upon the arrangement of notes and accents in one or two measures which give a characteristic swing to the entire composition. Rhythm is an altar upon which many idols are smashed. Sometimes one is inclined to regard rhythm as a kind of sacred gift. Whatever it may be, it is certainly most difficult to acquire or better to absorb. A good rhythm indicates a finely balanced musician—one who knows how and one who has perfect self-control. All the book study in the world will not develop it. It is a knack which seems to come intuitively or 'all at once' when it does come. My meaning is clear to anyone who has struggled with the problem of playing two notes against three, for at times it seems impossible, but in the twinkling of an eye the conflicting rhythms apparently jump into place, and thereafter the pupil has little difficulty with them.

"Rhythmic swing is different from rhythm, but is allied to it as it is allied to tempo. To get the swing— the impelling force—the student must have played many pieces which have a tendency to develop this swing. The big waltzes of Moszkowski are fine for this. If one of Leschetizky's pupils had difficulty with rhythm he almost invariably advised them to go to hear the concerts of that king of rhythm and dance, Eduard Strauss. Dances are invaluable in developing this sense of rhythm—swift-moving dances like the bolero and the tarantella are especially helpful. Certain pieces demand a particularly strict observance of the rhythm, as does the Opus 42 of Chopin, in which the left hand must adhere very strictly to the Valse rhythm.

THE ANALYSIS OF PHRASES

"The ability to see the phrases by which a composition is built, clearly and readily, simplifies the study of interpretation of a new piece wonderfully. This, of course, is difficult at first, but with the proper training the pupil should be able to see the phrases at a glance, just as a botanist in examining a new flower would divide it in his mind's eye into its different parts. He would never mistake the calyx for a petal, and he would be able to determine at once the peculiarities of each part. In addition to the melodic phrases the pupil should be able to see the metrical divisions which underlie the form of the piece. He should be able to tell whether the composition is one of eight-measure sections or four-measure sections, or whether the sections are irregular.

"What a splendid thing it would be if little children at their first lessons were taught the desirability of observing melodic phrases. Teachers lay great stress upon hand formation, with the object of getting the pupil to keep the hand in a perfect condition—a condition that is the result of a carefully developed habit. Why not develop the habit of noting the phrases in the same way? Why not a little mind formation? It is a great deal nearer the real musical aim than the mere digital work. The most perfectly formed hand in the world would be worthless for the musician unless the mind that operates the hand has had a real musical training."

Studying the Harmony

"Every piano student ought to have a knowledge of harmony. But this knowledge should be a practical one. What do I mean by a practical knowledge of harmony? Simply this—a knowledge of harmony which recognizes the ear as well as the eye. There are students of harmony who can work out some harmonic problem with the skill of an expert mathematician and yet they never for one single moment think of the music their notes might make. This is due to the great neglect of the study of ear-training in early musical education.

"To be able to recognize a chord when you see it on paper is not nearly such an acquisition as the ability to recognize the same chord when it is played. The student who can tell a diminished seventh, or an augmented sixth at a glance, but who could not identify the same chords when he saw them through his ears instead of his eyes is severely handicapped. But how many musicians can do this? Ear-training should be one of the first of all studies. It may be acquired more easily in childhood if the student is not naturally gifted with it, and it is the only basis of a thorough knowledge of harmony. The piano teacher cannot possibly find time to give sufficient instruction in the subject of harmony at the piano lesson. It demands a separate period, and in most cases it is necessary and advisable to have a separate teacher; that is, one who has made a specialty of harmony.

"The piano itself is of course a great help to the student in the study of harmony, providing the student listens all the time he is playing. Few adult piano students study string instruments, such as the violin or 'cello—instruments which cultivate the perception of hearing far more than can the piano. For this reason all children should have the advantage of a course in ear-training. This should not be training for pitch alone, but for quality of tone as well. It may be supplemented with exercises in musical dictation until the pupil is able to write down short phrases with ease after he has heard them once. A pupil who has had such a training would make ideal material for the advanced teacher, and because of the greatly developed powers of the pupil would be able to memorize quicker and make much better progress. In fact, ear-training and harmony lead to great economy of time. For instance, let us suppose that the pupil has a chord like the following in a sonata:

If the same chord appeared again in the piece it would probably be found in the key of the dominant, thus:

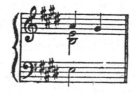

It seems very obvious that if the pupil could perceive the harmonic relationship between these two chords he would be spared the trouble of identifying an entirely different chord when he finds the repetition of it merely in another key. This is only one of scores of instances where a knowledge of the harmonic structure proves to be of constant importance to the student.

A CAREFUL ANALYSIS OF TOUCH EFFECTS

"Here again we find an interminable subject. Although there are only a few principal divisions into which the subject of touch might be divided, the number of different subdivisions of these best known methods of striking the keys to produce artistic effects is very considerable. The artist working day in and day out at the keyboard will discover some subtle touch effects which he will always associate with a certain passage. He may have no logical reason for doing this other than that it appeals to his artistic sense. He is in all probability following no law but that of his own musical taste and sense of hearing.

It is this more than anything else which gives individuality to the playing of the different virtuosos and makes their efforts so different from the playing of machines. Time and time again mechanical efforts have been made to preserve all these infinite subtilities and some truly wonderful machines have been invented, but not until the sculptor's marble can be made to glow with the vitality of real flesh can this be accomplished. Wonderful as the mechanical inventions are there is always something lacking.

"Here, again, ear-training will benefit the pupil who is studying with a virtuoso teacher. It is impossible to show exactly how certain touches produce certain effects. The ear, however, hears these effects, and if the pupil has the right kind of per-

sistence he will work and work until he is able to
reproduce the same effect that he has heard. Then
it will be found that the touch he employs will be
very similar to that used by the virtuoso he has heard.
It may take weeks to show a certain pupil a kind
of touch. The pupil with the trained ear and the
willingness to work might be able to pick up the
same touch and produce the same effect after a few
days. A highly developed sense of hearing is of
immense value to the student who attends concerts
for the purpose of promoting his musical knowledge.

The Responsibilities of the Teacher

"The more one contemplates this subject the more
one realizes the responsibilities of the teacher in
the first years of music study. Of all the pupils
who commence in the art there are but few who make
it a part of their lives; many of those who do continue
find themselves handicapped when they reach the
more advanced stages of the journey, owing to
inefficient early training. At the period when their
time is the most valuable to them they have to take
up studies which should have been mastered eight or
ten years before. The elementary teachers all over
the world have a big responsibility. If they belittle
their work with children and pine for the kind of
teaching which the virtuosos attempt to do, let them
realize that they are in a sense the foundation of the
structure, and although perhaps not as conspicuous as

the spire which towers up into the skies, they are certainly of equal importance."

QUESTIONS IN STYLE, INTERPRETATION, EXPRESSION AND TECHNIC OF PIANOFORTE PLAYING

SERIES IX

KATHARINE GOODSON

1. Is analysis natural to children?
2. When should the first steps in analysis be made?
3. Why is a knowledge of the different dance forms desirable?
4. What may be said of the poetic idea of the piece?
5. What indicates a finely balanced musician?
6. Should phrase analysis be taught at an early age?
7. Is the ability to identify a chord by hearing more important than the ability to identify it by sight?
8. Does a trained ear help in the acquisition of touch?
9. What may the pupil learn from concerts?
10. When is the teacher's responsibility greatest?

JOSEF HOFMANN

BIOGRAPHICAL

Josef Hofmann was born at Cracow, Russia, January 20, 1877. His father was an exceptionally successful teacher and was for a time Professor of Harmony and Composition at the Warsaw Conservatory. The elder Hofmann's talents were by no means limited to teaching, however, since he conducted the Opera at Warsaw for many performances. He undertook the training of his son with great care and since the child showed remarkable promise the musicians of Russia took an extraordinary interest in him. He appeared in public at the age of six and before he was ten years of age he was the most celebrated child prodigy of his time. He traveled thousands of miles, including tours of America, playing complicated classical compositions in a manner which surprised musicians everywhere. Fortunately for his health and education his tours were terminated in time for him to study for the advanced work of the more mature artist. Accordingly he was placed with the great Anton Rubinstein with whom he remained for two years. At seventeen he resumed his concert work again appearing in Dresden in 1894. By thoroughly dignified methods, scholarly analysis, and his natural poetical sense Hofmann introduced new ideas in virtuosoship which made him immensely popular at once.

12

PROGRESS IN PIANO STUDY
JOSEF HOFMANN

THE question of progress in pianoforte playing is
one that admits of the widest possible discussion.
One is frequently asked whether the manner of playing the pianoforte has undergone any change since
the time of Hummel, and, if it has advanced, of
what nature are the advances, and to what particular
condition are the advances due. Johann Nepomuk
Hummel, it will be remembered, was contemporary
with Beethoven, and was, in fact, a kind of bridge
between the old and the new. He made his début
at a concert given by Mozart at Dresden. For a
time he was a kind of assistant *kapellmeister* to Haydn,
and indeed many at that time thought his works
were quite on a par with those of the great master,
Beethoven. Hummel was a really great virtuoso,
and was noted for his remarkable improvisations.
His style of playing was taken as a model in his time,
and consequently we may safely start with this epoch
by way of example.

WHAT DETERMINES CHANGES IN PLAYING

It is sometimes said that the changes in the construction of the piano have caused a different treatment of it, but this reasoning is superficial, inasmuch

as the structural changes of the instrument itself are called forth by the ever-increasing demands of the *composer* made upon the instrument. So long as the tone quality, action and nature of the instrument sufficed for compositions of the type of those of Domenico Scarlatti, or François Couperin, or Rameau, there was little need for change, but as the more modern composers longed for new and more comprehensive effects, the piano-makers kept up with their desires and aims. Thus it is that after all is said and done, the composer, and the composer only, is responsible for the changes. The literature of the piano determines them. It is the same in the advancement of piano technic and interpretation. The composers conceive new and often radically different musical ideas. These in turn demand a new manner of interpretation. This kind of evolution has been going on continually since the invention of the instrument and is going on to-day, only it is more difficult for us to see it in the present than it is to review it in the past.

The general mental tendencies of the times, the artistic and cultural influences of the world taken as a whole, have also had a conspicuous though somewhat less pronounced share in these matters since they inevitably exert an influence upon the interpreter. Speaking from a strictly pianistic point of view, it is the player's individuality, influenced by the factors just stated, which is the determining element in producing new pianistic tendencies. It is thus very evident that progress in piano playing since the epoch of Hummel has been enormous.

THE NEW TECHNIC AND THE OLD

You ask me what are the essential differences between the modern technic and the technic of the older periods? It is very difficult to discuss this question off-hand and it is one which might better be discussed in an article of a different character. One difficulty lies in the regretable tendency of modern technic toward being a purpose in itself. Judging from the manner in which some ambitious young players work, their sole aim is to become human piano-playing machines quite without any real musical consciousness. Before radically condemning this tendency, however, it should be remembered that it has brought us many undeniable advantages. It cannot be doubted that we owe to the ingenious investigators of technical subjects greater possibilities in effective polyphonic playing, economy of power and arm motion, larger participation of the mind in the acquisition of technic, and numerous other praiseworthy factors in good piano playing. In the olden days, while technical exercises were by no means absent, they were not nearly so numerous, and more time was given to the real musical elements in the study of the musical compositions themselves. If the excellent technical ideas to be found in some of the systems of to-day are employed solely to secure real musical and artistic effects—that is, effects based upon known æsthetic principles—the new technic will prove valuable, and we should be very grateful for it. However, as soon as it becomes an objective point in itself and succeeds in eclipsing the higher purposes of musical interpretation, just so soon should it be abolished. If the black charcoal sketch which the artist puts upon canvas to use as an outline shows through the colors of the finished painting, no masterpiece will result. Really artistic piano playing is an impossibility until the outlines of technic have been erased to make way for true interpretation from the highest sense of the word. There is much more in this than most young artists think, and the remedy may be applied at once by students and teachers in their daily work.

Technic Since Liszt

Again you ask whether technic has made any significant advance since the time of Franz Liszt. Here again you confront me with a subject difficult to discuss within the confines of a conference. There is so much to be said upon it. A mere change in itself does not imply either progress or retrogression. It is for this reason we cannot speak of progress since the time of Liszt. To play as Liszt did—that is, exactly as he did, as a mirror reflects an object— would not be possible to anyone unless he were endowed with an individuality and personality exactly like that of Liszt. Since no two people are exactly alike, it is futile to compare the playing of any modern pianist with that of Franz Liszt. To discuss accurately the playing of Liszt from the purely technical standpoint is also impossible because so much of his technic was self-made, and also a mere manual expression of his unique personality and that which his own mind had created. He may perhaps never be equalled in certain respects, but on the other hand there are unquestionably pianists to-day who would have astonished the great master with their technics —I speak technically, purely technically.

DEFINITE METHODS ARE LITTLE MORE THAN STENCILS

I have always been opposed to definite "methods" —so-called—when they are given in an arbitrary fashion and without the care of the intelligent teacher to adapt special need to special pupils. Methods of this kind can only be regarded as a kind of musical stencil, or like the dies that are used in factories to produce large numbers of precisely similar objects. Since art and its merits are so strangely dependent upon individuality (and this includes anatomical individuality as well as psychological individuality), an inflexible method must necessarily have a deadening effect upon its victims.

The question of whether special technical studies of an arbitrary nature, such as scale studies, should be extensively used is one which has been widely debated, and I fear will be debated for years to come. Let us understand first, there is a wide difference between studying and practicing. They resemble each other only in so far as they both require energy and time. Many sincere and ambitious students make the great mistake of confounding these two very essential factors of pianistic success. Study and practice really are quite widely removed from each other, and at the same time they are virtually inseparable. The real difference lies in the amount and quality of the two elements. Practice means a large number of repetitions, with a fair amount of attention to mere correctness of notes, fingering, etc. Under ordinary circumstances and conditions it usually means a great sacrifice of time and a comparatively small investment of mentality.

Study, on the contrary, implies first of all mental activity of the highest and most concentrated type. It *presupposes* absolute accuracy in notes, time, fingerings, etc., and implies the closest possible attention to those things which are generally, though erroneously, regarded as lying outside of technic, such as tonal beauty, dynamic shading, rhythmical matters, and the like. Some have the happy gift of combining practice with study, but this is rare.

Hence, in the question of scale exercises, etc., if the word "study" is meant in the true sense, I can only say that the study of scales is more than necessary— it is indispensable. The pedagogical experts of the world are practically unanimous upon this subject. The injunction, "study," applies not only to scales, but to all forms of technical discipline, which only too often are "practiced" without being studied. I will not deny that mere practicing, as I have defined it, may bring some little benefit, but this benefit is gained at an enormous expenditure of time and physical and mental exertion. Oh! the endless leagues that ambitious fingers have traveled over ivory keys! Only too often they race like automobiles on a race-course—in a circle—and after having gone innumerable miles, and spent a tremendous amount of energy, they arrive at the same point from which they started, exhausted and worn, with very little to show for their work, and no nearer their real goal than when they started. The proportion in which mental and physical activity is compounded, determines, to my mind, the distinction between practicing and real study. One might also say that the proportion in which real study enters into the daily work of the student determines the success of the student.

The Study of Details Imperative

Study demands that the student shall delve into the minute details of his art, and master them before he attempts to advance. Only the most superficial students fail to do this in these days. All of the better trained teachers insist upon it, and it is hard for the pupil to skim through on the thinnest possible theoretical ice, as they did in past years. The separate study of embellishments, for instance, is decidedly necessary, especially in connection with the embellishments introduced by the writers of the early eighteenth century.

In the study of embellishments it is vitally important for the student to remember one or two very important points in connection with his investigation. One point is the understanding of the nature of the instrument for which the composer wrote when he had the embellishment in mind. The instruments of the early eighteenth century were characterized by a tone so thin and of such short duration that the composers and players (and it should be remembered that in those days practically all of the great composers played, and most of the great performers were composers) had to resort to all kind of subterfuges and tricks to produce the deception of a prolonged tone. For instance, they had a method of moving the finger to and fro (sideways) upon a key after it was struck. Thus they produced a sort of vibrato, not unlike that of which we have received an overdose in recent years from violinists and 'cellists. This vibrato (German, *Bebung*) was marked like our modern "shake," thus,

but if we interpret it as a "shake" we commit a grave error. We ought never to regard it as a "shake," unless it is obviously an integer of the melody.

The other point to be considered in the study of

embellishments is taste, or rather, let me say, "fashion," for the fashion of those times which over-indulged in ornamentation and over-loaded everything with it, from architecture to dress, was by no means an insignificant factor in music. The point is important because it involves the element of "concessions" which the composers, voluntarily or from habit, made to the public of their day. I seriously question the necessity of retaining these often superabundant embellishments in their entirety, for I contend that we study antique works on account of their musical substance and not for the sake of gewgaws and frills which were either induced by the imperfections of the instrument or by the vitiated taste of times to which the composer had to yield willy-nilly.

It is, of course, a very difficult and responsible task to determine what to retain and what to discard. This, to a large extent, must depend upon what part the ornament plays in the melody of the composition, whether it is really an integral part or an artificial excrescence. By all means never discard any embellishment which may serve to emphasize the melodic curve, or any one which may add to its declamatory character. A well-educated taste assisted by experience will be a fairly reliable guide in this matter. However, it is hardly advisable for amateurs with limited training to attempt any home editing of this kind.

Those embellishments which we do regain should in all cases be executed as the composer of the piece would desire to hear them executed if he could become acquainted with the instruments of to-day. This, of course, places the study of ornamentation with the many auxiliary musical branches which demand special and separate attention. Johann Sebastian Bach's son, Phillip Emanuel Bach, realized this, and gave years to the proper exposition of embellishments. However, the student should realize that the study of embellishments is only a part of the great whole and he should not be misled into accepting every little shake or other little frippery, and then magnifying it into a matter of more vital importance than the piece itself.

WELL-MEANING ADVISERS

The student should form the habit of determining things for himself. He will soon find that he will be surrounded with many well-meaning advisers who, if they have their own way, may serve to confuse him. Some virtuosos regard their well-meaning admirers and entertainers as the worst penalties of the virtuoso life. Whether they are or are not must, of course, depend upon the artist's character. If he accepts their compliments and courtesies as an expression of the measure of pleasure *they derived* from his playing, he has tacitly allowed for that share in their pleasure which is due to their power of appreciation, and he can therefore only rejoice in having provided something worthy of it. The manner of their expression, the observations they make, the very wording of their compliments will reveal, quickly enough, whether he has a case of real appreciation before him, or a mere morbid mania to hobnob with celebrities, or at least with people who by nature of their professional work are often compelled against their own desires to hold a more or less exposed position in the public eye. If he deals with the latter and still allows their compliments to go further than the physical ear, he must be a man of a character so weak as to make it doubtful that he will ever produce anything worthy of sincere and earnest appreciation. More young students are misled by blatant flattery than anything else. They become convinced that their efforts are comparable with those of the greatest artist, and the desire for improvement diminishes in direct ratio to the rate in which their opinion of their own efforts increases. The student should continually examine his own work with the same acuteness that he would be expected to show were he teaching another.

QUESTIONS IN STYLE, INTERPRETATION, EXPRESSION
AND TECHNIC OF PIANOFORTE PLAYING

SERIES X

JOSEF HOFMANN

1. Has piano playing progressed since the time of Hummel?

2. How have the changes in the structure of the instrument affected pianistic progress?

3. Why should students avoid becoming "piano-playing machines"?

4. What must be the sole aim in employing a technical exercise?

5. Will the technic of Liszt ever be excelled?

6. Why are stencil-like methods bad?

7. Is scale study indispensable?

8. Must the student know the characteristics of the instrument for which the composer wrote?

9. What part did fashion play in the introduction of embellishments?

10. Why should the student determine problems for himself?

JOSEF LHÉVINNE

BIOGRAPHICAL

Josef Lhèvinne is one of the last noted Russian
pianists to attain celebrity in America. At his first
appearance in New York he amazed the critics and
music lovers by the virility of his style, the comprehen-
siveness of his technic and by his finely trained artistic
judgment. Lhévinne was born at Moscow, in 1874.
His father was a professional musician, playing "all instruments except the piano." It is not surprising that
his four sons became professional musicians. Three
are pianists and one is a flutist. When Josef was four
his father discovered that he had absolute pitch, and
encouraged by this sign of musical capacity placed the
child under the instruction of some students from the
conservatory. At six Lhévinne became the pupil of a
Scandinavian teacher named Grisander. When eight
he appeared at a concert and aroused much enthusiasm
by his playing. At twelve he became the pupil of the
famous Russian teacher, Wassili Safonoff, at the conservatory at Moscow, remaining under his instruction
for six years. At the same time his teachers in theory
and composition were Taneieff and Arensky. In
1891 Rubinstein selected him from all the students
at the conservatory to play at a concert given under
the famous master's direction. After that Lhévinne
had frequent conferences with the great pianist, and
attributes much of his success to his advice. In 1895
he won the famous Rubinstein Prize in Berlin. From
1902 to 1906 he was Professor of Piano at the conservatory at Moscow. One year spent in military
service in Russia proved a compulsory setback in his
work, and was a serious delay in his musical progress.
Lhévinne came to America in 1907 and has been here
five times since then. His wife is also an exceptionally
fine concert pianist.

13

PIANO STUDY IN RUSSIA
JOSEF LHÉVINNE

RUSSIA'S MANY KEYBOARD MASTERS

"RUSSIA is old, Russia is vast, Russia is mighty. Eight and one-half million square miles of empire not made up of colonies here and there all over the world, but one enormous territory comprising nearly one hundred and fifty million people, of almost as many races as one finds in the United States, that is Russia. Although the main occupation of the people is the most peaceful of all labor—agriculture—Russia has had to deal with over a dozen wars and insurrections during a little more than a century. In the same time the United States has had but five. War is not a thing to boast about, but the condition reflects the unrest that has existed in the vast country of the Czar, and it is not at all unlikely that this very unrest is responsible for the mental activity which has characterized the work of so many artists of Russian birth.

Although Russia is one of the most venerable of the European nations, and although she has absorbed other territory possessed by races even more venerable than herself, her advance in art, letters and music is comparatively recent. When Scarlatti, Handel, and Bach were at their height, Russia, outside of court circles, was still in a state of serfdom. Tolstoi was born as late as 1828, Turgenieff in 1818 and Pushkin, the half-negro poet-humorist, was born in 1799. Contemporary with these writers was Mikhail Ivanovitch Glinka—the first of the great modern composers of Russia. Still later we come to Wassili Vereschagin, the best known of the Russian painters, who was not born until 1842. It may thus be seen that artistic development in the modern sense of the term has occurred during the lifetime of the American republic. Reaching back into the centuries, Russia is one of the most ancient of nations, but considered from the art standpoint it is one of the newest.

The folk songs that sprang from the hearts of the people in sadness and in joy indicated the unconcealable talent of the Russian people. They were longing to sing, and music became almost as much a part of their lives as food. It is no wonder then that we find among the names of the Russian pianists such celebrities as Anton Rubinstein, Nicholas Rubinstein, Essipoff, Siloti, Rachmaninoff, Gabrilowitsch, Scriabin, de Pachmann, Safonoff, Sapellnikoff and many others. It seems as though the Russian must be endowed by nature with those characteristics which enable him to penetrate the artistic maze that surrounds the wonders of music. He comes to music with a new talent, a new gift and finds first of all a great joy in his work. Much the same might be said of the Russian violinists and the Russian singers, many of whom have met with tremendous success.

With the Musical Child in Russia

The Russian parent usually has such a keen love for music that the child is watched from the very first for some indication that it may have musical talent. The parent knows how much music brings into the life of the child and he never looks upon the art as an accomplishment for exhibition purposes, but rather as a source of great joy. Music is fostered in the home as a part of the daily existence. Indeed, business is kept far from the Russian fireside and the atmosphere of most homes of intelligent people is that of culture rather than commerce. If the child is really musical the whole household is seized with the ambition to produce an artist. In my own case, I was taught the rudiments of music at so early an age that I have no recollection of ever having learned how to begin. It came to me just as talking does with the average child. At five I could sing some of the Schumann songs and some of those of Beethoven.

The Kind of Music The Russian Child Hears

The Russian child is spared all contact with really bad music. That is, he hears for the most part either the songs of the people or little selections from classical or romantic composers that are selected especially with the view of cultivating his talent. He has practically no opportunity to come in contact with any music that might be described as banal. America is a very young country and with the tension that one sees in American life on all sides there comes a tendency to accept music that may be most charitably described as "cheap." Very often the same themes found in this music, skilfully treated, would make worthy musical compositions. "Rag-time," and by this I refer to the peculiar rhythm and not to the bad music that Americans have come to class under this head, has a peculiar fascination for me. There is nothing objectionable about the unique rhythm, any more than there is anything iniquitous about the gypsy melodies that have made such excellent material for Brahms, Liszt and Sarasate. The fault lies in the clumsy presentation of the matter and its associations with vulgar words. The rhythm is often fascinating and exhilarating. Perhaps some day some American composer will glorify it in the Scherzo of a Symphony.

In Russia, teachers lay great stress upon careful grading. Many teachers of note have prepared carefully graded lists of pieces, suitable to each stage of advancement. I understand that this same purpose is accomplished in America by the publication of volumes of the music itself in different grades, although I have never seen any of these collections. The Russian teacher of children takes great care that the advancement of the pupil is not too rapid. The pupil is expected to be able to perform all the pieces in one grade acceptably before going to the next grade. I have had numerous American pupils and most of them seem to have the fault of wanting to advance to a higher step long before they are really able. This is very wrong, and the pupil who insists upon such a course will surely realize some day that instead of advancing rapidly he is really throwing many annoying obstacles directly in his own path.

INSTRUCTION BOOKS

Many juvenile instruction books are used in Russia just as in America. Some teachers, however, find that with pupils starting at an advanced age it is better to teach the rudiments without a book. This matter of method is of far greater importance than the average teacher will admit. The teacher often makes the mistake of living up in the clouds with Beethoven, Bach, Chopin, and Brahms, never realizing that the pupil is very much upon the earth, and that no matter how grandly the teacher may play, the pupil must have practical assistance within his grasp. The main duty in all elementary work is to make the piano study interesting, and the teacher must choose the course likely to arouse the most interest in the particular pupil.

OPPORTUNITIES FOR VIRTUOSO-STUDENTS IN RUSSIA

It may surprise the American student to hear that there are really more opportunities for him to secure public appearances right here in his own country than in Russia. In fact, it is really very hard to get a start in Russia unless one is able to attract the attention of the public very forcibly. In America the standard may not be so high as that demanded in the musical circles of Russia, but the student has many chances to play that would never come to him in the old world. There, the only chance for the young virtuoso is at the conservatory concerts. There are many music schools in Russia that must content themselves with private recitals, but the larger conservatories have public concerts of much importance, concerts that demand the attendance of renowned artists and compel the serious interest of the press. However, these concerts are few and far between, and only one student out of many hundreds has a chance to appear at them.

One singular custom obtains in Russia in reference to concerts. The pianist coming from some other European country is paid more than the local pianist. For instance, although I am Russian by birth, I reside in Germany and receive a higher rate when I play in Russia than does the resident artist. In fact, this rate is often double. The young virtuoso in the early stages of his career receives about one hundred roubles an appearance in Russia, while the mature artist receives from 800 to 1000. The rouble, while having an exchange value of only fifty cents in United States currency, has a purchasing value of about one dollar in Russia.

Why Russian Pianists Are Famed For Technic

The Russian pianist is always famed for his technical ability. Even the mediocre artists possess that. The great artists realize that the mechanical side of piano playing is but the basis, but they would no sooner think of trying to do without that basis than they would of dispensing with the beautiful artistic temples which they build upon the substantial foundation which technic gives to them. The Russian pianists have earned fame for their technical grasp because they give adequate study to the matter. Everything is done in the most solid, substantial manner possible. They build not upon sands, but upon rock. For instance, in the conservatory examinations the student is examined first upon technic. If he fails to pass the technical examination he is not even asked to perform his pieces. Lack of proficiency in technic is taken as an indication of a lack of the right preparation and study, just as the lack of the ability to speak simple phrases correctly would be taken as a lack of preparation in the case of the actor.

"Particular attention is given to the mechanical side of technic, the exercises, scales and arpeggios. American readers should understand that the full course at the leading Russian conservatories is one of about eight or nine years. During the first five years, the pupil is supposed to be building the base upon which must rest the more advanced work of the artist. The last three or four years at the conservatory are given over to the study of master works. Only pupils who manifest great talent are permitted to remain during the last year. During the first five years the backbone of the daily work in all Russian schools is scales and arpeggios. All technic reverts to these simple materials and the student is made to understand this from his very entrance to the conservatory. As the time goes on the scales and arpeggios become more difficult, more varied, more rapid, but they are never omitted from the daily work. The pupil who attempted complicated pieces without this preliminary technical drill would be laughed at in Russia. I have been amazed to find pupils coming from America who have been able to play a few pieces fairly well, but who wonder why they find it difficult to extend their musical sphere when the whole trouble lies in an almost total absence of regular daily technical work systematically pursued through several years.

"Of course, there must be other technical material in addition to scales, but the highest technic, broadly speaking, may be traced back to scales and arpeggios. The practice of scales and arpeggios need never be mechanical or uninteresting. This depends upon the attitude of mind in which the teacher places the pupil. In fact, the teacher is largely responsible if the pupil finds scale practice dry or tiresome. It is because the pupil has not been given enough to think about in scale playing, not enough to look out for in nuance, evenness, touch, rhythm, etc., etc.

Modern Russian Influence in Musical Art

"Most musicians of to-day appreciate the fact that in many ways the most modern effects sought by the composers who seek to produce extremely new effects have frequently been anticipated in Russia. However, one signal difference exists between the Russians with ultra-modern ideas and the composers of other nations. The Russian's advanced ideas are almost always the result of a development as were those of Wagner, Verdi, Grieg, Haydn and Beethoven. That is, constant study and investigations have led them to see things in a newer and more radical way. In the case of such composers as Debussy, Strauss, Ravel, Reger and others of the type of musical Philistine it will be observed that to all intents and purposes, they started out as innovators. Schönberg is the most recent example. How long will it take the world to comprehend his message if he really has one? Certainly, at the present time, even the admirers of the bizarre in music must pause before they confess that they understand the queer utterings of this newest claimant for the palm of musical eccentricity. With Debussy, Strauss and others it is different, for the skilled musician at once recognizes an astonishing facility to produce effects altogether new and often wonderfully fascinating. With Reger one seems to be impressed with tremendous effort and little result. Strauss, however, is really a very great master; so great that it is difficult to get the proper perspective upon his work at this time. It is safe to say that all the modern composers of the world have been influenced in one way or another by the great Russian masters of to-day and yesterday. Tchaikovsky, Rimsky-Korsakov, Cui, Glazounov, Rachmaninov, Moussorgsky, Arensky, Scriabine and others, have all had a powerful bearing upon the musical thought of the times. Their virility and character have been due to the newness of the field in which they worked. The influence of the compositions of Rubinstein and Glinka can hardly be regarded as Russian since they were so saturated with European models that they might be ranked with Gluck, Mendelssohn, Liszt and Meyerbeer far better than with their fellow-countrymen who have expressed the idiom of Russia with greater veracity."

QUESTIONS IN STYLE, INTERPRETATION, EXPRESSION
AND TECHNIC OF PIANOFORTE PLAYING

SERIES XI

JOSEF LHÉVINNE

1. Is music a part of the daily life of the child in the Russian home?

2. In what does the Russian teacher of children take great care?

3. Why are Russian pianists famed for their technical ability?

4. How are examinations conducted in Russia?

5. What would be thought of the Russian pupil who attempted pieces without the proper preliminary scale work?

6. Need the practice of scales be mechanical and uninteresting?

7. Why do some pupils find technical studies tiresome?

8. How does Russian musical progress in composition differ from that of other musical nations?

9. Has Russian music influenced the progress of other musical nations?

10. How may the compositions of Rubinstein and Glinka be regarded?

VLADIMIR DE PACHMANN

BIOGRAPHICAL

Vladimir de Pachmann was born at Odessa, Russia, July 27, 1848. His first teacher was his father, who was a musical enthusiast and a fine performer upon the violin. The elder de Pachmann was a Professor of Law at the University of Vienna and at first did not desire to have his son become anything more than a cultured amateur. In his youth de Pachmann was largely self taught and aside from hearing great virtuosos at concerts and modeling his playing to some extent after theirs he had no teachers until 1866 when he went to the Vienna Conservatory to study with the then celebrated teacher, Joseph Dachs. Dachs was a concert pianist of the old school. Academic perfection was his goal and he could not understand such a pupil as de Pachmann who was able to get results by what seemed un-academic means. After one year with Dachs de Pachmann toured Russia with great success and since then has made repeated tours of the entire musical world. He never gave any serious attention to musical composition. As an interpreter of the works of Chopin no one in recent times has ever excelled de Pachmann, but he also gave numerous recitals showing a great breadth of style in the performances of works of the other great masters particularly Brahms and Liszt.

(The following conference was conducted in English, German, French and Italian.)

14

SEEKING ORIGINALITY
VLADIMIR DE PACHMANN

THE MEANING OF ORIGINALITY

"ORIGINALITY in pianoforte playing, what does it really mean? Nothing more than the interpretation of one's real self instead of the artificial self which traditions, mistaken advisors and our own natural sense of mimicry impose upon us. Seek for originality and it is gone like a gossamer shining in the morning grass. Originality is in one's self. It is the true voice of the heart. I would enjoin students to listen to their own inner voices. I do not desire to deprecate teachers, but I think that many teachers are in error when they fail to encourage their pupils to form their own opinions.

"I have always sought the individual in myself. When I have found him I play at my best. I try to do everything in my own individual way. I work for months to invent, contrive or design new fingerings— not so much for simplicity, but to enable me to manipulate the keys so that I may express the musical thought as it seems to me it ought to be expressed. See my hand, my fingers—the flesh as soft as that of a child, yet covering muscles of steel. They are thus because I have worked from childhood to make them thus.

"The trouble with most pupils in studying a piece

is that when they seek individuality and originality, they go about it in the wrong way, and the result is a studied, stiff, hard performance. Let them listen to the voice, I say; to the inner voice, the voice which is speaking every moment of the day, but to which so many shut the ears of their soul.

"Franz Liszt—ah, you see I bow when I mention the name—you never heard Franz Liszt? Ah, it was the great Liszt who listened—listened to his inner voice. They said he was inspired. He was simply listening to himself.

MACHINE TEACHING

"*Nun, passen Sie mal auf!* I abominate machine teaching. A certain amount of it may be necessary, but I hate it. It seems so brutal—so inartistic. Instead of leading the pupil to seek results for himself, they lay down laws and see that these laws are obeyed, like *gendarmes*. It is possible, of course, by means of systematic training, to educate a boy so that he could play a concerto which he could not possibly comprehend intelligently until he became at least twenty years older; but please tell, what is the use of such a training? Is it artistic? Is it musical? Would it not be better to train him to play a piece which he could comprehend and which he could express in his own way?

"Of course I am not speaking now of the boy Mozarts, the boy Liszts or other freaks of nature, but of the children who by machine-made methods are made to do things which nature never intended that they should do. This forcing method to which some conservatories seem addicted reminds one of those men who in bygone ages made a specialty of disfiguring the forms and faces of children, to make dwarfs, jesters and freaks out of them. Bah!

ORIGINALITY THE ROAD TO PERMANENT FAME

"Originality in interpretation is of course no more important than originality in creation. See how the composers who have been the most original have been the ones who have laid the surest foundation for permanent fame. Here again true originality has been merely the highest form of self-expression. *Non é vero?* When the composer has sought originality and contrived to get it by purposely taking out-of-the-way methods, what has he produced? Nothing but a horrible sham—a structure of cards which is destroyed by the next wind of fashion.

"Other composers write for all time. They are original because they listen to the little inner voice, the true source of originality. It is the same in architecture. Styles in architecture are evolved, not created, and whenever the architect has striven for bizarre effects he builds for one decade only. The architects who build for all time are different and yet how unlike, how individual, how original is the work of one great architect from that of another.

THE MOST ORIGINAL COMPOSERS

"The most original of all composers, at least as they appear to me, is Johann Sebastian Bach. Perhaps this is because he is the most sincere. Next I should class Beethoven, that great mountain peak to whose heights so few ever soar. Then would come in order Liszt, Brahms, Schumann, Chopin, Weber, and Mendelssohn. Schumann more original than Chopin? Yes, at least so it seems to me. That is, there is something more distinctive, something more indicative of a great individuality speaking a new language.

"Compare these men with composers of the order of Abt, Steibelt, Thalberg, and Donizetti, and you will see at once what I mean about originality being the basis of permanent art. For over twenty years my great fondness for mineralogy and for gems led me to neglect in a measure the development of the higher works of these composers, but I have realized my error and have been working enormously for years to attain the technic which their works demand. Some years ago I felt that technical development must cease at a certain age. This is all idiocy. I feel that I have now many times the technic I have ever had before and I have acquired it all in recent years.

SELF-HELP THE SECRET OF MANY SUCCESSES

"No one could possibly believe more in self-help than I. The student who goes to a teacher and imagines that the teacher will cast some magic spell about him which will make him a musician without working, has an unpleasant surprise in store for him. When I was eighteen I went to Dachs at the Vienna Conservatory. He bade me play something. I played the *Rigoletto* paraphrase of Liszt. Dachs commented favorably upon my touch but assured me that I was very much upon the wrong track and that I should study the *Woltemperirtes Klavier* of Bach. He assured me that no musical education could be considered complete without an intimate acquaintance with the Bach fugues, which of course was most excellent advice.

"Consequently I secured a copy of the fugues and commenced work upon them. Dachs had told me to prepare the first prelude and fugue for the following lesson. But Dachs was not acquainted with my methods of study. He did not know that I had mastered the art of concentration so that I could obliterate every suggestion of any other thought from my mind except that upon which I was working. He had no estimate of my youthful zeal and intensity. He did not know that I could not be satisfied unless I spent the entire day working with all my artistic might and main.

"Soon I saw the wonderful design of the great master of Eisenach. The architecture of the fugues became plainer and plainer. Each subject became a friend and each answer likewise. It was a great joy to observe with what marvelous craftsmanship he had built up the wonderful structures. I could not stop when I had memorized the first fugue, so I went to the next and the next and the next.

A Surprised Teacher

"At the following lesson I went with my book under my arm. I requested him to name a fugue. He did, and I placed the closed book on the rack before me. After I had finished playing he was dumfounded. He said, 'You come to me to take lessons. You already know the great fugues and I have taught you nothing.' Thinking that I would find Chopin more difficult to memorize, he suggested that I learn two of the etudes. I came at the following lesson with the entire twenty-four memorized. Who could withstand the alluring charm of the Chopin etudes? Who could resist the temptation to learn them all when they are once commenced?

"An actor learns page after page in a few days, and why should the musician go stumbling along for months in his endeavor to learn something which he could master in a few hours with the proper interest and the burning concentration without which all music study is a farce?

"It was thus during my entire course with Dachs. He would suggest the work and I would go off by myself and learn it. I had practically no method. Each page demanded a different method. Each page presented entirely new and different technical ideas."

DEEP THOUGHT NECESSARY

"As a rule piano students do not think deeply enough. They skim over the really difficult things and no amount of persuasion will make them believe some very simple things difficult. Take the scale of C Major, for instance. This scale is by far the most difficult of all. To play it with true legato, at any desired degree of force or speed, in any desired rhythm and with any desired touch, is one of the most difficult achievements in all music. Yet the young pupil will literally turn up his nose at the scale of C Major and at the same time claim that he is perfectly competent to play a Beethoven Sonata.

"The scale of C should be learned step by step until the practice habits are so formed that they will reign supreme while playing all the other scales. This is the way to secure results—go deep into things. Pearls lie at the bottom of the sea. Most pupils seem to expect them floating upon the surface of the water. They never float, and the one who would have his scales shine with the beauty of splendid gems must first dive deep for the gems.

"But what is the use of saying all this? To tell it to young pupils seems to be a waste of words. They will go on making their mistakes and ignoring the advice of their teachers and mentors until the great teacher of all—experience—forces them to dive for the hidden riches.

Take Time To Do Things Well

"Every pianist advances at a rate commensurate with his personal ability. Some pianists are slow in development. Others with wonderful natural gifts go ahead very quickly. The student will see some pianist make wonderful progress and will sometimes imitate him without giving the time or effort to study that the other pianist has given. The artist will spend months upon a Chopin valse. The student feels injured if he cannot play it in a day.

"Look, I will play the wonderful Nocturne of Chopin in G, Opus No. 2. The legato thirds seem simple? Ah, if I could only tell you of the years that are behind those thirds. The human mind is peculiar in its methods of mastering the movements of the fingers, and to get a great masterpiece so that you can have supreme control over it at all times and under all conditions demands a far greater effort than the ordinary non-professional music lover can imagine.

Mastering Artistic Details

"Each note in a composition should be polished until it is as perfect as a jewel—as perfect as an Indian diamond—those wonderful scintillating, ever-changing orbs of light. In a really great masterpiece each note has its place just as the stars, the jewels of heaven, have their places in their constellations. When a star moves it moves in an orbit that was created by nature.

"Great musical masterpieces owe their existence to mental forces quite as miraculous as those which put the heavens into being. The notes in compositions of this kind are not there by any rule of man. They come through the ever mystifying source which we call inspiration. Each note must bear a distinct relation to the whole.

"An artist in jewels in making a wonderful work of art does not toss his jewels together in any haphazard way. He often has to wait for months to get the right ruby, or the right pearl, or the right diamond to fit in the right place. Those who do not know might think one gem just like another, but the artist knows. He has been looking at gems, examining them under the microscope. There is a meaning in every facet, in every shade of color. He sees blemishes which the ordinary eye would never detect.

"Finally he secures his jewels and arranges them in some artistic form, which results in a masterpiece. The public does not know the reason why, but it will instantly realize that the work of the artist is in some mysterious way superior to the work of the bungler. Thus it is that the mind of the composer works spontaneously in selecting the musical jewels for the diadem which is to crown him with fame. During the process of inspiration he does not realize that he is selecting his jewels with lightning rapidity, but with a highly cultivated artistic judgment. When the musical jewels are collected and assembled he regards the work as a whole as the work of another. He does not realize that he has been going through the process of collecting them. Schubert failed to recollect some of his own compositions only a few days after he had written them.

Something No One Can Teach

"Now the difficulty with students is that they do not take time to polish the jewels which the composers have selected with such keen æsthetic discernment. They think it enough if they merely succeed in playing the note. How horrible! A machine can play the notes, but there is only one machine with a soul and that is the artist. To think that an artist should play only the notes and forget the glories of the inspiration which came in the composer's mind during the moment of creation.

"Let me play the D flat Chopin Nocturne for you. Please notice how the notes all bear a relation to each other, how everything is in right proportion. Do you think that came in a day? Ah, my friend, the polishing of those jewels took far longer than the polishing of the Kohinoor. Yet I have heard young girls attempt to play this piece for me—expecting approbation, of course, and I am certain that they could not have practiced upon it more than a year or so. They evidently think that musical masterpieces can be brought into being like the cobwebs which rise during the night to be torn down by the weight of the dew of the following morning. *Imbecillità!*

The Best Teacher

"They play just as their teachers have told them to play, which is of course good as far as it goes. But they stop at that, and no worthy teacher expects his pupil to stop with his instruction. The best teacher is the one who incites his pupil to penetrate deeper and learn new beauties by himself. A teacher in the highest sense of the word is not a mint, coining pupils as it were and putting the same stamp of worth upon each pupil.

"The great teacher is an artist who works in men and women. Every pupil is different, and he must be very quick to recognize these differences. He should first of all teach the pupil that there are hundreds of things which no teacher can ever hope to teach. He must make his pupil keenly alert to this. There are hundreds of things about my own playing which are virtually impossible to teach. I would not know how to convey them to others so that they might be intelligently learned. Such things I have found out for myself by long and laborious experimentation. The control of my fifth finger in certain fingerings presented endless problems which could only be worked out at the keyboard. Such things give an individuality to the pianist's art, something which cannot be copied.

"Have you ever been in a foreign art gallery and watched the copyists trying to reproduce the works of the masters? Have you ever noticed that though they get the form, the design, and even tne colors and also that with all these resemblances there is something which distinguishes the work of the master from the work of the copyist, something so wonderful that even a child can see it? You wonder at this? *Pourquoi?* No one can learn by copying the secret the master has learned in creating.

THE BASIS OF GREATNESS

"Here we have a figure which brings out very clearly the real meaning of originality in piano playing and at the same time indicates how every pupil with or without a teacher should work for himself. Why was the great Liszt greater than any pianist of his time? Simply because he found out certain pianistic secrets which Czerny or any of Liszt's teachers and contemporaries had failed to discover.

"Why has Godowsky—*Ach! Godowsky, der ist wirklich ein grosser Talent*—how has he attained his wonderful rank? Because he has worked out certain contrapuntal and technical problems which place him in a class all by himself. I consider him the greatest master of the mysteries of counterpoint since the heyday of classical polyphony. Why does Busoni produce inimitable results at the keyboard? Simply because he was not satisfied to remain content with the knowledge he had obtained from others.

"This then is my life secret—work, unending work. I have no other secrets. I have developed myself along the lines revealed to me by my inner voice. I

have studied myself as well as my art.   I have learned
to study mankind through the sciences and through
the great literary treasures, you see; I speak many
languages fluently, I have stepped apace with the
crowd, I have drunk the bitter and the sweet from the
chalices of life, but remember, I have never stopped,
and to-day I am just as keenly interested in my progress as I was many years ago as a youth.   The new
repertoire of the works of Liszt and Brahms and other
composers demanded a different technic, a bigger
technic.   What exquisite joy it was to work for it.
Yes, *mio amico*, work is the greatest intoxication, the
greatest blessing, the greatest solace we can know.
Therefore work, work, work.   But of all things, my
good musical friends in America, remember the old
German proverb:

> " '*Das mag die beste Musik sein*
> *Wenn Herz und Mund stimmt überein.*' "

("Music is best when the heart and lips (mouth)
speak together.")

QUESTIONS IN STYLE, INTERPRETATION, EXPRESSION
AND TECHNIC OF PIANOFORTE PLAYING

SERIES XII

VLADIMIR DE PACHMANN

1. What does originality in pianoforte playing really mean?

2. State something of the evils of the forcing methods of training applied to young children.

3. Have the compositions of the most original composers been the most enduring?

4. Name seven of the most original composers for the pianoforte.

5. Must the pupil continually help himself?

6. What is considered the most difficult scale to learn?

7. Is a great virtuoso obliged to practice years in order to secure results?

8. How may piano study be compared with the polishing of beautiful jewels?

9. Tell what characteristics a great teacher must have.

10. What lies at the foundation of pianistic greatness?

MAX PAUER

BIOGRAPHICAL

Prof. Max Pauer was born in London, England, October 31, 1866, and is the son of the eminent musical educator, Ernst Pauer, who settled in England in 1851, and aside from filling many of the foremost positions in British musical life, also produced a great number of instructive works, which have been of immeasurable value in disseminating musical education in England. His work on *Musical Forms* is known to most all music students. Prof. Max Pauer studied with his father at the same time his parent was instructing another famous British-born pianist, Eugen d'Albert. At the age of fifteen he went to Karlsruhe, where he came under the instruction of V. Lachner. In 1885 he returned to London and continued to advance through self-study. In 1887 he received the appointment at the head of the piano department in the Cologne Conservatory. This position he retained for ten years, until his appointment at Stuttgart, first as head teacher in the piano department and later as director of the School. During this period the organization of the famous old conservatory has changed totally. The building occupied was very old and unfit for modern needs. The new conservatory building is a splendid structure located in one of the most attractive parts of the city. The old methods, old equipment, old ideas have been abandoned, and a wholly different atmosphere is said to pervade the institution, while all that was best in the old *régime* has been retained. Prof. Pauer made his *début* as a virtuoso pianist in London. Since then he has toured all Europe except the Latin countries. He has published several compositions for the piano. His present tour of America is his first in the New World

15

MODERN PIANISTIC PROBLEMS
MAX PAUER

Acquiring The Requisite Technic

"The preservation of one's individuality in playing is perhaps one of the most difficult, and at the same time one of the most essential tasks in the study of the pianoforte. The kind of technical study that passes the student through a certain process, apparently destined to make him as much like his predecessors as possible, is hardly the kind of technic needed to make a great artist. Technical ability, after all is said and done, depends upon nothing more than physiologically correct motion applied to the artistic needs of the masterpiece to be performed. It implies a clear understanding of the essentials in bringing out the composer's idea. The pupil must not be confused with inaccurate thinking. For instance, we commonly hear of the 'wrist touch.' More pupils have been hindered through this clumsy terminology than I should care to estimate. There cannot be a wrist touch since the wrist is nothing more than a wonderful natural hinge of bone and muscle. With the pupil's mind centered upon his wrist he is more than likely to stiffen it and form habits which can only be removed with much difficulty by the teacher. This is only an instance of one of the loose expressions with which the terminology of technic is encumbered. When the pupil comes to recognize the wrist as a *condition* rather than a thing he will find that the matter of the tight, cramped wrist will cease to have its terrors.   In fact, as far as touch itself is concerned, the motion of the arm as a whole is vastly more important than that of the wrist. The wrist is merely part of the apparatus which communicates the weight of the arm to the keyboard.

INNOVATORS SHOULD BE PIANISTS

"In my opinion the technical needs of the piano are likely to be far better understood by the virtuoso pianist than by one who has never been through the experiences which lead to the concert platform. Please do not infer that I would say that all teachers should be virtuoso pianists. I am referring particularly to the makers of methods.   I am continually confronted in my teaching with all manner of absurd ideas in piano technic. For instance, one pupil will come and exhibit an exercise which requires her to press hard upon the keyboard after the note is struck. Just why there should be this additional waste of nerve force when it can have no possible effect upon the depressed key I have never been able to find out. There is enough nervous energy expended in pianoforte study as it is without exacting any more from the pupil. Pupils are frequently carried away with some technical trick of this kind like a child with a new toy. They do these things without ever consulting their own judgment."

The whole idea of technic then is to achieve a position *through* conscious effort, where one may *dispense with* conscious effort. Not until this can be accomplished can we hope for real self-expression in playing. Nothing is so odious as the obtrusion of technic in any work of art. Technic is the trellis concealed beneath the foliage and the blossoms of the bower. When the artist is really great all idea of technic is forgotten. He must be absorbed by the sheer beauty of his musical message, his expression of his musical self. In listening to Rubinstein or to Liszt one forgot all idea of technic, and it must be so with all great artists in every branch of art in every age. What we claim when we attend a recital is the individual artist, unrestrained by mechanical bonds.

Very few of the great masters of pianoforte playing have delved very deeply into the technical pedagogical side of their art, as for instance have Tausig, Ehrlich or Joseffy, all of whom have produced remarkable works on technic. Liszt's contribution to the technic of the instrument was made through his pieces, not through exercises; his contributions to the Lebert and Stark Stuttgart Conservatory method consist of two well-known concert studies. Personally, I am opposed to set methods, that is, those that pretend to teach the pupil factory-wise. Of what value is the teacher if he is not to apply his knowledge with the discretion that comes with experience?

Deppe's influence to this day is far more theoretical

than practical.   This does not imply that Deppe did
not evolve some very useful ideas in pianoforte work.
All of present technic is a common heritage from many
investigators and innovators.   Pianoforte teaching,
as a matter of fact, is one of the most difficult of all
tasks.   It is easy to teach it along conventional
"cut and dried" method lines, but the teachers of
real importance are those who have the ability, the
gift, the inclination and the experience to make a
brand new method for every pupil.

In order to develop the means to communicate
one's message through one's art with the greatest
effectiveness, there must be a mastery of the delicate
balance between natural tendencies and discipline.
If the student is subjected to too much discipline,
stiff, angular results may be expected.   If the student
is permitted to play with the flabby looseness which
some confuse with natural relaxation, characterless
playing must invariably result.   The great desidera-
tum is the fine equilibrium between nature and discipline.   This may seem an unnecessary observation
to some, but many students never seem to be able to
strike the happy medium between marching over the
keys like a regiment of wooden soldiers, or crawling
over them like a lot of spineless caterpillars.

Avoid Machine-like Playing

There is a certain "something" which defines the
individuality of the player, and it seems well nigh
impossible to say just what this something is.   Let us

by all means preserve it. Imagine the future of music if every piece were to be played in the selfsame way by every player like a series of ordinary piano playing machines. The remarkable apparatus for recording the playing of virtuosos, and then reproducing it through a mechanical contrivance, is somewhat of a revelation to the pianist who tries it for the first time. In the records of the playing of artists whose interpretations are perfectly familiar to me, there still remain unquestioned marks of individuality. Sometimes these marks are small shortcomings, but which, nevertheless, are so slight that they do no more than give character. Look at a painting by Van Dyke, and then at one upon a similar subject by Rembrandt, and you will realize how these little characteristics influence the whole outward aspect of an art work. Both Van Dyke and Rembrandt were Dutchmen, and, in a sense, contemporaries. They used pigments and brushes, canvas and oil, yet the masterpieces of each are readily distinguishable by any one slightly familiar with their styles. It is precisely the same with pianists. All of us have arms, fingers, muscles and nerves, but what we have to say upon the keyboard should be an expression of our own minds, not a replica of some stereotyped model.

When I listened to the first record of my own playing, I heard things which seemed unbelievable to me. Was I, after years of public playing, actually making mistakes that I would be the first to condemn in any one of my own pupils? I could hardly believe my ears, and yet the unrelenting machine showed that in some places I had failed to play both hands exactly together, and had been guilty of other errors no less heinous, because they were trifling. I also learned in listening to my own playing, as reproduced, that I had unconsciously brought out certain nuances, emphasized different voices and employed special accents without the consciousness of having done so. Altogether it made a most interesting study for me, and it became very clear that the personality of the artist must permeate everything that he does. When his technic is sufficiently great it permits him to speak with fluency and self-expression, enhancing the value of his work a thousandfold.

Broad Understanding Necessary

"It would be a great mistake for the student to imagine that by merely acquiring finger dexterity and a familiarity with a certain number of pieces he may consider himself proficient. There is vastly more to piano-playing than that. He must add to his digital ability and his repertoire and comprehensive grasp of the principles of music itself. The pupil should strive to accomplish as much as possible through mental work. The old idea of attempting to play every single study written by Czerny, or Cramer or the other prolific writers of studies is a huge mistake. A judicious selection from the works of these pedagogical writers is desirable but certainly not all of them. They are at best only the material with which one must work for a certain aim, and that aim should be high artistic results. It should be realized by all students and teachers that this same study material, excellent in itself, may actually produce bad results if not properly practiced. I have repeatedly watched students practicing industriously, but becoming worse and worse and actually cultivating faults rather than approaching perfection. The student must always remember that his fingers are only the outward organs of his inner consciousness, and while his work may be mechanical in part he should never think mechanically. The smallest technical exercise must have its own direction, its own aim. Nothing should be done without some definite purpose in view. The student should have pointed out to him just what the road he must travel is, and where it leads to. The ideal teacher is the one who gives the pupil something to take home and work out at home, not the one who works out the student's lesson for him in the class room. The teacher's greatest mission is to raise the consciousness of the pupil until he can appreciate his own powers for developing an idea.

FREEDOM FROM CONVENTION

"Oh the horror of the conventional, the absolutely right, the human machine who cannot make an error! The balance between the frigidly correct and the abominably loose is a most difficult one to maintain. It is, of course, desirable that the young student pass through a certain period of strict discipline, but if

this discipline succeeds in making an automaton, of
what earthly use is it?   Is it really necessary to instruct our little folks to think that everything must be
done in a "cut and dried" manner?   Take the simple
matter of time, for instance.   Listen to the playing
of most young pupils and you will hear nothing but a
kind of "railroad train" rhythm.   Every measure
bumps along precisely like the last one.   The pupil
has been taught to observe the bar signs like stone
walls partitioning the whole piece off into sections.
The result as a whole is too awful to describe.   As a
matter of fact, the bar signs, necessary as they are as
guide-posts when we are learning the elements of
notation, are often the means of leading the poorly
trained pupil to a wholly erroneous interpretation.
For instance, in a passage like the following from
Beethoven's F minor Sonata, Opus 2, No. 1 (dedicated
to Joseph Haydn), Beethoven's idea must have been
the following:

before it was divided into measures by bar lines as
now found printed:

The trouble with the pupil in playing the above is that he seems inclined to observe the bar lines very carefully and lose all idea of the phrase as a whole. Music should be studied by phrases, not by measures. In studying a poem you strive first of all to get the poet's meaning as expressed in his phrases and in his sentences; you do not try to mumble a few words in an arbitrary manner. The pupil who never gets over the habit of playing in measures, who never sees the composer's message as a whole rather than in little segments can never play artistically. Many students fail to realize that in some pieces it is actually misleading to count the beats in the measure. The rhythm of the piece as a whole is often marked by a series of measures, and one must count the measures as units rather than the notes in the measures. For instance, the following section from a Chopin Valse, Opus 64, No. 1 (sometimes called the *Minute Valse*), may best be counted by counting the measures thus:

Every pupil knows that the first beat in each ordinary measure of four-quarter time carries a strong accent, the third beat the next strongest, and the second and fourth beats still weaker accents. In a series of measures which may be counted in fours, it will be found that the same arrangement often prevails. The pupil will continually meet opportunities to study his work along broader lines, and the wonderful part. of it all is that music contains so much that is interesting and surprising, that there need be no end to his investigations. Every page from a master work that has been studied for years is likely to contain some unsolved problem if the student can only see it right and hunt for it.

Questions in Style, Interpretation, Expression and Technic of Pianoforte Playing

SERIES XIII

MAX PAUER

1. Define technical ability.
2. Describe some useless technical tricks.
3. Do great pianists devote much time to writing upon piano technic?
4. State the evils of too much discipline.
5. How may machine-like playing be avoided?
6. State how faults are most frequently developed.
7. Why must one seek to avoid conventions?
8. Should music be studied by phrases or measures?
9. Play the Chopin Valse Opus 64, No 1, indicating how it may best be counted.
10. Where must the student find his problems?

S. V. RACHMANINOFF

BIOGRAPHICAL

Sergei Vassilievitch Rachmaninoff was born at Novgorod, Russia, April 1st, 1873. At the Moscow Conservatory he was placed under the instruction of Siloti who had been one of the favorite Russian pupils of Franz Liszt. This master imparted a very facile technic to Rachmaninoff and made him so thoroughly acquainted with the best literature of the instrument that his compositions became recognized at once as those of a thorough master of the keyboard. His teacher in composition was Arensky, who in addition to his skill in the technic of the art had a fund of melody which is a delight to all those who know his works. In 1891 Rachmaninoff won the great gold medal at the Moscow Conservatory and his work as a composer commenced to attract favorable attention throughout all Europe. In addition to this his ability as a pianist attracted wide notice and his tours have been very successful. His compositions have been cast in many different forms from opera to songs and piano pieces. His most popular work is *the Prelude in C Sharp Minor* which is in the repertoire of all advanced students. His appointment as Supervisor General of the Imperial conservatories of Russia was one of the highest distinctions that could be conferred in the land of the Czar. The correct pronunciation of the name as given by the composer is Rokh-mahn-ee-noff.

(The following conference was conducted in German.)

16

ESSENTIALS OF ARTISTIC PLAYING

S. V. RACHMANINOFF

FORMING THE PROPER CONCEPTION OF A PIECE

IT is a seemingly impossible task to define the number of attributes of really excellent pianoforte playing. By selecting ten important characteristics, however, and considering them carefully, one at a time, the student may learn much that will give him food for thought. After all, one can never tell in print what can be communicated by the living teacher. In undertaking the study of a new composition it is highly important to gain a conception of the work as a whole. One must comprehend the main design of the composer. Naturally, there are technical difficulties which must be worked out, measure by measure, but unless the student can form some idea of the work in its larger proportions his finished performance may resemble a kind of musical patchwork. Behind every composition is the architectural plan of the composer. The student should endeavor, first of all, to discover this plan, and then he should build in the manner in which the composer would have had him build.

You ask me, "How can the student form the proper conception of the work as a whole?" Doubtless the best way is to hear it performed by some pianist whose authority as an interpreter cannot be questioned.   However, many students are so situated that this course is impossible.   It is also often quite impossible for the teacher, who is busy teaching from morning to night, to give a rendering of the work that would be absolutely perfect in all of its details.   However, one can gain something from the teacher who can, by his genius, give the pupil an idea of the artistic demands of the piece.

If the student has the advantage of hearing neither the virtuoso nor the teacher he need not despair, if he has *talent*.   Talent!   Ah, that is the great thing in all musical work.   If he has talent he will see with the eyes of talent—that wonderful force which penetrates all artistic mysteries and reveals the truths as nothing else possibly can.   Then he grasps, as if by intuition, the composer's intentions in writing the work, and, like the true interpreter, communicates these thoughts to his audience in their proper form.

TECHNICAL PROFICIENCY

It goes without saying, that technical proficiency should be one of the first acquisitions of the student who would become a fine pianist.   It is impossible to conceive of fine playing that is not marked by clean, fluent, distinct, elastic technic.   The technical ability of the performer should be of such a nature that it can be applied immediately to all the artistic demands of the composition to be interpreted.   Of course, there may be individual passages which require some special technical study, but, generally speaking, technic is worthless unless the hands and the mind of the player are so trained that they can encompass the principal difficulties found in modern compositions.

In the music schools of Russia great stress is laid upon technic. Possibly this may be one of the reasons why some of the Russian pianists have been so favorably received in recent years. The work in the leading Russian conservatories is almost entirely under supervision of the Imperial Musical Society. The system is elastic in that, although all students are obliged to go through the same course, special attention is given to individual cases. Technic, however, is at first made a matter of paramount importance. All students must become technically proficient. None are excused. It may be interesting to hear something of the general plan followed in the Imperial music schools of Russia. The course is nine years in duration. During the first five years the student gets most of his technical instruction from a book of studies by Hanon, which is used very extensively in the conservatories. In fact, this is practically the only book of strictly technical studies employed. All of the studies are in the key of "C." They include scales, arpeggios, and other forms of exercises in special technical designs.

At the end of the fifth year an examination takes place. This examination is twofold. The pupil is examined first for proficiency in technic, and later for proficiency in artistic playing—pieces, studies, etc. However, if the pupil fails to pass the technical examination he is not permitted to go ahead. He knows the exercises in the book of studies by Hanon so well that he knows each study by number, and the examiner may ask him, for instance, to play study 17, or 28, or 32, etc. The student at once sits at the keyboard and plays.

Although the original studies are all in the key of "C," he may be requested to play them in any other key. He has studied them so thoroughly that he should be able to play them in any key desired. A metronomic test is also applied. The student knows that he will be expected to play the studies at certain rates of speed. The examiner states the speed and the metronome is started. The pupil is required, for instance, to play the E flat major scale with the metronome at 120, eight notes to the beat. If he is successful in doing this, he is marked accordingly, and other tests are given.

Personally, I believe this matter of insisting upon a thorough technical knowledge is a very vital one. The mere ability to play a few pieces does not constitute musical proficiency. It is like those music boxes which possess only a few tunes. The student's technical grasp should be all-embracing.

Later the student is given advanced technical exercises, like those of Tausig. Czerny is also very deservedly popular. Less is heard of the studies of Henselt, however, notwithstanding his long service in Russia. Henselt's studies are so beautiful that they should rather be classed with pieces like the studies of Chopin.

PROPER PHRASING

An artistic interpretation is not possible if the student does not know the laws underlying the very important subject of phrasing. Unfortunately many editions of good music are found wanting in proper phrase markings. Some of the phrase signs are erroneously applied. Consequently the only safe way is for the student to make a special study of this important branch of musical art. In the olden days phrase signs were little used. Bach used them very sparingly. It was not necessary to mark them in those times, for every musician who counted himself a musician could determine the phrases as he played. But a knowledge of the means of defining phrases in a composition is by no means all-sufficient. Skill in executing the phrases is quite as important. The real musical feeling must exist in the mind of the composer or all the knowledge of correct phrasing he may possess will be worthless.

REGULATING THE TEMPO

If a fine musical feeling, or sensitiveness, must control the execution of the phrases, the regulation of the tempo demands a kind of musical ability no less exacting. Although in most cases the tempo of a given composition is now indicated by means

of the metronomic markings, the judgment of the
player must also be brought frequently into requisi-
tion. He cannot follow the tempo marks blindly,
although it is usually unsafe for him to stray very
far from these all-important musical sign-posts.
The metronome itself must not be used "with closed
eyes," as we should say it in Russia. The player
must use discretion. I do not approve of continual
practice with the metronome. The metronome is
designed to set the time, and if not abused is a very
faithful servant. However, it should only be used
for this purpose. The most mechanical playing
imaginable can proceed from those who make themselves slaves to this little musical clock, which was
never intended to stand like a ruler over every minute
of the student's practice time.

Character in Playing

Too few students realize that there is continual
and marvelous opportunity for contrast in playing.
Every piece is a piece unto itself. It should, therefore, have its own peculiar interpretation. There
are performers whose playing seems all alike. It
is like the meals served in some hotels Everything brought to the table has the same taste. Of
course, a successful performer must have a strong
individuality, and all of his interpretations must
bear the mark of this individuality, but at the same
time he should seek variety constantly. A Chopin
ballade must have quite a different interpretation

from a Scarlatti Capriccio. There is really very little in common between a Beethoven Sonata and a Liszt Rhapsody. Consequently, the student must seek to give each piece a different character. Each piece must stand apart as possessing an individual conception, and if the player fails to convey this impression to his audience, he is little better than some mechanical instrument. Josef Hofmann has the ability of investing each composition with an individual and characteristic charm that has always been very delightful to me.

The Significance of the Pedal

The pedal has been called the soul of the piano. I never realized what this meant until I heard Anton Rubinstein, whose playing seemed so marvelous to me that it beggars description. His mastery of the pedal was nothing short of phenomenal. In the last movement of the B flat minor sonata of Chopin he produced pedal effects that can never be described, but for any one who remembers them they will always be treasured as one of the greatest of musical joys. The pedal is the study of a lifetime. It is the most difficult branch of higher pianoforte study. Of course, one may make rules for its use, and the student should carefully study all these rules, but, at the same time, these rules may often be skilfully broken in order to produce some very charming effects. The rules represent a few known principles that are within the grasp of our musical intelligence. They may be compared with the planet upon which we live, and about which we know so much.   Beyond the rules, however, is the great universe—the celestial system which only the telescopic artistic sight of the great musician can penetrate.   This, Rubinstein, and some others, have done, bringing to our mundane vision undreamt-of beauties which they alone could perceive.

THE DANGER OF CONVENTION

While we must respect the traditions of the past, which for the most part are very intangible to us because they are only to be found in books, we must, nevertheless, not be bound down by convention. Iconoclasm is the law of artistic progress.   All great composers and performers have built upon the ruins of conventions that they themselves have destroyed. It is infinitely better to create than to imitate.   Before we can create, however, it is well to make ourselves familiar with the best that has preceded us.   This applies not only to composition, but to pianoforte playing as well.   The master pianists, Rubinstein and Liszt, were both marvelously broad in the scope of their knowledge.   They knew the literature of the pianoforte in all its possible branches.   They made themselves familiar with every possible phase of musical advancement.   This is the reason for their gigantic prominence.   Their greatness was not the hollow shell of acquired technic.   THEY KNEW.   Oh, for more students in these days with the genuine thirst for real musical knowledge, and not merely with the desire to make a superficial exhibition at the keyboard!

REAL MUSICAL UNDERSTANDING

I am told that some teachers lay a great deal of stress upon the necessity for the pupil learning the source of the composer's inspiration. This is interesting, of course, and may help to stimulate a dull imagination. However, I am convinced that it would be far better for the student to depend more upon his real musical understanding. It is a mistake to suppose that the knowledge of the fact that Schubert was inspired by a certain poem, or that Chopin was inspired by a certain legend, could ever make up for a lack of the real essentials leading to good pianoforte playing. The student must see, first of all, the main points of musical relationship in a composition. He must understand what it is that gives the work unity, cohesion, force, or grace, and must know how to bring out these elements. There is a tendency with some teachers to magnify the importance of auxiliary studies and minimize the importance of essentials. This course is wrong, and must lead to erroneous results.

PLAYING TO EDUCATE THE PUBLIC

The virtuoso must have some far greater motive than that of playing for gain. He has a mission, and that mission is to educate the public. It is quite as necessary for the sincere student in the home

to carry on this educational work. For this reason
it is to his advantage to direct his efforts toward
pieces which he feels will be of musical educational
advantage to his friends. In this he must use judgment and not overstep their intelligence too far.
With the virtuoso it is somewhat different. He expects, and even demands, from his audience a certain
grade of musical taste, a certain degree of musical
education. Otherwise he would work in vain. If
the public would enjoy the greatest in music they must
hear good music until these beauties become evident.

It would be useless for the virtuoso to attempt a
concert tour in the heart of Africa. The virtuoso
is expected to give his best, and he should not be
criticized by audiences that have not the mental
capacity to appreciate his work. The virtuosos look
to the students of the world to do their share in the
education of the great musical public. Do not waste
your time with music that is trite or ignoble. Life
is too short to spend it wandering in the barren Saharas
of musical trash.

THE VITAL SPARK

In all good pianoforte playing there is a vital spark
that seems to make each interpretation of a masterpiece—a living thing. It exists only for the moment,
and cannot be explained. For instance, two pianists
of equal technical ability may play the same composition. With one the playing is dull, lifeless and sapless,
with the other there is something that is indescribably

wonderful. His playing seems fairly to quiver with life. It commands interest and inspires the audience. What is this vital spark that brings life to mere notes? In one way it may be called the intense artistic interest of the player. It is that astonishing thing known as inspiration.

When the composition was originally written the composer was unquestionably inspired; when the performer finds the same joy that the composer found at the moment the composition came into existence, then something new and different enters his playing. It seems to be stimulated and invigorated in a manner altogether marvelous. The audience realizes this instantly, and will even sometimes forgive technical imperfections if the performance is inspired. Rubinstein was technically marvelous, and yet he admitted making mistakes. Nevertheless, for every possible mistake he may have made, he gave, in return, ideas and musical tone pictures that would have made up for a million mistakes. When Rubinstein was over-exact his playing lost something of its wonderful charm. I remember that upon one occasion he was playing Balakireff's *Islamei* at a concert. Something distracted his attention and he apparently forgot the composition entirely; but he kept on improvising in the style of the piece, and after about four minutes the remainder of the composition came back to him and he played it to the end correctly. This annoyed him greatly and he played the next number upon the program with the greatest exactness, but, strange to say, it lost the wonderful charm of the interpretation of the piece in which his memory had failed him.   Rubinstein was really incomparable, even more so perhaps because he was full of human impulse and his playing very far removed from mechanical perfection.

While, of course, the student must play the notes, and all of the notes, in the manner and in the time in which the composer intended that they should be played, his efforts should by no means stop with notes. Every individual note in a composition is important, but there is something quite as important as the notes, and that is the soul.   After all, the vital spark is the soul.   The soul is the source of that higher expression in music which cannot be represented in dynamic marks.   The soul feels the need for the *crescendos* and *diminuendos* intuitively.   The mere matter of the duration of a pause upon a note depends upon its significance, and the soul of the artist dictates to him just how long such a pause should be held. If the student resorts to mechanical rules and depends upon them absolutely, his playing will be soulless.

Fine playing requires much deep thought away from the keyboard.   The student should not feel that when the notes have been played his task is done.   It is, in fact, only begun.   He must make the piece a part of himself.   Every note must awaken in him a kind of musical consciousness of his real artistic mission.

QUESTIONS IN STYLE, INTERPRETATION, EXPRESSION
AND TECHNIC OF PIANOFORTE PLAYING

SERIES XIV

S. V. RACHMANINOFF

1. Should the student gain an idea of the work as a whole before attempting detailed study?

2. How is the matter of digital technic regarded in Russia?

3. What part should the study of phrasing play in modern music education?

4. State how contrast in playing may be accomplished.

5. What may be considered the most difficult branch of pianoforte study?

6. What is the law of artistic progress?

7. How must real musical understanding be achieved?

8. What is the vital spark in piano playing?

9. Can one be overexact in playing?

10. What is the effect of too many mechanical rules?

ALFRED REISENAUER

BIOGRAPHICAL

Alfred Reisenauer was born at Königsberg, Germany, Nov. 1st, 1863. He was a pupil of his mother, Louis Köhler, and Franz Liszt. His début as a pianist was made in Rome, in 1881, at the palace of Cardinal Hohenlohe. After a concert tour in Germany and a visit to England he studied Law for one year at the Leipsic University. Not finding this altogether to his liking he resumed his concert work and commenced a long series of tours which included all the nooks and corners of the world where one might find a musical public. He was an accomplished linguist, speaking many languages very fluently. His work as a composer was not significant but in certain branches of pianoforte playing he rose to exceptional heights. He died October 31st, 1907.

17

SYSTEMATIC MUSICAL TRAINING
ALFRED REISENAUER

"I CAN never thank my mother enough for the splendid start she gave me in my early musical life. She was a wonderful woman and a veritable genius as a teacher. See, I have here to-day on my piano a copy of the Schumann Sonata in F sharp minor which she herself used and which she played with a feeling I have never heard equaled. There is one thing in particular for which I am everlastingly grateful to her. Before I was taught anything of notes or of the piano keyboard, she took me aside one day and explained in the simple and beautiful tongue which only a mother employs in talking to her child, the wonderful natural relationships of tones used in making music. Whether this was an inspiration, an intuition, or a carefully thought out plan for my benefit, I cannot tell, but my mother put into practice what I have since come to consider the most important and yet the most neglected step in the education of the child. The fault lies in the fact that most teachers at the start do not teach music, rather musical notation and the peculiarities of the instrument.

Nothing could possibly be more stultifying to the musical instinct of the child. For instance, the plan generally pursued is to let the child grope over the white keys of the piano keyboard and play exercises in the scale of C, until he begins to feel that the whole musical world lies in the scale of C, with the scales of F and G as the frontiers. The keys of F sharp, B, D flat and others are looked upon as tremendously difficult and the child mind reasons with its own peculiar logic that these keys being so much less used, must, of course be less important. The black keys upon the keyboard are a '*terra incognita*.' Consequently at the very start the child has a radically incorrect view of what music really is.

"Before notation existed,—before keyboards were invented,—people sang. Before a child knows anything of notation or a keyboard, it sings. It is following its natural, musical instinct. Notation and keyboards are simply symbols of music—cages in which the beautiful bird is caught. They are not music any more than the alphabet is literature. Unfortunately, our system of musical symbols and the keyboard itself are very complex. For the young child it is as difficult as are Calculus and Algebra for his older brother. As a matter of fact, the keys of F sharp, B, and D flat major, etc., are only difficult because fate has made them so. It would have served the musical purpose just as well if the pitch of the instruments employed had been adjusted so that what is now F sharp, would be the key of C major. That, however, would not have simplified matters and we have to receive our long established musical notation until we can exchange it for a better one.

"At a very early age, I was taken to Franz Liszt by my mother. Liszt immediately perceived my natural talent and strongly advised my mother to continue my musical work. At the same time he said 'As a child I was exposed to criticism as a Wunderkind (prodigy), through the ignorance of my parents, long before I was properly prepared to meet the inevitable consequences of public appearance. This did incalculable damage to me. Let your child be spared such a fate. My own experience was disastrous. Do not let your son appear in public until he is a mature artist.'

"My first teacher, Louis Köhler, was an artist and a great artist, but he was an artist-teacher rather than an artist-pianist. Compared with many of his contemporaries his playing suffered immensely, but he made an art of teaching as few other men have done. He did not play for his pupils to any extent, nor did he ask them to imitate him in any way. His playing was usually confined to general illustrations and suggestions. By these means the individuality of his pupils was preserved and permitted to develop, so that while the pupil always had an excellent idea of the authoritative traditions governing the interpretation of a certain piece, there was nothing that suggested the stilted or wooden performance of the brainless mimic. He taught his pupils to think. He was an indefatigable student and thinker himself. He had what many teachers would have considered peculiar ideas upon technic.

KÖHLER'S TECHNICAL SCHEME

"While he invented many little means whereby technical difficulties could be more readily overcome than by the existing plan he could not be called in any way radical. He believed in carrying the technical side of a pupil's education up to a certain point along more or less conventional lines. When the pupil reached that point he found that he was upon a veritable height of mechanical supremacy. Thereafter Köhler depended upon the technical difficulties presented in the literature of the instrument to continue the technical efficiency acquired. In other words, the acquisition of a technic was solely to enable the pupil to explore the world of music equipped in such a way that he was not to be overcome by anything. The everlasting continuance of technical exercises was looked upon by Köhler as a ridiculous waste of time and a great injury.

"I also hold this opinion. Let us suppose that I were to sit at the piano for six or seven hours and do nothing but play conventional finger exercises. What happens to my soul, psychologically considered, during those hours spent upon exercises which no man or woman could possibly find anything other than an irritation? Do not the same exercises occur in thousands of pieces but in such connection that the mind is interested? Is it necessary for the advanced pianist to punish himself with a kind of mental and physical penance more trying, perhaps, than the devices of the medieval ascetics or the oriental priests of to-day?   No, technic is the Juggernaut which has ground to pieces more musicians than one can imagine. It produces a stiff, wooden touch and has a tendency to induce the pianist to believe that the art of pianoforte playing depends upon the continuance of technical exercises whereas the acquisition of technical ability should be regarded as the beginning and not the end.   When pupils leave your schools you say that they are having a 'Commencement.'   The acquisition of a technic is only the commencement, unfortunately too many consider it the end.   This may perhaps be the reason why our conservatories turn out so many bright and proficient young people who in a few years are buried in oblivion.

With Liszt

"When I had reached a certain grade of advancement it was my great fortune to become associated with the immortal Franz Liszt.   I consider Liszt the greatest man I have ever met.   By this I mean that I have never met, in any other walk of life, a man with the mental grasp, splendid disposition and glorious genius.   This may seem a somewhat extravagant statement.   I have met many, many great men, rulers, jurists, authors, scientists, teachers, merchants and warriors, but never have I met a man in any position whom I have not thought would have proved the inferior of Franz Liszt, had Liszt chosen to follow the career of the man in question.   Liszt's personality can only be expressed by one word, 'colossal.' He had the most generous nature of any man I have ever met. He had aspirations to become a great composer, greater than his own measure of his work as a composer had revealed to him. The dire position of Wagner presented itself. He abandoned his own ambitions— ambitions higher than those he ever held toward piano virtuosity—abandoned them completely to champion the difficult cause of the great Wagner. What Liszt suffered to make this sacrifice, the world does not know. But no finer example of moral heroism can be imagined. His conversations with me upon the subject were so intimate that I do not care to reveal one word.

LISZT'S PEDAGOGICAL METHODS

His generosity and personal force in his work with the young artists he assisted are hard to describe. You ask me whether he had a certain method. I reply, he abhorred methods in the modern sense of the term. His work was eclectic in the highest sense. In one way he could not be considered a teacher at all. He charged no fees and had irregular and somewhat unsystematic classes. In another sense he was the greatest of teachers. Sit at the piano and I will indicate the general plan pursued by Liszt at a lesson. Reisenauer is a remarkable and witty mimic of people he desires to describe. The present writer sat at the piano and played at some length through several short compositions, eventually coming to the inevit-

able "Chopin Valse, Op. 69, No. 1, in A flat major."
In the meanwhile, Reisenauer had gone to another
room and, after listening patiently, returned, imitating the walk, facial expression and the peculiar
guttural snort characteristic of Liszt in his later years.
Then followed a long "kindly sermon" upon the
emotional possibilities of the composition. This was
interrupted with snorts and went with kaleidoscopic
rapidity from French to German and back again
many, many times. Imitating Liszt he said,

"First of all we must arrive at the very essence of
the thing; the germ that Chopin chose to have grow
and blossom in his soul. It is, roughly considered, this:

Chopin's next thought was, no doubt:

But with his unerring good taste and sense of
symmetry he writes it so:

Now consider the thing in studying it and while playing it from the composer's attitude. By this I mean

that during the mental process of conception, before the actual transference of the thought to paper, the thought itself is in a nebulous condition. The composer sees it in a thousand lights before he actually determines upon the exact form he desires to perpetuate. For instance, this theme might have gone through Chopin's mind much after this fashion:

"The main idea being to reach the embryo of Chopin's thought and by artistic insight divine the connotation of that thought, as nearly as possible in the light of the treatment Chopin has given it.

"It is not so much the performer's duty to play mere notes and dynamic marks, as it is for him to make an artistic estimate of the composer's intention and to feel that during the period of reproduction he simulates the natural psychological conditions which affected the composer during the actual process of composition. In this way the composition becomes a living entity—a tangible resurrection of the soul of the great Chopin. Without such penetrative genius a pianist is no more than a mere machine and with it he may develop into an artist of the highest type."

A Unique Attitude

Reisenauer's attitude toward the piano is unique and interesting. Musicians are generally understood to have an affectionate regard for their instruments, almost paternal. Not so with Reisenauer. He even goes so far as to make this statement: "I have aways been drawn to the piano by a peculiar charm I have never been able to explain to myself. I feel that I must play, play, play, play, play. It has become a second nature to me. I have played so much and so long that the piano has become a part of me. Yet I am never free from the feeling that it is a constant battle with the instrument, and even with my technical resources I am not able to express all the beauties I hear in the music. While music is my very life, I nevertheless hate the piano. I play because I can't help playing and because there is no other instrument which can come as near imitating the melodies and the harmonies of the music I feel. People say wherever I go, 'Ah, he is a master.' What absurdity! I the master? Why, there is the master (pointing to the piano), I am only the slave."

The Future of Pianoforte Music

An interesting question that frequently arises in musical circles relates to the future possibilities of the art of composition in its connection with the pianoforte. Not a few have some considerable apprehension regarding the possible dearth of new melodic material and the technical and artistic treatment of such material. "I do not think that there need be any fear of a lack of original melodic material or original methods of treating such material. The possibilities of the art of musical composition have by no means been exhausted. While I feel that in a certain sense, very difficult to illustrate with words, one great 'school' of composition for the pianoforte ended with Liszt and the other in Brahms, nevertheless I can but prophesy the arising of many new and wonderful schools in the future. I base my prophecy upon the premises of frequent similar conditions during the history of musical art.

"Nevertheless, it is yet my ambition to give a lengthy series of recitals, with programs arranged to give a chronological aspect of all the great masterpieces in music. I hope to be enabled to do this before I retire. It is part of a plan to circle the world in a manner that has not yet been done." When asked whether these programs were to resemble Rubinstein's famous historical recitals in London, years ago, he replied: "They will be more extensive than the Rubinstein recitals. The times make such a series possible now, which Rubinstein would have hesitated to give."

As to American composers, Reisenauer is so thoroughly and enthusiastically won over by Mac-Dowell that he has not given the other composers sufficient attention to warrant a critical opinion. I found upon questioning that he had made a genuinely sincere effort to find new material in America, but he said that outside of MacDowell, he found nothing but indifferently good salon-music. With the works of several American composers he was, however, unfamiliar. He has done little or nothing himself as a composer and declared that it was not his forte.

American Musical Taste

"I find that American musical taste is in many ways astonishing. Many musicians who came to America prior to the time of Thomas and Damrosch returned to Europe with what were, no doubt, true stories of the musical conditions in America at that time. These stories were given wide circulation in Europe, and it is difficult for Europeans to understand the cultured condition of the American people at the present time. America can never thank Dr. Leopold Damrosch and Theodore Thomas enough for their unceasing labors. Thanks to the impetus that they gave the movement, it is now possible to play programs in almost any American city that are in no sense different from those one is expected to give in great European capitals. The status of musical education in the leading American cities is surprisingly high. Of course the commercial element necessarily affects it to a certain extent; but in many cases this is not as injurious as might be imagined. The future of music in America seems very roseate to me and I can look back to my American concert tours with great pleasure.

Concert Conditions in America

"One of the great difficulties, however, in concert touring in America is the matter of enormous distances. I often think that American audiences rarely hear great pianists at their best. Considering the large amounts of money involved in a successful American tour and the business enterprise which must be extremely forceful to make such a tour possible, it is not to be wondered that enormous journeys must be made in ridiculously short time. No one can imagine what this means to even a man of my build." (Reisenauer is a wonderfully strong and powerful man.) "I have been obliged to play in one Western city one night and in an Eastern city the following night. Hundreds of miles lay between them. In the latter city I was obliged to go directly from the railroad depot to the stage of the concert hall, hungry, tired, travel worn and without practice opportunities. How can a man be at his best under such conditions?—yet certain conditions make these things unavoidable in America, and the pianist must suffer occasional criticism for not playing uniformly well. In Europe such conditions do not exist owing to the closely populated districts. I am glad to have the opportunity to make this statement, as no doubt a very great many Americans fail to realize under what distressing conditions an artist is often obliged to play in America."

QUESTIONS IN STYLE, INTERPRETATION, EXPRESSION
AND TECHNIC OF PIANOFORTE PLAYING

SERIES XV
ALFRED REISENAUER

1. What should be the first step in the musical education of the child?

2. Why was Köhler so successful as a teacher?

3. Did Liszt follow a method in teaching or was his work eclectic?

4. Give Liszt's conception of how Chopin developed one of his Valses.

5. Have the possibilities of the art of musical composition been exhausted?

6. Are other great schools of pianoforte playing likely to arise?

7. What was Reisenauer's opinion of the works of MacDowell?

8. What may be said of musical taste in America when Reisenauer was touring this country.

9. What may be said of the status of American musical education?

10. What great difficulties do the virtuosos visiting America encounter?

EMIL SAUER

Emil Sauer was born in Hamburg, Germany, October 8, 1862. His first teacher was his mother, who was a fine musician, and who took exceptional pains with her talented son. From 1879 to 1881 he studied with Nicholas Rubinstein, brother of the famous Anton Rubinstein. Nicholas Rubinstein was declared by many to be a far abler teacher than his brother, who eclipsed him upon the concert platform. From 1884 to 1885 Sauer studied with Franz Liszt. In his autobiographical work, "My Life," Sauer relates that Liszt at that time had reached an age when much of his reputed brilliance had disappeared, and the playing of the great Master of Weimar did not startle Sauer as it did some others. However, Liszt took a great personal interest in Sauer and prophesied a great future for him.

In 1882 Sauer made his first tour as a virtuoso, and met with such favor that numerous tours of the music-loving countries ensued. The critics praised his playing particularly for his great clarity, sanity, symmetrical appreciation of form, and unaffected fervor. For a time Sauer was at the head of the Meisterschule of Piano-playing, connected with the Imperial Conservatory in Vienna.

(The following conference was conducted in German and English.)

18

THE TRAINING OF THE VIRTUOSO

EMIL SAUER

ONE of the most inestimable advantages I have ever had was my good fortune in having a musical mother. It is to her that I owe my whole career as an artist. If it had not been for her loving care and her patient persistence I might have been engaged in some entirely different pursuit. As a child I was very indifferent to music. I abhorred practice, and, in fact, showed no signs of pronounced talent until my twelfth year. But she kept faithfully pegging away at me and insisted that because my grandfather had been a noted artist and because she was devoted to music it must be in my blood.

My mother was a pupil of Deppe, of whom Miss Amy Fay has written in her book "Music Study in Germany." Deppe was a remarkable pedagogue and had excellent ideas upon the foundation of a rational system of touch. He sought the most natural position of the hand and always aimed to work along the line of least resistance. My mother instilled Deppe's ideas into me together with a very comprehensive training in the standard etudes and classics within my youthful technical grasp. For those years I could not have had a better teacher. Lucky is the child, who like Gounod, Reisenauer and others, has had the invaluable instruction that a patient, self-sacrificing mother can give. The mother is the most unselfish of all teachers, and is painstaking to a fault.

SLOW SYSTEMATIC PRACTICE

She insisted upon slow systematic regular practice. She knew the importance of regularity, and one of the first things I ever learned was that if I missed one or two days' practice, I could not hope to make it up by practicing overtime on the following days. Practice days missed or skipped are gone forever. One must make a fresh start and the loss is sometimes not recovered for several days.

I was also made to realize the necessity of freshness at the practice period. The pupil who wants to make his practice lead to results must feel well while practicing. Practicing while tired, either mentally or physically, is wasted practice.

Pupils must learn to concentrate, and if they have not the ability to do this naturally they should have a master who will teach them how. It is not easy to fix the mind upon one thing and at the same time drive every other thought away. With some young pupils this takes much practice. Some never acquire it—it is not in them. Concentration is the vertebræ of musical success. The student who cannot concentrate had better abandon musical study. In fact, the young person who cannot concentrate is not likely to be a conspicuous success in any line of activity. The study of music cultivates the pupil's powers of concentration perhaps more than any other study. The notes to be played must be recognized instantaneously and correctly performed. In music the mind has no time to wander. This is one of the reasons why music is so valuable even for those who do not ever contemplate a professional career.

One hour of concentrated practice with the mind fresh and the body rested is better than four hours of dissipated practice with the mind stale and the body tired. With a fatigued intellect the fingers simply dawdle over the keys and nothing is accomplished. I find in my own daily practice that it is best for me to practice two hours in the morning and then two hours later in the day. When I am finished with two hours of hard study I am exhausted from close concentration. I have also noted that any time over this period is wasted. I am too fatigued for the practice to be of any benefit to me.

The Necessity for a Good General Education

Parents make a great mistake in not insuring the general education of the child who is destined to become a concert performer. I can imagine nothing more stultifying or more likely to result in artistic disaster than the course that some parents take in neglecting the child's school work with an idea that if he is to become a professional musician he need only devote himself to music. This one-sided cultivation should be reserved for idiots who can do nothing else. The child-wonder is often the victim of some mental disturbance.

I remember once seeing a remarkable child mathematician in Hungary. He was only twelve years of age and yet the most complicated mathematical problems were solved in a few seconds without recourse to paper. The child had water on the brain and lived but a few years. His usefulness to the world of mathematics was limited solely to show purposes. It is precisely the same with the so-called musical precocities. They are rarely successful in after life, and unless trained by some very wise and careful teacher, they soon become objects for pity.

The child who is designed to become a concert pianist should have the broadest possible culture. He must live in the world of art and letters and become a naturalized citizen. The wider the range of his information, experience and sympathies, the larger will be the audience he will reach when he comes to talk to them from the concert platform. It is the same as with a public speaker. No one wants to hear a speaker who has led a narrow, crabbed intellectual existence, but the man who has seen and known the world, who has become acquainted with the great masterpieces of art and the wonderful achievements of science, has little difficulty in securing an audience providing he has mastered the means of expressing his ideas.

CLEAN PLAYING VS. SLOVENLY PLAYING

In the matter of technical preparation there is, perhaps, too little attention being given to-day to the necessity for clean playing. Of course, each individual requires a different treatment. The pupil who has a tendency to play with stiffness and rigidity may be given studies which will develop a more fluent style. For these pupils' studies, like those of Heller, are desirable in the cases of students with only moderate technical ability, while the splendid "etudes" of Chopin are excellent remedies for advanced pupils with tendencies toward hard, rigid playing. The difficulty one ordinarily meets, however, is ragged, slovenly playing rather than stiff, rigid playing. To remedy this slovenliness, there is nothing like the well-known works of Czerny, Cramer or Clementi.

I have frequently told pupils in my "Meisterschule" in Vienna, before I abandoned teaching for my work as a concert pianist, that they must learn to draw before they learn to paint. They will persist in trying to apply colors before they learn the art of making correct designs. This leads to dismal failure in almost every case. Technic first—then interpretation. The great concert-going public has no use for a player with a dirty, slovenly technic no matter how much he strives to make morbidly sentimental interpretations that are expected to reach the lovers of sensation. For such players a conscientious and exacting study of Czerny, Cramer, Clementi and others of similar design is good musical soap and water. It washes them into respectability and technical decency. The pianist with a bungling, slovenly technic, who at the same time attempts to perform the great masterpieces, reminds me of those persons who attempt to disguise the necessity for soap and water with nauseating perfume.

Health a Vital Factor

Few people realize what a vital factor health is to the concert pianist. The student should never fail to think of this. Many young Americans who go abroad to study break down upon the very vehicle upon which they must depend in their ride to success through the indiscretions of overwork or wrong living. The concert pianist really lives a life of privation. I always make it a point to restrict myself to certain hygienic rules on the day before a concert. I have a certain diet and a certain amount of exercise and sleep, without which I cannot play successfully.

In America one is overcome with the kindness of well-meaning people who insist upon late suppers, receptions, etc. It is hard to refuse kindness of this description, but I have always felt that my debt to my audiences was a matter of prime importance, and while on tour I refrain from social pleasures of all kinds. My mind and my body must be right or failure will surely result.

I have often had people say to me after the performance of some particularly brilliant number "Ah!

You must have taken a bottle of champagne to give a performance like that." Nothing could be further from the truth. A half a bottle of beer would ruin a recital for me. The habit of taking alcoholic drinks with the idea that they lead to a more fiery performance is a dangerous custom that has been the ruin of more than one pianist. The performer who would be at his best must live a very careful, almost abstemious life. Any unnatural excess is sure to mar his playing and lead to his downfall with the public. I have seen this done over and over again, and have watched alcohol tear down in a few years what had taken decades of hard practice and earnest study to build up.

Judicious Use of Technical Exercises

The field of music is so enormous that I have often thought that the teacher should be very careful not to overdo the matter of giving technical exercises. Technical exercises are, at best, short cuts. They are necessary for the student. He should have a variety of them, and not be kept incessantly pounding away at one or two exercises. As Nicholas Rubinstein once said to me, "Scales should never be dry. If you are not interested in them work with them until you become interested in them." They should be played with accents and in different rhythms. If they are given in the shapeless manner in which some teachers obliged their unfortunate pupils to practice them they are worthless. I do not believe in working out technical exercises at a table or with a dumb piano. The brain must always work with the fingers, and without the sound of the piano the imagination must be enormously stretched to get anything more than the most senseless, toneless, soulless touch.

Technic with many is unmistakably a gift. I say this after having given the matter much careful thought. It is like the gift of speech. Some people are fluent talkers, precisely as some people can do more in two hours' technical work at the keyboard than others could accomplish with four. Of course, much can be accomplished with persistent practice, and a latent gift may be awakened, but it is certainly not given to all to become able technicalists. Again some become very proficient from the technical standpoint, but are barren, soulless, uninspired and vapid when it comes to the artistic and musicianly interpretation of a piece.

There comes a time to every advanced pianist when such exercises as the scales, arpeggios, the studies of Czerny and Cramer are unnecessary. I have not practiced them for some years, but pray do not think that I attempt to go without exercises. These exercises I make by selecting difficult parts of famous pieces and practicing them over and over. I find the concertos of Hummel particularly valuable in this connection, and there are parts of some of the Beethoven concertos that make splendid musical exercises that I can practice without the fatal diminution of interest which makes a technical exercise valueless.

STUDY ABROAD

In the matter of foreign study I think that I may speak without bias, as I am engaged in teaching and am not likely to resume for some years. I am *absolutely convinced* that there are many teachers in America who are as good as the best in Europe. Nevertheless, I would advise the young American to secure the best instruction possible in his native land, and then to go abroad for a further course. It will serve to broaden him in many ways.

I believe in patriotism, and I admire the man who sticks to his fatherland. But, in art there is no such thing as patriotism. As the conservatory of Paris provides, through the "Prix de Rome," for a three years' residence in Italy and other countries for the most promising pupil, so the young American music students should avail themselves of the advantages of Old World civilization, art, and music. There is much to be learned from the hustle and vigorous wholesome growth of your own country that would be of decided advantage to the German students who could afford a term of residence here. It is narrowing to think that one should avoid the Old World art centers from the standpoint of American patriotism.

VERSATILITY

Few people recognize the multifarious requirements of the concert pianist. He must adjust himself to all sorts of halls, pianos and living conditions.

The difference between one piano and another is often very remarkable. It sometimes obliges the artist to readjust his technical methods very materially. Again, the difference in halls is noteworthy. In a great hall, like the Albert Hall of London, one can only strive for very broad effects. It is not possible for one to attempt the delicate shadings which the smaller halls demand. Much is lost in the great hall, and it is often unjust to determine the pianist's ability by his exclusively bravura performances in very large auditoriums.

Cultivating Finger Strength

The concert pianist must have great endurance. His fingers must be as strong as steel, and yet they must be as elastic and as supple as willow wands. I have always had great faith in the "Kleine Pischna" and the "Pischna Exercises" in cultivating strength. These exercises are now world famous, and it would be hard for me to imagine anything better for this particular purpose. They are somewhat voluminous, but necessarily so. One conspicuous difficulty with which teachers have to contend is that pupils attempt pieces requiring great digital strength without ever having gone through such a course as I advocate above. The result is that they have all sorts of troubles with their hands through strain. Some of these troubles are irremediable, others are curable, but cause annoying delays. I have never had anything of this sort and attribute my immunity from weeping sinews, etc., to correct hand positions, a loose wrist and slow systematic work in my youth.

VELOCITY

Velocity depends more upon natural elasticity than strength. Some people seem to be born with the ability to play rapidly. It is always a matter of the fingers, but is more a matter of the brain. Some people have the ability to think very rapidly, and when these people have good supple hands they seem to be able to play rapidly with comparatively little study. When you fail to get velocity at first, do not hesitate to lay the piece aside for several weeks, months or years. Then you will doubtless find that the matter of velocity will not trouble you. Too much study upon a piece that fails for the time being to respond to earnest effort is often a bad thing. Be a little patient. It will all come out right in the end. If you fuss and fume for immediate results you may be sadly disappointed.

TALENT

Talent is great and immutable. Take the case of Liszt, for instance. I recently heard from a reliable source the following interesting story: One day Liszt was called away from his class at Wiemar by an invitation to visit the Grand Duke. Von Bülow, then a mature artist, was present, and he was asked by Liszt to teach the class for the day. Liszt left the room, and a young student was asked to play one of Liszt's own compositions. Von Bülow did not like the youth's interpretation, as he had been accustomed to play the same work on tour in a very different manner. Consequently he abused the student roundly, and then sat at the keyboard and was playing to his great satisfaction when the tottering old master broke in the room and with equal severity reprimanded Von Bülow, and sat down at the keyboard and gave an interpretation that was infinitely superior to that of Von Bülow. It was simply a case of superiority of talent that enabled the aged and somewhat infirm Liszt to excel his younger contemporary.

BE NATURAL

In closing, let me enjoin all young American music students to strive for naturalness. Avoid ostentatious movements in your playing. Let your playing be as quiet as possible. The wrist should be loose. The hands, to my mind, should be neither high nor low, but should be in line with the forearm. One should continually strive for quietness. Nothing should be forced. Ease in playing is always admirable, and comes in time to all talented students who seek it. The Deppe method of hand position, while pedantic and unnecessarily long, is interesting and instructive.

Personally, I advocate the use of the Etudes of Chopin, Moscheles and the *Etudes Transcendante* to all advanced pupils. I have used them with pupils with invariable success. I have also a series of thirteen Etudes of my own that I have made for the express purpose of affording pupils material for work which is not adequately covered in the usual course.

Young Americans have a great future before them. The pupils I have had have invariably been ones who progress with astonishing rapidity. They show keenness and good taste, and are willing to work faithfully and conscientiously, and that, after all, is the true road to success.

TALENT COUNTS

If you think that talent does not count you are very greatly mistaken. We not infrequently see men who have been engaged in one occupation with only very moderate success suddenly leap into fame in an entirely different line. Men who have struggled to be great artists or illustrators like du Maurier astonish the world with a previously concealed literary ability. It is foolish not to recognize the part that talent must play in the careers of artists. Sometimes hard work and patient persistence will stimulate the mind and soul, and reveal talents that were never supposed to exist, but if the talent does not exist it is as hopeless to hunt for it as it is to seek for diamonds in a bowl of porridge.

Talented people seem to be born with the knack or ability to do certain things twice as well and twice as quickly as other people can do the same things.

I well remember that when all Europe was wild over the "Diabolo" craze my little girl commenced to play with the sticks and the little spool. It looked interesting and I thought that I would try it a few times and then show her how to do it. The more I tried the more exasperated I became. I simply could not make it go, and before I knew it I had wasted a whole morning upon it. My little daughter took it up and in a few minutes' practice she was able to do it as well as an expert. It is precisely the same at the keyboard. What takes some pupils hours to accomplish others can do in a few seconds with apparently less effort. The age of the pupil seems to have little to do with musical comprehension. What does count is talent, that peculiar qualification which seems to lead the student to see through complex problems as if he had been solving them through different generations for centuries.

Questions in Style, Interpretation, Expression and Technic of Pianoforte Playing

SERIES XV
EMIL SAUER

1. Can missed practice periods ever be made up?
2. Does piano study cultivate concentration?
3. What is a good arrangement of practice hours?
4. What are some remedies for slovenly playing?
5. How is one's playing affected by health?

6. Are stimulants good or bad?
7. Is listening important in pianoforte playing?
8. How may finger strength be cultivated?
9. Upon what does velocity depend?
10. What part does talent play in the artist's success?

XAVER SCHARWENKA

BIOGRAPHICAL

Franz Xaver Scharwenka was born at Samter, Posen (polish Prussia), January 6, 1850. He was a pupil of Kullak and Würst at Kullak's Academy in Berlin, from which he graduated in 1868. Shortly thereafter he was appointed a teacher in the same institution. The next year he made his début as a virtuoso at the *Singakademie*. For many years thereafter he gave regular concerts in Berlin in connection with Sauret and Grünfield. In 1874 he gave up his position in the famous Berlin music school and commenced the career of the touring virtuoso. In 1880 he founded the Scharwenka Conservatory in Berlin together with his brother Philipp Scharwenka, an able composer.

In 1891 Scharwenka came to New York to establish a conservatory there. This, however, was closed in 1898 when Scharwenka returned to Berlin as Director of the Klindworth-Scharwenka conservatory. He has been the recipient of numerous honors from the governments of Austria and Germany. He received the title of "Professor" from the King of Prussia (Emperor Wilhelm II) and that of Court Pianist from the emperor of Austria.

His many concert tours in America and in Europe have established his fame as a pianist of great intellectual strength as well as strong poetical force. His compositions, including his four Concertos, have been widely played, and his opera, *Mataswintha*, has received important productions. One of his earlier works, the *Polish Dance*, has been enormously popular for a quarter of a century.

(The following conference was conducted in German and English.)

19

ECONOMY IN MUSIC STUDY
XAVER SCHARWENKA

It is somewhat of a question whether any time spent in music study is actually wasted, since all intellectual activity is necessarily accompanied by an intellectual advance. However, it soon becomes apparent to the young teacher that results can be achieved with a great economy of time if the right methods are used. By the use of the words "right methods" I do not mean to infer that only one right method exists. The right method for one pupil might be quite different from that which would bring about the best results with another pupil. In these days far more elasticity of methods exists than was generally sanctioned in the past, and the greatness of the teacher consists very largely of his ability to invent, adapt, and adjust his pedagogical means to the special requirements of his pupil. Thus it happens that the teacher, by selecting only those exercises, etudes and teaching pieces demanded by the obvious needs of the pupil, and by eliminating unnecessary material, a much more rapid rate of advancement may be obtained. One pupil, for instance, might lack those qualities of velocity and dexterity which many of the etudes of Czerny develop in such an admirable manner, while another pupil might be deficient in the singing tone, which is almost invariably improved by the study of certain Chopin etudes.

TIME LOST IN EARLY STUDY

Although my educational work for many years has been almost exclusively limited to pupils preparing for careers as teachers and as concert pianists, I nevertheless have naturally taken a great interest in those broad and significant problems which underlie the elementary training of the young music student. I have written quite extensively upon the subject, and my ideas have been quite definitely expressed in my book, *Methodik des Klavierspiels: Systematische Darstellung der technischen und æsthetischen Erfordernisse für einen rationellen Lehrgang.* I have also come in close contact with this branch of musical work in the Klindworth-Scharwenka Conservatory in Berlin.

My observations have led to the firm conviction that much of the time lost in music study could be saved if the elementary training of the pupil were made more comprehensive and more secure. It is by no means an economy of time to hurry over the foundation work of the pupil. It is also by no means an economy of money to place the beginner in the hands of a second-rate teacher. There is just as much need for the specialist to train the pupil at the start as there is for the head of the "meisterschule" to guide the budding virtuoso. How can we expect the pupil to make rapid progress if the start is not right? One might as well expect a broken-down automobile to win a race. The equipment at the beginning must be of the kind which will carry the pupil through his entire career with success. If any omissions occur, they must be made up later on, and the difficulty in repairing this neglect is twice as great as it would have been had the student received the proper instruction at the start.

EAR-TRAINING

The training of the ear is of great importance, and if teachers would only make sure that their pupils studied music with their sense of hearing as well as with their fingers, much time would be saved in later work. Young pupils should be taught to listen by permitting them to hear good music, which is at the same time sufficiently simple to insure comprehension. Early musical education is altogether too one-sided. The child is taken to the piano and a peculiar set of hieroglyphics known as notation is displayed to him. He is given a few weeks to comprehend that these signs refer to certain keys on the keyboard. He commences to push down these keys faithfully and patiently and his musical education is thus launched in what many consider the approved manner. Nothing is said about the meaning of the piece, its rhythm, its harmonies, its æsthetic beauties. Nothing is told of the composer, or of the period in which the piece was written. It would be just about as sensible to teach a pupil

to repeat the sounds of the Chinese language by
reading the Chinese word-signs, but without comprehending the meaning of the sounds and signs.
Is it any wonder that beginners lose interest in their
work, and refuse to practise except when compelled
to do so?

I am most emphatically in favor of a more rational,
a more broad, and a more thorough training of the
beginner.   Time taken from that ordinarily given to
the senseless, brainless working up and down of
the fingers at the keyboard, and devoted to those
studies such as harmony, musical history, form, and
in fact, any study which will tend to widen the pupil's
knowledge and increase his interest, will save much
time in later work.

WASTE IN TECHNICAL STUDY

Geometrically speaking, the shortest distance between two points is a straight line.   Teachers should
make every possible effort to find the straight line
of technic which will carry the pupil from his first
steps to technical proficiency without wandering
about through endless lanes and avenues which lead
to no particular end.   I suppose that all American
teachers hear the same complaint that is heard by
all European teachers when any attempt is made to
insist upon thorough practice and adequate study
from the *dilettante*.   As soon as the teacher demands
certain indispensable technical studies, certain necessary investigations of the harmonic, æsthetic or

historical problems, which contribute so much to the excellence of pianistic interpretations, he hears the following complaint: "I don't want to be a composer" or "I don't want to be a virtuoso—I only want to play just a little for my own amusement." The teacher knows and appreciates the pupil's attitude exactly, and while he realizes that his reasoning is altogether fatuous, it seems well-nigh impossible to explain to the amateur that unless he does his work right he will get very little real pleasure or amusement out of it.

The whole sum and substance of the matter is that a certain amount of technical, theoretical and historical knowledge must be acquired to make the musician, before we can make a player. There is the distinction. Teachers should never fail to remember that their first consideration should be to make a musician. All unmusical playing is insufferable. No amount of technical study will make a musician, and all technical study which simply aims to make the fingers go faster, or play complicated rhythms, is wasted unless there is the foundation and culture of the real musician behind it.

To the sincere student every piece presents technical problems peculiar to itself. The main objection to all technical study is that unless the pupil is vitally interested the work becomes monotonous. The student should constantly strive to avoid monotony in practicing exercises. As soon as the exercises become dull and uninteresting their value immediately depreciates. The only way to avoid this is to seek variety. As I have said in my *Methodik des Klaverspiels:* "The musical and tonal monotony of technical exercises may be lessened in a measure by progressive modulations, by various rhythmical alterations, and further through frequent changes in contrary motion." Great stress should be laid upon practice in contrary motion. The reason for this is obvious to all students of harmony. When playing in contrary motion all unevenness, all breaks in precision and all unbalanced conditions of touch become much more evident to the ear than if the same exercises were played in parallel motion. Another important reason for the helpfulness of playing in contrary motion is not to be undervalued. It is that a kind of physical 'sympathy' is developed between the fingers and the nerves which operate them in the corresponding hands. For instance, it is much easier to play with the fifth finger of one hand and the fifth finger of the other hand than it is to play with the third finger of one hand and the fifth finger of another."

WASTE IN UNIMPORTANT SUBJECTS

There is a general impression among teachers to-day that much time might be saved by a more careful selection of studies, and by a better adaptation of the studies to particular pupils. For instance, Carl Czerny wrote over one thousand opus numbers. He wrote some of the most valuable studies ever written, but no one would think of demanding a pupil to play all of the Czerny studies, any more than the student should be compelled to play everything that Loeschhorn, Cramer and Clementi ever wrote. Studies must be selected with great care and adapted to particular cases, and if the young teacher feels himself incapable of doing this, he should either use selections or collections of studies edited by able authorities or he should place himself under the advice of some mature and experienced teacher until the right experience has been obtained. It would not be a bad plan to demand that all young teachers be apprenticed to an older teacher until the right amount of experience has been obtained. The completion of a course in music does not imply that the student is able to teach. Teaching and the matter of musical proficiency are two very different things. Many conservatories now conduct classes for teachers, which are excellent in their way. In the olden days a mechanic had to work side by side with his master before he was considered proficient to do his work by himself. How much more important is it that our educators should be competently trained. They do not have to deal with machinery, but they do have to deal with the most wonderful of all machines—the human brain.

Some studies in use by teachers are undeserving of their popularity, according to my way of thinking. Some studies are altogether trivial and quite dispensable. I have never held any particular fondness for

Heller for instance. His studies are tuneful, but they seem to me, in many cases, weak imitations of the style of some masters such as Schumann, Mendelssohn, etc., who may be studied with more profit. I believe that the studies of Loeschhorn possess great pedagogical value. Loeschhorn was a born teacher: he knew how to collect and present technical difficulties in a manner designed to be of real assistance to the student. The studies of Kullak are also extremely fine.

This is a subject which is far more significant than it may at first appear. Whatever the student may choose to study after he leaves the teacher, his work while under the teacher's direction should be focused upon just those pieces which will be of most value to him. The teacher should see that the course he prescribes is unified. There should be no waste material. Some teachers are inclined to teach pieces of a worthless order to gain the fickle interest of some pupils. They feel that it is better to teach an operatic arrangement, no matter how superficial, and retain the interest of the pupil, than to insist upon what they know is really best for the pupil, and run the risk of having the pupil go to another teacher less conscientious about making compromises of this sort. When the teacher has come to a position where he is obliged to permit the pupil to select his own pieces or dictate the kind of pieces he is to be taught in order to retain his interest, the teacher will find that he has very little influence over the pupil. Pupils who insist upon mapping out their own careers are always stumbling-blocks.   It is far better to make it very clear to the pupil in the first place that interference of this kind is never desirable, and that unless the pupil has implicit confidence in the teacher's judgment it is better to discontinue.

Brain Technic versus Finger Technic

Few pupils realize that hours and hours are wasted at the piano keyboard doing those things which we are already able to do, and in the quest of something which we already possess.   When we come to think of it, every one is born with a kind of finger dexterity. Any one can move the fingers up and down with great rapidity;   no study of the pianoforte keyboard is necessary to do this.   The savage in the African wilds is gifted with that kind of dexterity, although he may never have seen a pianoforte.   Then why spend hours in practicing at the keyboard with the view of doing something we can already do?   It may come as a surprise to many when I make the statement that they already possess a kind of dexterity and velocity which they may not suspect.   One does not have to work for years to make the fingers go up and down quickly.   It is also a fact that a few lessons under a really good teacher and a few tickets for high-class piano recitals will often give the feeling and "knack" of producing a good touch, for which many strive in vain for years at the keyboard.

No, the technic which takes time is the technic of the brain, which directs the fingers to the right place at the right time. This may be made the greatest source of musical economy. If you want to save time in your music study see that you comprehend your musical problems thoroughly. You must see it right in your mind, you must hear it right, you must feel it right. Before you place your fingers on the keyboard you should have formed your ideal mental conception of the proper rhythm, the proper tonal quality, the æsthetic values and the harmonic content. These things can only be perfectly comprehended after study. They do not come from strumming at the keyboard. This, after all, is the greatest possible means for saving time in music study.

A great deal might be said upon the subject of the teacher's part in saving time. The good teacher is a keen critic. His experience and his innate ability enable him to diagnose faults just as a trained medical specialist can determine the cause of a disease with accuracy and rapidity. Much depends upon the diagnosis. It is no saving to go to a doctor who diagnoses your case as one of rheumatism and treats you for rheumatic pains, whereas you are really suffering from neurasthenia. In a similar manner, an unskilled and incompetent teacher may waste much treasured time in treating you for technical and musical deficiencies entirely different from those which you really suffer. Great care should be taken in selecting a teacher for with the wrong teacher not only time is wasted, but talent, energy, and sometimes that jewel in the crown of success—"ambition."

A Case in Point

An illustration of one means of wasting time is well indicated in the case of some pedagogs who hold to old ideas in piano-playing simply because they are old. I believe in conservatism, but at the same time I am opposed to conservatism which excludes all progressiveness. The world is continually advancing, and we are continually finding out new things as well as determining which of the older methods will prove the best in the long run. All musical Europe has been upset during the last quarter of the century over the vital subject of whether the pressure touch is better than the angular blow touch. There was a time in the past when an apparent effort was made to make everything pertaining to pianoforte technic as stiff and inelastic as possible. The fingers were trained to hop up and down like little hammers—the arm was held stiff and hard at the side. In fact, it was not uncommon for some teachers to put a book under the armpit and insist upon their pupils holding it there by pressing against the body during the practice period.

H. Ehrlich, who in his day was a widely recognized authority, wrote a pamphlet to accompany his edition of the Tausig technical studies in which this system is very clearly outlined. He asserts that Tausig insisted upon it. To-day we witness a great revolution. The arms are held freely and rigidity of all kind is avoided. It was found that the entire system of touch was under a more delicate and sensitive control when the pressure touch was employed than when the mechanical "hitting" touch was used. It was also found that much of the time spent in developing the hitting touch along mechanical lines was wasted, since superior results could be achieved in a shorter time by means of pressing and "kneading" the keys, rather than delivering blows to them. The pressure touch seems to me very much freer and I am emphatically in favor of it. The older method produced cramped unmusical playing and the pupil was so restricted that he reminded one for all the world of the new-fangled skirts ("hobble-skirts") which seem to give our ladies of fashion so much difficulty just now.

The American pupils who have come to Germany to study with me have been for the most part exceedingly well trained. In America there are innumerable excellent teachers. The American pupil is almost always very industrious. His chief point of vantage is his ability to concentrate. He does not dissipate his time or thought. In some instances he can only remain in Europe for two years—sometimes less. He quite naturally feels that a great deal must be done in those two years, and consequently he works at white heat. This is not a disadvantage, for his mental powers are intensified and he is faithful to his labor.

The young women of America are for the most part very self-reliant. This is also very much to their advantage. As a rule, they know how to take care of themselves, and yet they have the courage to venture and ask questions when questions should be asked. My residence in America has brought me many good friends, and it is a pleasure to note the great advance made in every way since my last visit here. I am particularly anxious to have some of my later compositions become better known in America, as I have great faith in the musical future of the country. I wish that they might become familiar with such works as my *Fourth Concerto*. I should deeply regret to think that Americans would judge my work as a composer by my "Polish Dance" and some other lighter compositions which are obviously inferior to my other works.

QUESTIONS IN STYLE, INTERPRETATION, EXPRESSION AND TECHNIC OF PIANOFORTE PLAYING

SERIES XVII

XAVER SCHARWENKA

1. Is any time spent in music study really wasted?

2. How may the pupil's elementary work be made more secure?

3. State the importance of ear-training.

4. What additional musical studies should be included in the work of the pupil?

5. What should be the teacher's first consideration?

6. Why must monotony be avoided in technical study?

7. State the value of practice in contrary motion.

8. May time be wasted with unprofitable studies?

9. What is the difference between brain technic and finger technic?

10. State how a revolution in methods of touch has come about.

ERNEST SCHELLING

BIOGRAPHICAL

Ernest Schelling was born at Belvidere, New Jersey, 1875. His first musical training was received from his father. At the age of four and one-half years he made his début at the Philadelphia Academy of Music. At the age of seven he entered the Paris Conservatoire, with the famous Chopin pupil, Georges Mathias, as his teacher. He remained with Mathias for two years. However, he commenced giving concerts which took him to France, England, and Austria when he was only eight years old. At ten he was taken to Stuttgart and placed under the educational guidance of Pruckner and the American teacher, Percy Götschius, who attained wide fame abroad. Shortly thereafter he was placed for a short time under the instruction of Leschetizky, but this was interrupted by tours through Russia and other countries. At twelve he was taken to Basle, Switzerland, and Hans Huber undertook to continue his already much varied training. Here his general education received the attention which had been much neglected. At fifteen he went to study with Barth in Berlin, but the strain of his previous work was so great that at seventeen he was attacked with neuritis and abandoned the career of a virtuoso. An accidental meeting with Paderewski led to an arrangement whereby Paderewski became his teacher for three years during which time Paderewski had no other pupils. Since then Schelling has made numerous tours at home and abroad.

20

LEARNING A NEW PIECE

ERNEST SCHELLING

Preliminary Study

In studying a new musical composition experience has revealed to me that the student can save much time and get a better general idea of the composition by reading it over several times before going to the instrument. While this is difficult for very young pupils to do before they have become accustomed to mentally interpreting the notes into sounds without the assistance of the instrument, it is, nevertheless, of advantage from the very start. It saves the pupil from much unprofitable blundering. To take a piece right to the keyboard without any preliminary consideration may perhaps be good practice for those who would cultivate ready sight reading, but it should be remembered that even the most apt sight readers will usually take the precaution of looking a new piece through at least once to place themselves on guard for the more difficult or more complicated passages. By forming the habit of reading away from the piano the pupil soon becomes able to hear the music without making the sounds at the keyboard and this leads to a mental conception of the piece as a whole, which invariably produces surprisingly good results.

THE TECHNICAL DEMANDS OF THE PIECE

"The next consideration should be the execution of the right notes. A careless prima-vista reading often leads the pupil to play notes quite different from those actually in the piece. It is astonishing how often some pupils are deceived in this matter. Until you have insured absolute accuracy in the matter of the notes you are not in condition to regard the other details. The failure to repeat an accidental chromatic alteration in the same bar, the neglect of a tie, or an enharmonic interval with a tie are all common faults which mark careless performances. After the piece has been read as a whole and you have determined upon the notes so that there is no opportunity for inaccuracy from that source you will find that the best way to proceed is to take a very small passage and study that passage first. For the inexperienced student I should suggest two measures or a phrase of similar length. Do not leave these two measures until you are convinced that you have mastered them. This will take a great amount of concentration. Many pupils fail because they underestimate the amount of concentration required. They expect results to come without effort and are invariably disappointed. After the first two measures have been mastered take the next two measures and learn these thoroughly. Then go back and learn measures two and three so that there may be no possibility of a break or interruption between them. Next proceed in the same way with the following four measures and do not stop until you have completed the piece.

This kind of study may take more time than the methods to which you have become accustomed, but it is by all means the most thorough and the most satisfactory. I found it indispensable in the preparation of pieces for public performances. It demands the closest kind of study, and this leads to artistic results and a higher perception of the musical values of the composition being studied. Take for instance the C Major Fantasie of Schumann, one of the most beautiful and yet one of the most difficult of all compositions to interpret properly. At first the whole work seems disunited, and if studied carelessly the necessary unity which should mark this work can never be secured. But, if studied with minute regard for details after the manner in which I have suggested the whole composition becomes wonderfully compact and every part is linked to the other parts so that a beautiful unity must result.

Formal Divisions

"Many works have formal divisions, such as those of the sonata, the suite, etc. Even the Liszt 'Rhapsodies' have movements of marked differences in tempo and style. Here the secret is to study each division in its relation to the whole. There must be an internal harmony between all the parts. Otherwise the interpretation will mar the great masterpiece. The difficulty is to find the bearing of one movement upon

another.   Even the themes of subjects of the conventional sonata have a definite interrelation.   How to
interpret these themes and yet at the same time produce contrast and unity is difficult.   It is this difference of interpretation that adds charm to the piano
recitals of different virtuosos.   There is no one right
way and no one best way, but rather an indefinite
margin for personal opinion and the exhibition of
artistic taste.   If there was one best way, there are
now machines which could record that way and there
the whole matter would end.   But we want to hear
all the ways and consequently we go to the recitals
of different pianists.   How can I express more emphatically the necessity for the pianist being a man of
culture, artistic sensibilities and of creative tendencies?
The student must be taught to think about his interpretations and if this point is missed and he is permitted to give conventional, uninspired performances
he need never hope to play artistically.

The Touch Required

"In studying a new piece, as soon as the style of
the piece has been determined and the accuracy of
the notes secured, the pupil should consider the
all-important matter to touch.   He should have been
previously instructed in the principles of the different kinds of touch used in pianoforte playing.   I
am a firm believer in associating the appropriate
kind of touch with the passage studied from the very
beginning.   If the passage calls for a staccato touch

do not waste your time as many do by practicing it legato. Again, in a cantabile passage do not make the mistake of using a touch that would produce the wrong quality of tone. The wrists at all times should be in the most supple possible condition. There should never be any constraint at that point. When I resumed my musical studies with Paderewski after a lapse of several years he laid greatest emphasis upon this point. I feel that the most valuable years for the development of touch and tone are those which bind the natural facility of the child hand with the acquired agility of the adult. To my great misfortune I was not able to practice between the ages of twelve and eighteen. This was due to excessive study and extensive concert tours as a prodigy. These wrecked my health and it was only by the hardest kind of practice in after life that I was able to regain the natural facility that had marked my playing in childhood. In fact I owe everything to the kind persistence and wonderful inspiration of M. Paderewski.

The Right Tempo

"The right tempo is a very important matter for the student. First of all, he must be absolutely positive that his time is correct. There is nothing so barbarous in all piano-playing as a bad conception of time. Even the inexperienced and unmusical listener detects bad time. The student should consider this matter one of greatest importance and demand perfect time from himself. With some students this can only be cultivated after much painful effort. The metronome is of assistance, as is counting, but these are not enough. The pupil must create a sense of time, he must have a sort of internal metronome which he must feel throbbing within all the time.

"Always begin your practice slowly and gradually advance the tempo. The worst possible thing is to start practicing too fast. It invariably leads to bad results and to lengthy delays. The right tempo will come with time and you must have patience until you can develop it. In the matter of 'tempo rubato' passages, which always invite disaster upon the part of the student, the general idea is that the right hand must be out of time with the left. This is not always the case, as they sometimes play in unison. The word simply implies 'robbing the time,' but it is robbed after the same manner in which one 'robs Peter to pay Paul,' that is, a ritard in one part of the measure must be compensated for by an acceleration in another part of the measure. If the right hand is to play at variance with the left hand the latter remains as a kind of anchor upon which the tempo of the entire measure must depend. Chopin called the left hand the *chef d'orchestre* and a very good appellation this is. Take, for instance, his *B flat minor Prelude*. In the latter part of this wonderful composition the regular rhythmic repetition in octaves in the bass makes a rhythmic foundation which the most erratic and nervous right hand cannot shake.

RHYTHMIC PECULIARITIES

"Rhythm is the basis of everything. Even the silent mountain boulders are but the monuments of some terrible rhythmic convulsion of the earth in past ages. There is a rhythm in the humming bird and there is a rhythm in the movements of a giant locomotive. We are all rhythmic in our speech, our walk, and in our life more or less. How important then is the study of the rhythmic peculiarities of the new piece. Every contributing accent which gives motion and characteristic swing to the piece must be carefully studied. It is rhythm which sways the audience. Some performers are so gifted with the ability to invest their interpretations with a rhythmic charm that they seem to fairly invigorate their audiences with the spirit of motion. I cannot conceive of a really great artist without this sense of rhythm.

THE COMPOSER'S INSPIRATION

"Personally I believe in 'pure music,' that is music in the field of pianoforte composition that is sufficient unto itself and which does not require any of the other arts to enhance its beauty. However, in the cases of some of our modern composers who have professedly drawn their musical inspiration from tales, great pictures or from nature, I can see the desirability of investigating these sources in order to come closer to the composer's idea.   Some of the works of Debussy demand this.   Let me play you his '*Night in Granada*,' for instance.   The work is most subtle and requires an appreciation of Oriental life, and is indeed a kind of tonal dream picture of the old fortified palace of Moorish Spain.   I feel that in cases of this kind it helps the performer to have in mind the composer's conception and in playing this piece in public I always follow this plan.

STUDYING THE PHRASING

"Each phrase in a piece requires separate study. I believe that the student should leave nothing undone to learn how to phrase or rather to analyze a piece so that all its constituent phrases become clear to him.   Each phrase must be studied with the same deference to detail that the singer would give to an individual phrase.   This is by no means an easy matter.   More important still is the interrelation of phrases.   Every note in a work of musical art bears a certain relation to every other note.   So it is with the phrases.   Each phrase must be played with reference to the work as a whole or more particularly to the movement of which it is a part.

MARKING THE FINGERING

"It seems hardly necessary to say anything about the fingering when so much attention is being given to the matter by the best teachers of the country, but certainly one of the most essential considerations

in the study of a new piece is the study of the fingering. A detailed study of this should be made and
it should be clearly understood that the fingering
should be adapted to fit the hand of the player. It
is by no means necessary to accept the fingering
given in the book as 'gospel.' The wise student
will try many fingerings before deciding upon the
one that suits him best. Students who go to these
pains are the ones who invariably succeed. Those
who take anything that is presented to them without considering its advisability rarely attain lofty
musical heights.

"When a fingering has once been determined upon
it should never be changed. To change a fingering
frequently means to waste many hours of practice.
This may be considered a mechanical method but
it is the method invariably employed by successful
artists. Why? Simply because one fingering closely
adhered to establishes finger habits which give
freedom and certainty and permits the player to
give more consideration to the other details of artistic
interpretation.

"I ofttimes find it expedient to adapt a more difficult fingering of some given passage for the reason
that the difficult fingering frequently leads to a
better interpretation of the composer's meaning. I
know of innumerable passages in the piano classics
which illustrate this point. Moreover a fingering
that seems difficult at first is often more simple than
the conventional or arbitrary fingering employed

by the student, after the student has given sufficient time to the new fingering. The required accent often obliges the performer to employ a different fingering. The stronger fingers are naturally better adapted to the stronger accents. Otherwise it is best to use a similar fingering for similar passages.

MEMORIZING

"I should like to add a few words with regard to committing pieces to memory. There are three ways. 1, By sight; that is, seeing the notes in your mind's eye; 2, memorizing by 'ear,' the way which comes to one most naturally; 3, memorizing by the fingers, that is training the fingers to do their duty no matter what happens. Before performing in public the student should have memorized the composition in all of these ways. Only thus can he be absolutely sure of himself. If one way fails him the other method comes to his rescue.

"After careful attention has been given to the various points of which I have spoken and the details of the composition satisfactorily worked out the student should practice with a view to learning the piece as a whole. Nothing is so distressing to the musician as a piece which does not seem to have coherence and unity. It should be regarded aurally as the artist regards his work visually. The painter stands off at some distance to look at his work in order to see whether all parts of his painting harmonize. The pianist must do much the same thing.

He must listen to his work time and time again and if it does not seem to 'hang together' he must unify all the parts until he can give a real interpretation instead of a collection of disjointed sections. This demands grasp, insight and talent, three qualifications without which the pianist cannot hope for large success."

QUESTIONS IN STYLE, INTERPRETATION, EXPRESSION AND TECHNIC OF PIANOFORTE PLAYING

SERIES XVIII
ERNEST SCHELLING

1. What should be the preliminary study of a new composition'?

2. How should the mechanical difficulties of the piece be studied?

3. How may one find the bearing of one movement upon another?

4. State the importance of deciding upon the appropriate touch.

5. How may the right tempo be established?

6. What did Chopin call the left hand?

7. What is it in playing that sways the audience?

8. How should the fingering of a new piece be studied?

9. Why is a more difficult fingering sometimes preferable?

10. Give a practical plan for memorizing.

SIGISMUND STOJOWSKI

BIOGRAPHICAL

Sigismund Stojowski was born at Strelce, Poland, May 2, 1870. He studied piano with L. Zelenski at Cracow and with Diémer at the Paris Conservatoire. At the same institution he studied composition with Léo Delibes. His talent both as a composer and as a pianist was considered extraordinary at that time and he was successful in carrying off two first prizes, one for piano and one for composition (1889). At that time Stojowski's great fellow countryman, Paderewski, assumed the educational supervision of his career and became his teacher in person.

Stojowski's orchestral compositions attracted wide attention in Paris and he met with pronounced success as a virtuoso. Mr. Stojowski came to America in 1906 and he entered immediately into the musical life of the country, taking foremost rank as a composer, pianist and teacher. Aside from his musical talent he is a remarkable linguist and speaks many languages fluently. His articles written in English, for instance, are unusually graphic and expressive. Once when complimented upon his linguistic ability he remarked "We Poles are given the credit of being natural linguists because we take the trouble to learn many languages thoroughly in our youth." In 1913 Mr. Stojowski made a highly successful tour abroad, his compositions meeting with wide favor.

21

WHAT INTERPRETATION REALLY IS

SIGISMUND STOJOWSKI

THE COMPOSER'S LIMITATIONS IN HIS MEANS OF EXPRESSION

IT is difficult for some people who are not versed in the intricate mysteries of the art of music to realize how limited are the means afforded the composer for communicating to the interpreter some slight indication of the ideal he had in mind when writing the composition. It may be said that, while every great composer feels almost God-like at the moment of creation, the merest fraction of the myriad beauties he has in mind ever reach human ears. The very signs with which the composer is provided to help him put his thoughts down on paper are in themselves inadequate to serve as a means of recording more than a shadow of his masterpiece as it was originally conceived. Of course, we are speaking now in a large sense—we are imagining that the composer is a Beethoven with an immortal message to convey to posterity. Of all composers, Beethoven was perhaps the one to employ the most perfect means of expression. His works represent a completeness, a poise and a masterly finish which will serve as a model for all time to come. It must also be noted that few composers have employed more accurate marks of expression—such as time marks, dynamic marks, etc.

In all these things Beethoven was obliged to adhere to the conventions adopted by others for this purpose of attempting to make the composer's meaning clearer to other minds. These conventions, like all conventions, are partly insufficient to convey the full idea of the composer, and partly arbitrary, in that they do not give the interpreter adequate latitude to introduce his own ideas in expression. The student should seek to break the veil of conventions provided by notation and seek a clearer insight into the composer's individuality as expressed in his compositions. From this point of view the so-called subjective interpretation seems the only legitimate one. In fact, the ones who pretend to be objective in the sense of being literal and playing strictly according to the marks of expression and admitting little elasticity in the interpretation of these are also, as Rubinstein pointed out, subjective at heart. This may be more concisely expressed thus: Since all things of permanent value in music have proceeded from a fervid artistic imagination, they should be interpreted with the continual employment of the performer's imagination.

On the other hand, the subjective method, right as it is in principle, can become, of course, according to the Italian saying, *Traduttore, traditore*— that is, an absolute treachery to the composer's ideal, if the performer's understanding and execution of the composition is not based upon long and careful investigation of all the fundamental laws and associated branches of musical study, which are designed to give him a basis for forming his own opinions upon the best method of interpreting the composition. Inadequate training in this respect is the Chinese Wall which surrounds the composer's hidden meaning. This wall must be torn down, brick by brick, stone by stone, in a manner which we would call "analytical practice." It is the only way in which the student may gain entrance to the sacred city of the elect, to whom the ideal of the composer has been revealed.

The Interpreter Must Coöperate with the Composer

In a certain sense the interpreter is a coöperator with the composer, or, more definitely expressed, he is the "continuer" along the line of the musical thought and its adequate expression. Music, of all arts, is the unfinished art. When a great painting is completed, time, and time only, will make the changes in its surface. When the great masterpieces left the brushes of Raphael, Rubens, Holbein, Correggio or Van Dyck they were finished works of art. When Bach, Beethoven, Chopin, and Brahms put their thoughts down upon paper they left a record in ink and paper which must be born again every time it is brought to the minds of men. This rebirth is the very essence of all that is best in interpretative skill. New life goes into the composition at the very moment it passes through the soul of the master performer. It is here that he should realize the great truth that in music, more than in any other art, "the letter kills and the spirit vivifies." The interpreter must master the "letter" and seek to give "rebirth" to the spirit. If he can do this he will attain the greatest in interpretative ability.

From the literal or objective standpoint, then, an insight is gained into the nature of the composer's masterpiece,—by close and careful study of the work itself, by gaining a knowledge of the musical laws underlying the structure and composition of a work of its kind as well as the necessary keyboard technic to give expression to the work,—but the veil is torn from the composer's hidden meaning, only becoming intimate with his creative personality as a master, by studying his life environments, by investigating the historical background of the period in which he worked, by learning of his joys and his sufferings, by cultivating a deep and heartfelt sympathy for his ideals and by the scrupulous and constant revision of one's own ideals and conceptions of the standards by which his masterpieces should be judged.

STUDYING THE HISTORICAL BACKGROUND

To exemplify what I mean, I could, for instance, refer to Paderewski's interpretations of Liszt and Chopin. During the time I was associated with the master pianist as a pupil I had abundant opportunities to make notes upon the very individual, as well as the highly artistically differentiated expressions of his musical judgment. It was interesting to observe that he played the Rhapsodies with various extensions and modifications, the result of which is the glorification of Liszt's own spirit. On the contrary, in order to preserve Chopin's spirit, the master would always repudiate any changes, like those of Tausig, for instance, by which some virtuosos pretend to "emphasize" or "modernize" Chopin's personal and perfect pianism. Differences in treatment are the outcome of deep insight as well as the study of the time and conditions under which the work was produced.

The study of musical history reveals many very significant things which have a direct bearing not only upon the interpretation of the performer, but upon the degree of appreciation with which the listener is able to enjoy a musical work. It was for this reason that I prefaced the first two recitals of my course of historical recitals given at Mendelssohn Hall, New York, during the past season, with a lecture upon the historical conditions which surrounded the masters at the time the compositions were composed.

The Inadequacy of Musical Signs

I have already referred to the inadequacy of musical signs. Even the mechanical guide, the metronome, is not always to be depended upon to give the exact tempo the composer had in mind. Let me cite a little instance from the biography of Ries, the friend of Beethoven. Ries was preparing to conduct a performance of the Beethoven Ninth Symphony.   He requested Beethoven to make notes upon paper regarding the metronomic marks of speed at which the composition should be played.   The metronome at that time was a comparatively new instrument. Maelzel, its inventor (or, rather, its improver, since the principle of the metronome was of Dutch origin), was a friend of Beethoven.   At times they were on the best of terms, and at other times they were literally "at swords' points."   Nevertheless, Maelzel, who had a strong personality, succeeded in inducing Beethoven to put metronomic markings upon several of his compositions.   Naturally, the metronome was immediately accorded an important place in the musical world even at that day.   Ries was consequently very anxious to give the Choral Symphony according to Beethoven's own ideas.   Beethoven had complied with the publisher's desire and sent a slip of paper with the tempi marked metronomically.   This slip was lost.   Ries wrote to Beethoven for a duplicate. Beethoven sent another.   Later the lost slip was found, and, upon comparing it with the second slip, it was found that Beethoven had made an entirely different estimate of the tempi at which he desired the Symphony to be played.

Even with the most elaborate and complete marks of expression, such as those, for instance, employed by Beethoven and by Wagner, the composer is confronted with his great poverty of resources to present his views to the mind of the interpreter.   Extensive as some of the modern dictionaries of musical terminology seem to be, they are wholly inadequate from the standpoint of a complete vocabulary to give full expression to the artist's imagination. It also gives full scope to an infinite variety of error in the matter of the shades or degrees of dynamic force at which the conventional marks may be rendered.

One might venture to remark that composers are the most keen, most conscious judges of their own works, or, rather, of the garments which fit them best. There is in all composition a divine part and also a conscious part. The divine part is the inspiration. The conscious part has to do with dressing the inspiration in its most appropriate harmonic, polyphonic, and rhythmic garments. These garments are the raiment in which the inspiration will be viewed by future generations. It is often by these garments that they will be judged. If the garments are awkward, inappropriate and ill-fitting, a beautiful interpretation of the composer's ideal will be impossible. Nevertheless, it is the performer's duty in each case to try to see through even unbecoming garments and divine the composer's thought, according to the interpreter's best understanding.

LEARNING THE MUSICAL LANGUAGE

Where interpretation is concerned, one is too often inclined to forget that while there is a higher part, the secrets of which are accessible only to the elect, there is also an elementary part which involves the knowledge of musical grammar, and beyond that the correct feeling of musical declamation—since music, after all, is a language which is at all times perfectly teachable, and which should be most carefully and systematically taught. I consider the book of Mathis Lussy, *Rhythm and Musical Expression*, of great value to the student in search of truths pertaining to intelligent interpretation. Lussy was a Swiss who was born in the early part of the last century. He went to Paris to study medicine, but, having had a musical training in the country of his birth, he became a good pianoforte teacher and an excellent writer upon musical subjects. While teaching in a young ladies' school, he was confronted with the great paucity of real knowledge of the rudiments of expression, and he accordingly prepared a book upon the subject which has since been translated into several languages. This book is most helpful, and I advocate its use frequently. It should be in the hands of every conscientious piano student.

Mistakes Peculiar to the Pianoforte Player

The nature of the keyboard of the piano, and the ease with which certain things are accomplished, make it possible for the performer to make certain errors which the construction of other instruments would prevent. The pianist is, for instance, entirely unlike the violinist, who has to locate his keyboard every time he takes up his instrument, and, moreover, locate it by a highly trained sense of position. In a certain way I sometimes feel somewhat ashamed for the pianist profession when I hear players, even those with manifest technical proficiency, commit flagrant mistakes against elementary rules of accentuation and phrasing, such as, for instance, an average violinist acquainted with good bowing is accordingly prevented from making upon his instrument.

The means of discovering the composer's hidden meaning are, in fact, so numerous that the conscientious interpreter must keep upon continuous voyages of exploration. There are many easily recognizable paths leading to the promised land—one is the path of harmony, without an understanding of which the would-be performer can never reach his goal; another is musical history; others are the studies of phrasing, rhythm, accentuation, pedaling, etc., etc., *ad infinitum*. To fail to traverse any one of these roads will result in endless exasperation. Find your guide, press on without thinking of failure, and the way to success may be found before you know it.

QUESTIONS IN STYLE, INTERPRETATION, EXPRESSION AND TECHNIC OF PIANOFORTE PLAYING

SERIES XIX

SIGISMUND STOJOWSKI

1. What composer preserved the most perfect balance between artistic conception and expression?

2. How may the student break the veil of conventions?

3. What fundamental laws should underlie interpretation?

4. How may master works be born again?

5. Is one ever warranted in altering a masterpiece?

6. Tell of Beethoven's attitude toward the metronome.

7. How may errors arise in the use of the terms of expression?

8. How may one be helped in learning the musical language?

9. State some mistakes peculiar to the pianoforte.

10. What voyages of exploration must the student make?

IGNAZ JAN PADEREWSKI

Biographical

Ignaz Jan Paderewski was born at Kurylowka, Podolia, Poland, November 6, 1860. At the Warsaw Conservatory he was a pupil of Raguski. His first concert tour occurred when he was sixteen years of age. Three years later he became a teacher at the Warsaw Conservatory. Thereafter he went to Berlin where he studied under Urban and Wuerst. He did not go to Leschetizky until he was twenty-four years of age. For a short time he was a professor at the Strasburg Conservatory at a very small salary. He returned to Leschetizky, and shortly thereafter he commenced making public appearances. His success was soon triumphant. In 1890 he made his first appearances in England, and became immensely popular. In 1891 he visited America, and has since made many tours of the United States. His pianoforte playing has been so frequently appraised by great critics that it is unnecessary to comment upon it here. By many he is regarded as the greatest composer of his race with the exception of Chopin. His many noteworthy compositions for the piano are heard far too rarely from the keyboards of other virtuosos. There is a charm and originality about his works such as the *Chants du Voyager*, the *Concerto in A Minor*, the *Humoresques* and the *Toccata* that command permanent attention from the musical world. His opera *Manru* has been given occasionally in Europe and in America. It is a work of force and distinctiveness. His *Symphony in B Minor*, first given by the Boston Symphony Orchestra in 1909, is a work of large dimensions and fresh inspiration. During the great war Paderewski gave enormously from his wealth and income to stricken Poland. In 1900 Paderewski gave by Deed of Trust a sum of $10,000 to establish a prize to be given every three years for the best compositions submitted by native Americans. Among those who have won the prizes in the past have been H. K. Hadley, H. W. Parker, Arthur Bird and Arthur Shepherd.

22

BREADTH IN MUSICAL ART

IGNAZ JAN PADEREWSKI

THE call for breadth in musical art has been insistent since the earliest days of its history. Yet one can not help being conscious of the fact that the public in general is inclined to look upon all art workers as idealists confined to a narrow road very much apart from the broad pathway of life itself. As a matter of fact, the art-worker never approaches the great until he has placed himself in communication with life in all its wonderful manifestations. Take, for instance, the case of the remarkable Florentine painter Leonardo da Vinci. The average reader would probably remember him as the creator of the much discussed Mona Lisa, but he was far more than a painter. He was an architect, an engineer, a sculptor, a scientist, a mechanician, and he even made excursions into the art of music, to say nothing of that of aerial navigation. Da Vinci lived over four centuries ago, and yet even in our own time, one now and then finds well meaning individuals who fail to realize that unless the artist has the element of breadth in all his work, his productions must be, to say the least, transient in value.

Again, we encounter the case of another great Italian artist, Michelangelo, painter, sculptor, ar-

chitect and poet. Could the creator of so many
amazingly beautiful art works have been as great
had he not possessed the universal quality of mind
which must have compelled him to develop the
technic of expression in many different forms of
his art? This can not be attributed so much to a
kind of natural versatility as to his great breadth
of vision, his communion with life in many different forms. The case of Richard Wagner is likewise one in which our attention is drawn to a remarkable exhibition of breadth. In his earliest
works Wagner followed the traditions of the
Italian and French opera composers. *Rienzi* is
quite as spectacular in its *mise en scène* as anything
that Meyerbeer ever wrote, but Wagner's broad
outlook upon life soon led him to reach out for
larger works. While it is frequently averred by
man-critics that Wagner's music is greatly superior
to his verse, we must nevertheless remember that
the music of one of his earlier operas was rejected
at the Paris opera and the libretto accepted for the
use of another composer. In Wagner one finds not
only the composer, but the poet and the creator
of immortal stage pictures.

Many of the great composers of the past have
been men of such pronounced musical breadth that
they could not have confined themselves to the
creative branches of their work. Bach, Handel,
Mozart, Beethoven, Weber, Mendelssohn, Brahms

and others took great pride in their public performances. Indeed, in the early days of musical art, when the literature of the piano, for instance, was insignificant in comparison with its great present wealth, the interpreter was in many cases identical with composer. Interest centered in him because of the fact that he was gifted with the creative faculty. Bach, indeed, was not only a masterly organist but could play the violin and the clavichord in a manner which attracted wide attention. Since the time of Bach, however, the score of music has increased so enormously that if one masters the literature of one instrument he will have accomplished a great task. But he should not, however, permit this accomplishment to obliterate everything else in his life, as so many apparently think he must do. If he possesses the mind of a creator he owes it to himself and to society to develop that as well. He must keep in touch with the great movements of his time and of the past in art, science, history and philosophy. The student who sacrifices these things can never hope to climb to fame on a ladder of technic.

SERIOUS INTEREST IN STUDY

The need for technic must, nevertheless, not be underrated. Technic demands patient, painstaking, persistent study. Art without technic is invertebrate, shapeless, characterless. You ask me whether the Poles, for instance, are a musical people. I can only say that one constantly meets in Poland young men and women with the most exceptional musical talent—but what is talent without serious, earnest study leading to artistic and technical perfection?

For more than one hundred years Poland has been woefully restricted in its devlopment. Without national resources and with limited school facilities little progress of a broad character has been possible. In the conservatory at Warsaw, for instance, we meet at once a decided difference between that institution and the great music schools at Moscow and St. Petersburg. In the Russian conservatories general educational work goes hand in hand with music, and the result is that the students receive a comprehensive course leading to high culture. If the same studies were introduced in the Warsaw schools, instruction would have to be in the Russian language and the Polish opposition to this is so great that such a plan could only meet with failure. One can but take pride in a nation that has been divided for a century, yet still maintains the integrity of its mother tongue.

As a consequence of the educational conditions in Poland there has been in the past what might be described as a lack of ambition to develop serious works of art. The people strive to be light-hearted and much of the music one hears in the home takes its complexion from this spirit. However, there has developed in Poland during the last twenty or twenty-five years what many now regard as the new Polish school of music. Much of this is due to the efforts of that remarkable man Sigismund Noszkowski.

Noszkowski was born in 1848. He was early fired with an intense zeal to develop the melodic resources of his native land. For a time he studied under Kiel and Raif at Berlin, but in the late eighties he became a professor at the Warsaw Conservatory. His noble attitude toward his art may be estimated from the fact that his efforts for a time were confined to the invention of a system of musical notation for the blind. His example soon inspired many younger men to work at musical creation and as a result we can point at the present moment to distinguished younger composers with really remarkable accomplishments as musicians. Among the best known I may quote such names as Szymanowski, Rozycki, Melcer. The composer Fitelberg is frequently classed among the members of the new Polish school, despite the fact that he is properly of Russian-Jewish origin.

By the use of themes suggesting those of the folk music of Poland, these younger men, all finely equipped for their careers through exhaustive technical training, have produced new musical works which must contribute much to the fame of Poland

and to the pride of the Poles. This has been accomplished, it should be remembered, despite the
political and educational restrictions and notwithstanding the fact that the scarcity of means for
promoting musical culture in Poland is almost lu-
dicrous. The conservatory, for instance, has a
subvention of only about four thousand dollars
a year.

BREADTH THROUGH PRACTICE

While there are many extremely gifted musicians
in Poland, the young people, like the young people
of many lands, are far too inclined to look upon
music as a pastime rather than as a serious study.
This does not mean that the student should elimi-
nate the joy or the pleasure from his work at the
keyboard, but he should rather find his true happiness in labor of a more serious kind. In Poland
the general state of the musical development is not
very great, but this is not due to lack of talent. In
fact the quantity of talent is in some cases surprisingly high. This is particularly the case among
executive artists. They have rich imaginations and
great temporary zeal, but lack the inclination or
ability to regard music as a serious art worthy of a
great life struggle.

Students spend too much time in playing and too
little in work. It seems beyond the comprehension
of many that hour after hour may be thrown away

at the keyboard and little or nothing accomplished. The very essence of success is, of course, practice. But students who are gifted are very likely to be so enchanted with a composition that they dream away the priceless practice minutes without any more definite purpose than that of amusing themselves. It is human to crave pleasure and the more musical the student the more that student is inclined to revel in the musical beauties of a new work rather than to devote the practice time to the more laborious but vastly more productive process of real hard music study.

Music Study Is Work

This is often especially true of exercises, scales, arpeggios, etc. Students with monstrous technical shortcomings neglect all exercises with the sublime conceit that they are different from other mortals and can afford to do without them. They are quite willing to attempt the most difficult things in the piano repertoire. The highest peaks are nothing to them. They will essay anything before they are able to climb and the result is almost invariably disastrous. Music study is work. Those who work are the only ones in any art who ever win the greatest rewards. What could be more obvious? Still it is one of the greatest truths in all music study. It is very delightful to sit at the keyboard and revel in some great masterpiece, but when it comes to the

systematic study of some exacting detail of fingering, pedaling, phrasing, touch, dynamics: that is
work, and nothing but work. One can not be too
emphatic on this point.

PRACTICE THAT LEADS TO BREADTH

One is often importuned for suggestions to help
aspiring pianists in their practice. While one may
welcome an opportunity to help others in this particular, there is very little that can be said. System
is perhaps the most essential thing in practice. I
do not mean a system that is so inelastic that it can
not be instantly adapted to changing needs, but I
do refer to the fact that the student who wishes
to progress regularly must have some system in his
daily work. He must have some design, some
chart, some plan for his development. A bad plan
is better than no plan. In his daily practice, however, he should see to it that he does not narrow
himself. His plan should be a comprehensive one
and should embrace as many things as he can
possibly do superlatively well, and no more.

MUSICAL CULTURE IN THE HOME

Music in itself is one of the greatest forces for
developing breadth in the home. Far too many students study music with the view to becoming great
virtuosi. Music should be studied for itself without
any great aim in view except in the cases of marvel-

ously talented children. Again, many children might be developed into teachers or composers who would never make virtuosos. This should be very carefully considered. Most of the students assume that the career of the virtuoso is easier, more illustrious, and last but not least, more lucrative than that of the composer. But is it not better to start out to be a great composer or a great teacher and become one, rather than to strive to be a virtuoso and prove a fiasco?

The intellectual drill which the study of music gives the child is of great educational value. There is nothing which will take its place and it is for this reason that many of the greatest educators have advocated it so highly. In addition to this the actual study of music results in almost limitless gratification in later life in the understanding of great musical masterpieces.

I am very much impressed with the educational value of the mechanical means for representing music, such as the best piano players with the best rolls and the sound-reproducing machines with the best records. I know of one instance of a man who possessed a high class player-piano. At first he refused to have anything to do with music except that of the most popular description, such as popular songs and light operas. Gradually his taste was revolutionized and now he will not permit any trashy music in his home. This was accomplished in such a short time that I was astonished. Naturally such a man would want his children, or anyone in whom he was interested, to attend the best concerts, the best operas and secure instruction in the art of music. In other words, a person addicted to very trivial music was won over to music of the best description. His whole outlook upon the art was changed and he was made a broader man in this sense.

I can not but feel that these mechanical means of reproducing music, in addition to carrying masterpieces to thousands who might not otherwise be able to become acquainted with them, will at the same time develop a more widespread demand for musical instruction, for the mysteries of the most beautiful of arts will always have their fascination as well as their educational benefits.

Questions in Style, Interpretation, Expression and Technic of Pianoforte Playing

SERIES XX

IGNAZ JAN PADEREWSKI

1. How does the art worker approach the great in his art?
2. Name seven master composers who were also noted for their ability at the keyboard?
3. What instruments did Bach play?

4. How has the conservatory at Warsaw differed in the past from the leading conservatories of Russia?

5. What is the essence of pianistic success?

6. What is one of the dangers of gifted students?

7. State the value of a plan in piano study.

8. What should be the principal aim of music in the home?

9. Of what value as an intellectual drill is music?

10. Is there any subject that will take the place of music in general educational work?

YOLANDA MÉRÖ

BIOGRAPHICAL

Although Mme. Mérö's first American tour was as recent as 1910, she has already become one of the best known of the artists touring America. This is particularly noteworthy, as she came to this country unsupported by the name of any famous teacher to help her in gaining recognition with the American public. She was not a pupil of Liszt or of Leschetizky or Rubinstein, but of teachers whose names are known to but very few Americans. Unknown, she won upon her own merits, and her position has constantly advanced by the same means. Her career is an illustration of the fact that the teacher with a great career is not necessary to the student's success. Mme. Mérö was born in Budapest in 1887. Her first teacher was her father. At six she entered the *National Concervatory* and remained there for eight years. Her pianoforte teacher was Augusta Rennebaum, a pupil of Liszt. Mme. Mérö has met with significant success in all of the European music centres. Just at this time, when the world is amazed at the wonderful efficiency of the methods in all phases of activity in the countries under Teutonic influence, the following interview should prove very interesting indeed.

23

THOROUGHNESS IN HUNGARIAN MUSIC STUDY

MME. YOLANDA MÉRÖ

COMPARATIVELY few American tourists visit Budapest after the manner in which they go in veritable droves to London, Berlin, Paris, Munich, Venice and Nuremberg. The reason probably is that the city is something over one hundred miles further than Vienna, and American tourists are fearful that they might not be so readily understood. As a matter of fact Budapest is the most hospitable of cities and the tourist has less difficulty there in making himself understood than he does in some of the western centres of culture in Europe.

Musically speaking, Budapest has the advantage of the so-called German efficiency and the Hungarian *Zal*, or spirit which is eternally identified with all phases of Magyar art. Part of the Hungarian capital reaches back to the middle ages, and other parts are as modern, or if you please as "up-to-date," as any American city. Education is revered and the University has in the vicinity of five thousand students. It is a city of very nearly one million inhabitants and what an interesting city it is with its cosmopolitan ancestry and its cosmopolitan present. Life lacks little in variety and color in the old city on the Danube. There people

of all nations meet. The predominating spirit is
Hungarian, although there are thousands of Ger-
mans and Austrians in the city, as indeed there are
French and English and orientals. Please get out
of your head the idea that Hungarians are necessarily gipsies. As a matter of fact the gipsy popu-
lation of Hungary is comparatively small. There
are, however, many influences from the Orient
which one cannot fail to note. As late as the time
of the birth of Bach, Budapest was under Turkish
control and was the seat of a Turkish Pasha. It is
desirable to review the character of Hungary in
order to understand the nature of Hungarian musical education. In no city of the world do exactly
the same conditions exist.

Hungary's Great Music Schools

In Budapest there are two great musical institutions both of which were founded by Franz Liszt.
One is the Royal Academy and the other is the
National Conservatory. Liszt's pupil, Count Zichy,
who in young manhood lost his right arm and then
startled the world with his wonderful left hand
playing, has been the artistic executor of Liszt in
these great undertakings in that he has given of his
time and energies in a most generous manner to
the National Conservatory of which he is the president.

While there are many private teachers in Budapest, the government institutions set the standard and all other teachers are obliged to live up to that standard. The schools begin at the very beginning. Every step is taken up and nothing is left out. The pupil is not permitted to advance until the examiners have become convinced that everything has been comprehended. Women have played a very interesting part in Hungarian musical education. Lina Ramann, although born in Bavaria, devised a system of training for the young which has influenced Hungarian music teachers in that it demanded that little children should sing songs as a part of their training. Lina Ramann was a pupil of Liszt and was his biographer. It is understood that she was advised by Liszt in many of the reforms that she instituted. My own teacher, Mme. Augusta Rennebaum, had the greatest regard for her common sense ideas pointing to musical development along artistic lines. Unfortunately her valuable essays upon elementary musical training have not been translated into English.

While the general line of musical instruction in the Hungarian schools is not so very different from that of the German schools, the pupils are characterized by the enthusiastic Hungarian temperament and the interest in the work is intense in the extreme. There is constant rivalry among the pupils even in such matters as technic or simple scale playing. The pupils are kept at a white heat of interest and competition is very severe. The concerts that occur with great frequency are of immense help to the student. How is the student to gain his orchestral repertoire unless he has a chance to perform his concertos with orchestras? This opportunity the Budapest conservatories give in liberal measure. When I went out into the professional world I did not have merely a theoretical knowledge of the actual work of the concert platform for I had played the great works with the conservatory orchestra,—not an amateur orchestra stumbling along with me as a hindrance but a finely drilled body of players capable of taking the most difficult music and doing it well. It is one thing to be able to play the Liszt E flat major Concerto or the Chopin F minor Concerto with a second piano accompaniment and quite another thing to play them with a full orchestra. There are great numbers of most excellent teachers in America including some of the finest living masters, but the student who aspires to play with the great orchestras of the country (every touring virtuoso of the present day must do that in addition to his solo playing) should have practical drill with a real orchestra or run the chance of making a fiasco at the first concert.

A Fault in American Musical Training

One fault I would find with American musical

training, and that is that the pupils run after so many different teachers. I saved years by sticking to one good teacher. American music students should cultivate more respect for their teachers and teachers should be so thorough and so sincere that they will command respect. A teacher is not a suit of clothes that can be changed every day or every half hour. The selection of a good teacher is a serious problem but once you have found a good one and find yourself progressing properly, don't think of changing because someone suggests that you might do better under another teacher. The Hungarian musical students are spared such unfortunate changes because their musical training is intelligently guided. The parents have respect for the judgment of musicians of established reputation and do not as a rule attempt to interfere in things about which they know little or nothing. I have a feeling that many American parents of pupils who could be put to shame musically by Hungarian parents of the same station meddle needlessly with the musical education of their children, sending them from teacher to teacher until the child has nothing but a muddled idea of what he is doing. Why cannot Americans see fit to leave the direction of the careers of their children to specialists?

In much the same manner Americans have been sent in hordes to Europe for the benefits of the efficient training in some centers only to find that they could have accomplished as much if they had gone to the right teachers in America. Why send pupils to Europe half-trained to have the thorough European teachers laugh at them and gain a contemptuous idea of American musical training when as a matter of fact the right teachers in America would have given them quite as thorough a drilling as they could have gotten in any European country.

THE LAND OF LISZT

It is natural that in the land of Liszt the piano should be the most popular instrument. The interesting cembalo that one sees in Hungarian bands is comparatively rare,—as the zither is rare in modern Germany. It is a national instrument, but the most popular instrument of Hungary is unquestionably the piano, with the violin as second. Pianists' concerts in Budapest are attended with the same interest with which the people of New York flock to the opera. The student is of course influenced by this. If one lives in a community where the piano is respected only as a piece of machinery, as one would respect a steam boiler or a threshing-machine, the interest in the instrument is not likely to be very uplifting to the student. Liszt was, and still is, one of the great national heroes of Hungary, and Liszt was first and foremost a pianist. In no country of the world has the piano a higher station than it has in Hungary. The interest in

everything pianistic is serious and deep. The
pianist is somebody. This principle needs no explanation. It is human to crave appreciation. Nobody is impelled to spend a lifetime in developing
something that will be rejected by the public. For
this reason the Hungarian music student, even
though he is at the same time a violinist, usually
plays the piano and plays it well.

GIPSY INFLUENCES

In Hungary the peasants still invent folk songs
for their own entertainment. They have no idea
of ever doing anything more than amusing their
own circle of friends with the pretty tunes. Many
of the themes that are believed by the public to be
Gipsy themes are no more nor less than these Magyar folk songs that have been appropriated by the
Gipsies and played by them as they roamed around
the country. The Hungarian themes have had a
great influence upon Hungarian music of the more
developed kind. Liszt was among the first to utilize
this material. But it is a great mistake to believe
that the themes are Gipsy in their origin. One
hears it said that modern Hungarian composers
such as Bartok and Kedaly, who are as advanced in
their methods as Debussy, have employed Gipsy
themes. They have been subject to Hungarian influences but their Gipsy influence is limited to the
exploitation of Hungarian themes by the roaming

Gipsy players. This is a distinction which Hungarians are proud to make as they do not wish to be classed as nomads any more than the Bohemians wish to be thought the free and easy habitués of the studio districts which the misuse of the name Bohemian has given to them.

QUESTIONS IN STYLE, INTERPRETATION, EXPRESSION AND TECHNIC OF PIANOFORTE PLAYING

SERIES XXI

MME. YOLANDO MÉRÖ

1. Who founded the leading musical institutions of Hungary?

2. What famous Bavarian woman had much to do with the development of music in Hungary?

3. State one of the advantages of public performance in Hungarian conservatories?

4. What is one of the serious faults in American musical education?

5. What is one of the dangers in sending American pupils to Europe?

6. How is the piano regarded in Hungary?

7. Have the Hungarian Folk Themes originated in Gypsy music?

RUDOLF GANZ

Biographical

Mr. Rudolph Ganz has made repeated tours of the United States, gaining continual favor every year. He has the unique distinction of being one of the few musicians of Swiss birth who have come to renown in the United States. Mr. Ganz was born in Zurich, February 24, 1877. His first studies in music were received at the Zurich Conservatory under Robert Freund (piano) and Joh. Hegar ('cello). He was then placed under the instruction of his uncle, Carl Eschmann-Dumur, in Lausanne. It was at this time that he made his first appearance as a pianist, a 'cellist and organist and as a composer. Then he went to Strasburg, where he became the pupil of Fritz Blumer at the local conservatory. Thereafter he went to Berlin and studied a short time with Ferruccio Busoni. His teachers in composition were Charles Blanchet (at Lausanne) and Heinrich Urban (at Berlin). In 1899 he appeared several times as a pianist with the Berlin Philharmonic Orchestra and also directed his own First Symphony. In 1900 he was called to Chicago, where he remained for five years as a teacher in a leading conservatory. Then he returned to Europe with the view of giving more time and attention to his concert work and to composition. He has produced many original works, including a *Konzertstück* for piano and orchestra, numerous male choruses and many songs. He has given particular attention on his concert programs to the works of modern masters.

24

OPPORTUNITIES AND LIMITATIONS IN PIANOFORTE PLAYING

RUDOLF GANZ

CHANGING CONDITIONS IN PIANOFORTE PLAYING

THE tendency in modern pianoforte playing is to bring about the best results with the least possible effort. Twenty-five years ago it really seemed as though the opposite were true. Then the virtuous student was estimated by the huge amount of practice that was done. Whether that practice was really aimed at any definite accomplishment seemed to matter very little indeed. It was done like penance, and each repetition was supposed to expiate some technical sin. The result was that with that kind of practice and very arbitrary courses of study the pupil was able to do a certain number of set tasks and nothing else. There was not enough musical or pianistic *culture*. The pupils were a manufactured product and little else. Like all fabricated contrivances, they were limited to one set of operations and lacked independence. In this manner these pupils could play certain set sonatas, certain études and certain brilliant concert pieces, but the moment they ventured beyond this limited repertoire they were miserably lost. Indeed, the training of some teachers and some schools was so arbitrary that it was easily possible for an acute observer to determine the identity of the teacher by hearing a pupil play a given work. I know of one teacher whose pupils play a certain Beethoven sonata so much after the same fashion that one might think that they had swallowed the same piano-player roll, and that the perforations were going through their automatic intellects with the same mechanical precision that they would through a piano-player. It seemed to be a case of making *pupils* out of *would-be-young-artists* instead of making *young artists* out of *pupils*, which is the *new* idea of teaching.

For instance, the theme of the *Rondo* in the Sonata Opus 53 of Beethoven is as follows:

No. I.

I have heard this Sonata played by innumerable pupils of a great European teacher and they invariably play it thus:

No. 2.

There is no æsthetic reason why the passage should be altered, but that is not the main question here, but rather to demonstrate the deadly uniformity of set or forced interpretation. It is as though a teacher of acting with a peculiar nasal whine should insist upon the pupil imitating him in every detail.

THE RIGHTFUL PRESCRIPTION OF TECHNIC

One cannot always prescribe technic as one does medicine, but there are certain things which the teacher should take into account in rounding out the pupil's work. For instance, the pupil with an inclination to be sentimental is to be developed by having music that is heroic in style. Again the pupil who is robust and ponderous in type should have the delicate side of his nature cultivated. At all times, however, the semblance of the machine in playing should be fought through the culture of personality,—individuality. Let the teacher ask the pupil (I am speaking here of the well-prepared and well-advanced student): "What is your feeling about this passage? In the light of what you know, how do you think it ought to be interpreted?" In almost every case this will bring about a far better and higher form of interpretation than if the teacher lays down ironclad rules and insists upon their observance.

THE LIMITATIONS OF THE PIANOFORTE

Some piano enthusiasts seem to be happiest when they are trying "to make the piano whisper" or make it sound like a cyclone. After all, so few have considered the individuality of the piano itself and the gentle art of making it sound like a piano. Indeed, there is a difference in pianos, and the different pianos and the different auditoriums in which they are heard all require a different treatment. The parlor grand is to my mind the best balanced instrument, more so than the great concert grand. The piano is suited to medium-sized halls far better than large halls, and when one plays in such a great room as Carnegie Hall the nature of the piano is necessarily strained. The player must be able to adapt himself to his instrument and the size of his instrument. Some do this and some never think of it. The huge concert hall is only suitable for *al fresco* playing and such sensational performances should be given in a great winter garden.

There is a need for more reserve and sensitiveness in piano playing, so that the pianistic values may be better observed. The piano is not an anvil, as many seem to imagine. It is not the poor piano's fault that it is a piano, and it shouldn't be made to suffer for it. Why deceive our ears and our intelligence about musical instruments, when their characteristics are so very obvious to all? I can always get far more out of the treble in a parlor grand than I can out of the treble in a concert grand because the proportion of tone between treble and

bass is more even. I have, however, great faith in
the new invention of an Englishman (Clutsam)
called the "cradle key" action, which has been applied to different pianos of different makes as an
experiment, and which should become the piano
action of the future. This is a real innovation to
my mind, and induces far greater sensitiveness of
touch with much less effort than any previous form
of action.

OPPORTUNITIES IN TONE VALUE

This is an age of tone values in piano playing.
To my mind, Busoni is the only one of the modern
pianists who has introduced new tone values. He
has not a "touch;" he has "touches." He realized
that there was no expression in touch *per se,* but
that expression comes from regulating tonal values
in a series of notes. No painter can take a brush
and splash one brushful of color on a canvas and
express anything by it,—at least he cannot express
anything that anyone other than a futurist would
recognize as beautiful. He needs to make innumerable strokes all of varying color values, and the
result is an artistic whole. So in piano playing, the
study of each note struck and the manner in which
it is struck depends upon the relation of that tone
to the whole.

In Thalberg's day it was doubtless possible to
sing far more readily at the keyboard than in this

day, when the actions of pianos are very much
heavier. This is the principal reason for the complete revolutionizing of ideas in playing; instead of
so-called perfect relaxation we have weight playing
and "set finger," "wrist," "forearm," etc., positions.

TASTE

As certain classes of cultured people are trained
to love Chopin, Schumann and Debussy, so there
will always be hordes of people climbing up the
cultural staircases, who for the time being must
survive on music very near to their intellectual and
emotional capacity. It is well for them to be frank
about their likes and dislikes, and I have far more
respect for the man who candidly says that he pre-
fers Lange's *Flower Song* to Richard Strauss'
Elektra than I have for the individual who endures
Elektra like a surgical operation merely because it
is fashionable to do so. The need for the music
of yesterday is shown in a remarkable way by the
tremendous amount of piano player records of old-
fashioned pieces. I have recently heard pieces on
the piano player that I imagined were extinct, only
to learn that there is a great market for such pieces
among purchasers who have had no specific training
in piano playing. Think of it! So much bad music
is written and not enough to supply the market! It
does not pay for anyone to be snobbish or "patron-
ize" the musical taste of others. This is a big

world, and while it is incumbent upon all artists to
help in raising the taste of the public as a whole, it
is not going to be done by snatching away Gottschalk's *Dying Poet* or Jungmann's *Heimweh* from
the person who is reveling in them, but by leading
them to see that the music of abler composers has
a refinement and character absent in the pieces of
the more superficial writers.

OPPORTUNITIES IN SHADING

The pianist is learning new ideas upon the subject of shading.   There was a time in our art when
nothing but a very definite tune would satisfy the
taste of the cultured musician.   The day of melody
is not past by any means, and Wagner, Schumann
and Brahms showed us that the definition of a tune
was a very elastic one.   It remained for Debussy
and his confrères, however, to point out that there
was a beauty in atmosphere and color just as there
is a beauty in masses of clouds or in sunsets.   I
have all of my pupils play the Debussy *Preludes,*
and the Ravel and Scott pieces so that they may
learn that one kind of beauty may be obtained by
the exquisite shading of tone masses in what might
be termed fluid form.   From these they learn how
to shade in Chopin.   Without shading the modern
French is nothing.   Ravel in some ways is greater
than Debussy in the opportunity his works offer
for polyphonic and polyharmonic shading.   This is

instanced in his wonderfully exotic *Le Gibet,* which I consider the most complete example of modern music. It is one of the most ambitious things ever written for the instrument. Indeed, it would seem to me one of the most difficult compositions of all pianoforte literature,—much more difficult for the interpreting musician than the famous *Don Juan Fantaisie of Mozart* as arranged by Liszt.

Opportunities in Phrasing

There are, of course, no new opportunities in phrasing except that the student of today realizes the necessity for intelligent phrasing far more than the student of twenty years ago. There are, however, still some people who believe that anyone can play the piano without being a musician. That is, they seem to think that all one need do is to cultivate a digital cleverness to succeed as a pianist. Of course, one may learn a great deal from certain books on phrasing, but the master pianist gets his outlook upon phrasing by being as familiar with the laws of the composer as the composer himself. A smattering of information on the subject will never satisfy him. I advise my pupils to go to hear the concerts of great orchestras and learn how to listen to the careful phrasing of each instrument. The playing of concertos with accompaniment of the teacher at the second piano is to be recommended most highly. The standard of musical interpretation lies within the performances of a perfect orchestral organization.

OPPORTUNITIES IN PEDALING

I pedal Chopin quite differently since I have played the compositions of the modern French school. It is strange how the new illuminates the old. There were certain prescribed methods which held me back from playing the new things to my satisfaction until I felt the new "light." The idea of pedaling for what is known as atmosphere was new and not easy to master. Just as the master artist disdains the sharp, definite outline of the photographic lines and seeks the softness of an artistic blending of his surfaces and colors, so does the pianist of the modern school pedal his works at times so that the tone masses are blended without being blurred. Indeed, even a blur of tone is now conceded to have its artistic values when properly introduced, and I personally make it a point to teach with utter enjoyment what—years ago—I considered to be "bad" pedaling. The modern musician must be able to "hear with his eyes" and "see with his ears." He then can live in the new conquered land.

QUESTIONS IN STYLE, INTERPRETATION, EXPRES-
SION AND TECHNIC OF PIANOFORTE PLAYING

SERIES XXII

RUDOLF GANZ

1. What is the tendency of modern pianoforte playing?

2. What danger should the student fight in his piano playing?

3. What type of piano is the best-balanced instrument?

4. Upon what does the manner of striking a single note depend?

5. Has the day of melody passed?

6. What is Debussey's signal accomplishment?

7. How does the master pianist get his artistic outlook?

8. Why are orchestral concerts desirable for the piano student?

9. How has the modern French school affected the study of pedaling?

ERNEST HUTCHESON

Mr. Ernest Hutcheson is one of a group of young men who have within recent years brought the name of Australia into the musical firmament. Although the better part of his life has been spent in foreign lands, Mr. Hutcheson is a native of Melbourne, where he was born July 20, 1871. He was a pupil of the Rev. G. W. Torrance, Mus.Doc. (Dublin), and of Max Vogrich. At the age of fourteen he went to the Leipsic Conservatory, where he studied under Zwintscher, Reinecke and Jadassohn, remaining under these masters for four years. Thereafter he went to Weimar, where he placed himself under the tuition of Stavenhagen, the well-known Liszt pupil. Although he had played all over Australia at the age of five as a child pianist, his mature debut was made in Berlin, 1894. After successful appearances abroad he came to America, where he was engaged for some time teaching at the Peabody Conservatory in Baltimore and at Chautauqua, New York. He then returned to Germany, where he remained for some years teaching and playing. In America he has appeared with all of the leading orchestras and in a great number of recitals.

25

UNIVERSALITY IN PIANO TEACHING METHODS

ERNEST HUTCHESON

THE NEED FOR PRACTICAL INSTRUCTION

WHEN one contemplates the vast number of things that have been said about piano playing and piano study one is tempted to be silent upon the subject, but as a matter of fact there is still a great deal that one may observe and a great deal that one may say. The tendency just now is away from theory, in piano pedagogical matters. People do not ask to know useless opinions upon piano technic, but rather prefer to find out how the best playing is done from actual observation.

The need for practical instruction has in a way created a new class of piano teachers who do not write essays about what they intend to do, but who actually play and teach, and through their experiences evolve means of their own to fit particular needs.

Leschetizky has been called the greatest piano teacher of the nineteenth century and this is no exaggeration. He was great because he was always practical. He indicated certain methods for help in establishing the main priciples of elementary technic, but beyond that he was above methods.

Technic Required

Technic has always adapted itself to the need of the times and to the character of the instrument. In the early days of keyboard instruments the action and the music to be played made little demands upon the strength of the player; accordingly, with the spinet we find that it was the custom to play with extended fingers, the motion coming principally from the nailjoint, and to avoid the thumbs. The spinet was a delicate instrument meant for delicate ears. It tinkled delightfully but had little sonority. A few modern chords would smash such an instrument.

At the next step of the historical development of the instrument a newer and stronger technic came in vogue through the use of the harpsichord and early pianoforte, coincidently with the writings of Bach, Scarlatti, Haydn, Mozart and Beethoven. Freer use of the thumb, a stronger finger-action (from the knuckle-joint, with curved fingers), and the hand-action from the wrist for staccato work characterize the progress of this period.

Finally came the technic of Franz Liszt, and with it a piano of iron and steel frame, deepened touch and immensely magnified resources of tone. Again pianists modified their methods, the chief points of novelty being an arched position of the hand (to give greater scope to the finger-action), and the free use of the upper arm.

Piano touch, however, is merely a necessary means of creating piano tone, and in considering the external movements of the arms and fingers it is all too easily possible to lose sight of their true object.

After all, music is the art of the ear. It reaches the individual solely through that organ, and that being the case the first consideration of the pianist should be beautiful, varied and expressive tone.

THE STUDY OF TONE

The analysis of tone must be an ear analysis. No matter how carefully the student may have attended to all the outward technical directions regarding hand position, fingers, etc., if the tone is not right his whole technic is faulty. I rarely watch the fingers of a pupil, nor indeed do I watch my own fingers very closely when playing, but I listen incessantly. If I hear a particular kind of tone I know that the elbow is stiff—another kind might betray wobbly fingers, and so on.

"One of the most common defects in the technic of the average pupil is lack of freedom in the upper arm. It is surprising what mischief can be brought about by a tightness of the muscles above the elbow. It prohibits a proper concentration of weight in the finger tips and infallibly hardens the tone in forte passages of all kinds, especially strong chords and octaves. Save for quite extraordinary effects, the whole playing mechanism except the nail-joints should be in a state of relaxation.

It is important to observe that the physical freedom of the player is directly communicated to the action of the instrument itself. The sensitiveness of the piano is, I am convinced, seldom realized by the student or the public. The tone of a piano is affected by cold or heat, by dampness or dryness of the air, by its acoustic surroundings, and not least by the physical expression of the player's mood. Treat a piano badly, and it will sulkily lock up its treasures of tone. Treat it lovingly and understandingly, and it is one of the most responsive of instruments; its harp of over two hundred strings, its great sounding board and frame, and its system of pedals are all susceptible to the minutest variations of sound for musical purposes, to such a degree that very slight and apparently unimportant motions at the keyboard affect the tonal mass.

The Sensitiveness of the Piano

The sensitiveness of the piano, then, is one of the first things which should command the attention of the student. As long as he regards it as a kind of tub or as an anvil which may be drummed on or hammered at pleasure he will not secure musical results. On the other hand, respect for the instrument is no small step toward a better understanding and treatment of it.

I am often asked why pianists move the wrist up and down *after* playing a note; it is agreed that nothing can be done to modify the tone when the key is held down. First, I answer, practically all pianists do it, therefore it is *prima facie* right and must have a meaning. Secondly, a tone undoubtedly can be modified in many ways after its initial sounding, by pedalling, by 'Bebung' and echo effects, and by this very oscillation of the wrist. Just watch me for a moment while I do it and then watch that vase of flowers on the other end of the piano. You see that every rose nods its head in sympathy with my slight movements. That means that I am communicating vibration to the entire case of the piano and reinforcing the effect of the sounding board. Again, do you know that the thunderous, echoing roll of big chords in a great concert hall is largely caused by strong vibration imparted to the whole body of the piano by pedal action? Once more, are you aware that if one note is played with singing tone and another lightly, as in accompaniment, the hammers may seem to behave differently after leaving the strings? But now let us leave these instances of the delicacy of the instrument and return to technic.

TYPICAL TOUCHES

The student, in my opinion, should begin by mastering certain typical forms of touch which may at first be definitely associated with simple movements. These touches are what might be called the primary colors of piano playing and they should be understood by the player and intelligently applied. I have often found the following table of great use to beginners:

These, of course, are only the broadest of types, and I do not mean to say that a portamento cannot be executed by the fingers, or that the wrist takes no part in legato playing. A staccato, for instance, may be performed by finger-action, by hand-action from the wrist, by movement of the wrist itself, by arm-action from the elbow or shoulders, or by combined action of finger and hand or hand and arm. In fact, an almost infinite variety of touch is possible, according to the tonal effect desired, and it is largely this which gives charm to expressive interpretation. Nevertheless, the three typical touches should first be studied and developed, not only in technical exercises but also in musical performance. The study of Mozart's Fantasias and Sonatas may be especially recommended in this connection.

The extension of piano literature has made a giant technic necessary. Yet it is obviously impossible to prepare for every difficulty which may occur in modern music. Teachers now realize that a command of certain technical formulæ and elementary principles opens the way to the more intricate problems. They know that technic is at best a means to an end. They consider how the exercises and scales are played rather than the mere task of playing them an infinite number of times. Any fool can play a five-finger exercise but it takes a wise man to adapt what he has learned from playing such an exercise to the uses of his interpretative work.

It is surprising how certain pedagogical materials survive in the pianoforte study of today. Of course, new and excellent materials come from the printing presses all the time, but only the best survives. Take the case of Czerny and Cramer. Teachers find themselves turning back to those able étude writers all the time. Czerny was a contemporary of both Hummel and Steibelt and in their day Hummel and Steibelt were looked upon as the equals of Beethoven. Now their music is largely a memory but Czerny and Cramer are both used to this hour.

So it is with scales and arpeggios. The wise teacher is the experienced teacher, and the experienced teacher knows that a certain fluency and easiness and general intuitive intimacy with the keyboard can be obtained through the use of these materials that cannot be obtained as easily in other ways. In other words, the pianist's mind has to be hitched up to the instrument so that he is able to do a great deal of his keyboard work without conscious effort. Drill in scale playing seems to accomplish this. Scales and arpeggios seem to do away with the incessant need for watching the keys and give the player a grasp upon the possibilities of his instrument. There is really nothing like them for this purpose, and if they are not used some other much longer and much more circuitous path must be taken. Don't sniff at the man who swears by Cramer, Czerny, scales and arpeggios. He is dangerous only when his vision stops with these purely technical means to an end.

Modern technic aims to free the player from mechanical bonds so that his musical intuitions may be given the widest reign. The mind acts subconsciously to the great advantage of the student who has put the necessary technical work behind him in his race for musical success. I am told by a man who uses a typewriter constantly in his daily work, that the warning bell which indicates that the end of a line is reached, may ring a thousand times and not be noted audibly by the person operating the machine. Nevertheless the bell makes an impression and the operator unconsciously or subconsciously obeys it and sends the carriage back for the beginning of a new line. This is illustrative of the many acts which the pianist must do and which becomes habitual.

The human mind is not great enough to carry consciously more than a mere fraction of the many things which a pianist must remember in playing a complicated masterpiece. The mind must direct at all times, but its chief concern must be the artistic import of the passage and never the mechanical details. All modern methods recognize this and seek to have these details accomplished by wisely planned technical drill. This in a measure accounts for the great improvement in pianoforte playing in general during the last twenty-five years.

QUESTIONS IN STYLE, INTERPRETATION, EXPRESSION AND TECHNIC OF PIANOFORTE PLAYING

SERIES XXIII

ERNEST HUTCHESON

1. Why was Leschetizky regarded as the greatest piano teacher of the nineteenth century?

2. State the differences in the touch demanded by the spinet, the harpsichord and the piano.

3. How must tone be analyzed?

4. What is the effect of tightening the muscles above the elbow?

5. What should the student know about the sensitiveness of the piano?

6. How is the piano tone affected by pressure upon the keys after they have been struck?

7. State the characteristic touches of the fingers, the hand and the arm.

8. What is the value of scales and arpeggios in piano practice?

9. State how the subconscious mind helps in piano study.

The Three Primary Colors in Pianoforte Playing

As indicated by Mr. Ernest Hutcheson

Typical Touch	Meaning	Marking	Typical Movement	Description
Portamento	*" carried "*	⌒	**Arm**	*Notes held to their full value but not connected [usually involving use of the pedal.]*
Staccato	*detached*	. . . . or ! ! ! !	**Hand**	*Notes shortened of their written value and disconnected.*
Legato	*bound*	⌒	**Finger**	*Notes held to their full value and connected.*

OLGA SAMAROFF

Biographical

Olga Samaroff (Mrs. Leopold Stokowski) was born on August 8, 1882, in San Antonio, Texas. Her mother, the daughter of George Loening, a native of Bremen, Germany, was born in Munich but educated in America. Her father is of Holland Dutch extraction. Mme. Samaroff received her first instruction from her maternal grandmother and mother, both fine musicians. At the age of fourteen she entered the Paris Conservatory, being, so far as the writer knows, the first American woman to be admitted to the classes of that famous institution. After graduating from the Paris Conservatory she studied with Jedliczka (a pupil of Rubinstein and Tschaikowsky) in Berlin. It may be mentioned that at various times Mme. Samaroff studied the piano for a short time under Constantin von Sternberg, Ludovic Breitner, Ernest Hutcheson, and the organ with Hugo Riemann.

In spite of her serious studies and ever prominent passion for music Mme. Samaroff did not intend to make a public career. It was not until January 18, 1905, that she made her first appearance on any stage, at Carnegie Hall in New York, with the New York Symphony Orchestra. Her success was so rapid that many concert-goers are under the impression that she has played for a much longer period. It was not until her success was thoroughly established in America that she played in Europe, and it is significant of the prestige which an American success now gives an artist that Mme. Samaroff at once obtained engagements with the leading orchestras in the cities where she played, and made her *début* in Paris, Vienna, London, Munich and elsewhere as soloist at the most important orchestral concerts of those cities.

After this single season in Europe and four seasons in America, Mme. Samaroff's career was interrupted by a very serious illness, which forced her to abandon all concert work for nearly four years. Three years ago she became the wife of Leopold Stokowski, then conductor of the Cincinnati Orchestra, now filling the same position with the Philadelphia Orchestra. It may be added that the very Russian sounding name of Olga Samaroff is a *nom de Plume* name—the name of Mme. Samaroff's maternal great-grandmother, who was a Russian.

26

CONCENTRATION IN MUSIC STUDY

OLGA SAMAROFF

THE subject of concentration in music study has been discussed so many times that it would seem well nigh impossible to say anything about it approaching novelty. Yet concentration is a matter of such great consequence to all students, particularly music students, that there are few artists who would hesitate to place it at the very foundation of all serious work. Successful concentration is a mental process attained only after much intellectual effort. There is unfortunately a tendency among certain American students to look upon anything intellectual connected with music with more or less contempt. They do not hesitate to criticize certain great artists in such a way that one readily discovers that the students make "intellect" synonymous with inferiority. One realizes how absurd this is when one remembers that all higher musical work is based upon a development of the individual's intellectuality.

The precious divine spark which the artist must keep flaring on his high altar is not to be dimmed by higher mental culture. But the emotional content of the artist's interpretation will not be lessened because he uses his brain every second during his study hours. It is true that we often hear music performed with a kind of technical coldness which many ascribe to a superior intellectual attitude—the divine spark quite extinct. We can but say that the warmth of emotion, the fervor of interpretative genius, never existed in the soul of the performer. If it had, no amount of so-called "intellectual effort" would have done away with it. The *bete noir* "intellect" has misled many a careless student who has imagined that by some mysterious process musical success will come to him without any special mental industry. I would in fact almost be inclined to say that while an intellectual "performer" may lack the divine spark, the performer with the divine spark in the highest sense cannot be lacking in intellect, but on the contrary is one of the highest manifestations of the possibilities of intellectual achievement.

We have today, as there have been in the past, artists who have attained wide popularity through a certain instinctive musical quality such as that one often finds in the Italian and Slavic peasants. Their music seems to come to them apparently without study, as though they work entirely through the sub-conscious mind. Such musicians combine a certain amount of fire and natural breadth of tone, and, for want of a better term, "magnetism." Often such a musician succeeds in casting a spell over an audience, particularly an undiscriminating one. Such a performer was Blind Tom, a mere freak of nature. To my mind, however, these performers do not deserve to be seriously considered as artists. The truly great artist is one who not only possesses all the gifts which the natural performer may have, but who also combines these with intellectual breadth achieved through years of intelligent study and experience.

MAKING ONE'S PRACTICE A THOUSANDFOLD MORE VALUABLE

The student then should have a high regard for all intellectual work demanded by his music study, technical mastery, and all those faculties which make for a refined understanding of music considered from the highest aspect. Let us repeat to those who hesitate to consider the intellectual processes in their work—if the flame of genius within the musician is so feeble that it could be extinguished by the development and use of his grey matter it would scarcely in any case be capable of producing distinguished artistic results. Of all the intellectual processes none is more helpful to the student than concentration—directing one's thinking powers toward one thing and keeping them upon that thing until some definite purpose is accomplished. The student should always fasten upon the conviction that whatever is his in the way of natural talent is there to remain. Concentration upon technical details will enhance the value of his

natural talent a thousand fold.   There are doubtless hundreds of students now who are struggling
along hopelessly because they do not know how to
concentrate their forces.   Why will some students
persist in being so short-sighted in this particular?
The playing of Bach demands concentration in a
remarkable degree.   Yet I have students come to
me and say, "If I play Bach I shall not be able to
play Chopin."   One might as well say, "If I read
Shakespeare I shall not be able to read Maeter-
linck."   Can anyone imagine anything more absurd?   The qualities which one develops through
playing Bach are of incalculable benefit in playing
Chopin.

No Patent Rules for Concentration

By concentration the student must not imagine
that I have any proprietary methods in mind.
There are no patents, no rules, no schemes.   What
is needed is everyday common sense.   Common
sense ought to reveal to the average student that if
he can play a passage once correctly he should be
able to play it again and again correctly, if only he
reproduces the same degree of concentration which
insured perfection in the first case.   That is to say,
if the student's technical ability and musical understanding encompass a passage in question once, it
is largely a matter of mind control if the student
succeeds in reproducing the passage without the

customary needless and wastful repetitions through which so many students go before they seem to get results. Every time the passage you have selected for practice fails to "go right" after you have once succeeded in playing it to your satisfaction, just tell yourself that you are not concentrating. Some misguided young musicians seem to fail in realizing that in order to insure results one must invariably preserve that intimate connection between the brain and the fingers that spells concentration. They seem to think that they may dream away at the keyboard and let their blundering digits take care of themselves. Years of study are wasted in this way and the ears of students, to say nothing of others who are obliged to listen, are tortured by bungling practice that never in all the world can possibly lead to real success.

The first mistake, like all first offences, is the beginning of the end unless the student takes great care to avoid such a custom. Mistake making in most cases is an entirely avoidable habit, often resulting from not checking the matter at the very start. If the student would only learn to stop the very moment that the first mistake is made and give himself a severe lecture on the lack of concentration he would stand a far better chance of ultimate success than if he blindly continued to conceal his blunders under that most deceptive of legends "Practice makes Perfect." Practice does make perfect, it is true, but only right practice brought about by concentration can lead to the perfection which all young musicians aspire to attain. It is not lack of talent, not lack of opportunity, not lack of atmosphere which stands in the way of many students—it is wool-gathering. In the olden time the shepherd boys used to run far and wide over the hills and dales for little clumps of wool left hanging on bushes. It was a task with slender profit that demanded thousands of steps for very little wool. In some similar manner some pupils run through miles of scales, arpeggios and finger passages in order to get very little out of them. The successful performer has not time for this wasteful practice. He must get his results with as few wasted notes as possible.

A Famous Actor's Power of Concentration

This does not mean, however, that numerous repititions are undesirable or unnecessary. I recollect a story told to me by an old friend, Ernest Coquelin, the famous French actor, which illustrates how a great artist, even in another branch of interpretative art, realizes the necessity for concentration upon detail. In the play of "Thermidor," in which Coquelin gave a really marvelous performance, there was a little passage in which he was obliged to get up and walk around a chair. All the while he was obliged to signify the dawning realization of a great danger. Coquelin told me that in order to master the ways and means leading to an impressive theatrical effect that the audience would at once perceive and comprehend, he once practiced the little bit some two hundred times. With every repetition he became more and more absorbed, so that he entirely forgot everything else. Not only did several important engagements escape his mind, but he also failed to remember that he was to take a certain train for the south of France, where he was engaged to appear, thus losing his last chance for a lucrative performance. It seems needless to say that all those who saw his performance were especially impressed by this particular passage.

To the artist who has once gained complete control of himself and his medium there is such a thing as a sub-conscious governing or directing by the mind which gives him sureness and a kind of technical liberty, permitting his imagination to have the freest possible play. But this sub-conscious governing of our work comes only with the complete control resulting from years and years of right practice habits at the keyboard. Most of the problems confronting the average student and performer may be solved by the kind of concentrated thinking which comes through the habit of collecting one's thoughts and focusing them upon one point until something is actually accomplished.

In preparing a passage for public performance the student should endeavor to keep in mind the ultimate manner in which the passage will be performed. That is to say, he will gain nothing by practicing the passage in any other way. The idea surprisingly advocated by some otherwise fine teachers of always practicing things as they are *not* to be played eventually, has always struck me as preposterous. Some teachers tell their pupils to disregard the phrasing, the pedaling, the expression marks, etc. It is easy to see how the student can, by giving special attention to any one of these phases of his playing through concentration develop that phase, but at the same time he must realize that in playing a single measure he is called upon not to do one thing only, but to control many different things all occurring at the same instant. That is one of the things that makes music study so fascinating. The mind is given one short moment to perform a number of different actions and these must be executed with perfection of digital detail, fine appreciation of artistic values and correspondence with the rest of the composition. The artist with the brush may stand before his easel for months, painting, painting, painting, erasing one color here and supplying a line there, but he has all eternity in which to complete his task if he chooses to take it. The canvas of the interpretative musician is the attention of his listener. He paints at a miracuously rapid rate and his mind must be trained to think with a speed demanded in no other art except perhaps that of the stage. This in itself should emphasize the necessity for concentration in study so that the student will realize how very vital it is to his progress.

I find pupils who will completely learn and produce the notes of a work and expect by some mysterious means to be able to supply all the fine points of phrasing, accenting, pedaling and correct tempo, at the moment of playing, without any detailed concentration upon these matters before the hour of the concert. Before the student permits his work to reach the ears of the auditor he must have studied it not only in all its parts but he must have played it many, many times just as he expects to play it on the evening of its ultimate performance. He must concentrate upon his work so that he can sit at the keyboard with supreme confidence and paint a tonal picture that will leave a permanent artistic impression upon the mind of the hearer. If the student would only keep before him the fact that he has such a very short time in which to create a master work in interpretation, he will surely see that he can not afford to waste any moments during his practice periods in wool-gathering.

Don't Try To Do Too Much At Once

Some students attempt to learn a whole composition at one time. This usually results in a succession of disasters. The student works prodigiously

and produces nothing.   For instance, in the Beethoven Sonata in D Minor (Opus 31, No. 2), there
are 232 measures in the first movement.   The right
way to proceed after a general idea of the movement has been obtained through a cursory survey of
the piece is to take, let us say eight measures.   In
this case we will take the first eight measures which
appear thus:

Very simple you will say, but let us make a little
catalog of the things you must observe in this little
passage which takes only a few seconds to play.
Considering them in order we must learn:

Seventy-three notes.

Thirteen marks of phrasing.

Three marks of tempo.

Three important pedaling marks.

Sixteen marks indicating a certain kind of touch.

Nine marks pertaining to dynamics (*cres., sf.,* etc.).

Twenty-three fingerings specified by some painstaking editor.

Two significant pauses.

An embellishment which must be properly interpreted. And all in eight measures! Yet the student has only skimmed over the surface of the measures. He must study the nature of the phrasing not indicated in the phrasing marks; he must know how the opening arpeggio is to be played; he must note the extent of the main theme before the second theme is introduced; in fact there are many things yet to be considered in this little passage of eight measures. Some people have the gift of observing, comprehending and fixing these technical and artistic points so that they are able to do the work in a much shorter time. These people are those who have learned to concentrate.

How Concentration Helps Memorizing

Concentration helps immensely in memorizing—indeed it hardly seems necessary to mention this very obvious fact. One little device I have em-

ployed in memorizing may be of assistance to the
student.   In studying a new phrase with the view
to fixing it in the mind one should not merely study
the phrase alone but also part of the preceding
phrase.   The actor in studying his parts lays great
stress upon his cues.   He learns the last words of
the previous speech so that the moment he hears
them his own lines come out automatically—that is
without apparent thought or effort.   In memorizing, I apply a similar method which seems to help
me immensely in works of a complicated nature.
In studying a new phrase I always commence in the
middle of the previous phrase.   For instance, in
a section of the sonata to which we have just referred we find these two phrases:

In memorizing the second phrase I would practice it as follows:

This gives to the musical memory the same assistance upon which the actor depends for his security in reciting his lines on the stage.

A great deal may be gained by watching the fingers on the keyboard. Of course this refers only to the work of the pianist playing from memory. It may be necessary at the outstart for the student to practice with his eyes away from the keyboard, but after the student has gained a sense of location he will find that his eyes will help him immensely in preserving accuracy. One famous virtuoso, one of the very greatest, always keeps his eyes upon the keys. The superficial student might think that this would make the playing of the virtuoso stilted, and lacking in the abandon of the old type of pianist, who focused his eyes on the ceiling, and his fingers on the wrong notes. However, there is something in the attraction of the keyboard that becomes almost hypnotic and the eye learns to help make the playing more definite, more dependable, while at the same time the poet interpreter's imagination is not robbed of any of its phantasy.

It is gratifying to note that American artists are gaining more and more recognition in their own land. No symbol of our musical progress could be more wholesome and the American's ability to focus his efforts upon the business at hand has had much to do with this change in public musical appreciation.

QUESTIONS IN STYLE, INTERPRETATION, EXPRESSION AND TECHNIC OF PIANOFORTE PLAYING

SERIES XXIV

OLGA SAMAROFF

1. What qualities must the truly great artist possess?

2. Which composer's works demand a superior degree of concentration?

3. What is usually the trouble when passages fail to go right?

4. State one way in which the work of the painter differs from that of the pianist.

5. Give a good way of classifying difficulties.

6. How does concentration help the student to memorize?

7. Should the pianist watch the fingers at the keyboard?

MARK HAMBOURG

BIOGRAPHICAL

Mark Hambourg is a member of a very musical family. His father, Michael Hambourg, is himself a noted teacher; his brother Boris is a 'cellist of renown, while another brother of Mark is the brilliant violinist, Jan Hambourg. Mark Hambourg was born at Bogutchar, Southern Russia, June 1st, 1879. At first the pupil of his father, he became the pupil of Leschetizky at the age of twelve. As a prodigy he made numerous very successful appearances, but his parents wisely foresaw the necessity of developing his general education until he became a mature artist. Accordingly he was withdrawn from public work for many years, but since then he has toured all of the civilized countries, meeting with great success. In 1907 he married Dorothea, daughter of Sir Kenneth Muir Mackenzie, G. C. B., Permanent Clerk to the House of Lords.

27

INSURING PROGRESS IN MUSIC STUDY

MARK HAMBOURG

In these days of dreadnaught technique, when the modern pianist must have an equipment as powerful and as invulnerable as a battleship, to ward off the projectiles of the critical public and press, there is so very much to be accomplished that not a moment's time must be lost if the career of the virtuoso is chosen as a life work. The standard of playing has become high because one part of the public has been educated to expect perfection and because another part has a really well developed appreciation of what is and what is not good taste in interpretation. Therefore it may easily be seen that the career of the virtuoso is becoming more and more exacting as time goes on. Think for a moment of the immense number of pieces with which the successful pianist must be familiar to say nothing of those which he must have at his finger's ends—his repertoire. Nowadays one must have a veritable library not on one's bookshelves but in one's head. In what other profession are such enormous demands made upon the memory alone? The work before the student, then, is staggering in its aspects. No wonder many are discouraged before they have traveled more than a short distance along the road. If real progress is to be insured no time at all can be wasted. The need for expert instruction in the case of the student expecting to become a virtuoso is really very great. A poor teacher wastes not only time but that more scarce if not more valuable commodity, money. The good teacher uses only what is needed in each particular case; and thus the pupil is not weighted down with a vast amount of unnecessary luggage.

ESSENTIALS THAT COUNT

Great erudition and great keyboard skill never make a successful teacher unless there is that precious gift for divining just what is right at the right time. Common sense in little things in teaching is far better than a complicated view of musical complexities. For instance, the pupil should learn at the outstart that he has four main channels through which his musical training may be brought to him, namely

Visual
Aural
Harmonic
Mechanical

That is, he must use his eyes to fix in his mind everything that can be determined by the eye. Nothing on the printed page must escape him— nothing in hand, arm and body position must elude the close scrutiny of his eyes. His eyes must be like two ever-present teachers making every hour of practice an instructive hour and nothing but an instructive hour. His ears are likewise teachers, and when the aural sense is so developed that he can hear music when he sees it, as though it was being played and enjoy it with the same ease with which he reads a book, he is to be congratulated. By synchronizing as it were the visual sense and the aural sense a vast amount of waste time may be saved. Yet thousands struggle with the keyboard for years and never acquire this sense.

Next, the student must understand the family of chords and know how they are related. Practice in harmony should be as regular as practice in keyboard exercises. The brain must have a kind of harmonic technic. The reason why I emphasize this is simply because with such a technic the student can save hours of silly finger dawdling at the keys—hours that never produce anything but calloused finger tips.

Finally, we have the mechanical, which, indispensable as it is, sometimes results in excesses altogether unwarranted. Please do not think that I am trying to say anything so stupid as declaring that keyboard practice and lots of it is not necessary. Quite the contrary is true. What I am trying to point out is that it is not the time that one spends at the keyboard that counts but what is brought to the keyboard by the brain of the pupil, and how the time is spent at the keyboard. I do my best practice away from the keyboard. That is, I work out the musical problems and get them straight in my mind so that no time is lost in fumbling over keys.

A CONVINCING ILLUSTRATION

In order to point out very clearly what I mean when I say that it is what is done at the keyboard rather than how much time is spent there that really counts, one need not go any further than the case of the child prodigy. Here we have an instance where there has not been time for an enormous amount of practice yet there are continually brought before the public children of ten, eleven and twelve with astonishing technical ability. In my own case I remember very well that my father, a very busy man, let me have as a first teacher one of his own pupils who was gifted in playing rather than teaching. This was a well meaning person of eighteen or twenty who took a perfunctory interest in teaching, but did not do everything possible to advance me. Consequently, I came to hate my music lessons and detested practice. This hate became so violent that I remember as a very little tot running splinters into my fingers to prevent taking a music lesson. My father was quick to note my attitude and soon took me in hand himself. He was a natural born teacher who loved children, and inside of a few weeks my enthusiasm was so great that it was difficult to keep me away from the piano. In a little more than a year I acquired a technic which seems surprising to me at this day. In a very short time I was considered ready to make a public appearance and soon found myself before the public playing in many cities with success. Obviously, it was not years that gave me that technic but a well-planned course carefully worked out and filled full of that priceless enthusiasm without which musical success is unthinkable. My father's logical explanations instead of dogmatic directions gave me delight in everything I did. In no other way could I have been enabled to play with orchestra at the age of eight. Ordinary instruction was carrying me farther and farther away from the right path. MORAL: Have as good a teacher as you can possibly secure and afford. It always pays in the end.

How Reflection Saves Time

In studying a new piece, experience has shown me that it is possible to save a great deal of time through reflection. First I play the piece through carefully to hear how it sounds. Then I analyze it carefully down to its finest points. This serves to fix the piece in the mind and saves hours of practice drudgery. Then comes the practice itself which is followed by a period of reflection. During this period of reflection the piece is, as it were, digested musically.   It is only by some such process that the student can really be said to master a work.   The great trouble is that the fingers are magnified in their importance and the brain is minimized.

Teachers seem to fail to realize that pupils have brains, and that these brains must be directed as carefully in music as in any educational work.   More "talents" have been ruined by failing to consider the brain side of the work than in any other way.   In no other art but music is anybody and everybody permitted to teach.   To preserve the talent of the child and insure regular progress, by all means secure a good teacher at the start.   Forget about the method that the teacher teaches and see that you get the right individual.   Of course, the work must be methodical but it need not be somebody's patent plan that is supposed to apply in all cases with magic precision.   With all other thinking pianists, Leschetizky included, I am emphatically against the proprietary method idea in music study.   A poor teacher with the best method in the world could not produce good results.   To paraphrase a line of Shakespeare "The teacher's the thing," and by this I mean the individual.   To hold to a weak teacher with a much advertised method would be like retaining an incompetent doctor in a dangerous case just because he was a homeopathist, an allopath or a Christian Scientist.   The main thing is to get the right individual who has repeatedly shown his efficiency so that there can be no mistaking his claims. Let proprietary methods go to the wind. All really good teachers use much from many, many different methods.

ADVANCED WORK

Naturally the pupil must expect to work with a teacher who will criticize his efforts with relentless severity, if he expects his advanced work to be profitable. Anyone who has faced the fire of Leschetizky has always realized that after this experience one was ready to face almost anything. Nothing could have been more exacting than the demands of Leschetizky. Yet everything he said was tempered with such good common sense, and often with biting wit, that part of the sting was taken away. While with him I always tried to create opportunities to play. Every week I learned a new piece and it seemed as though Leschetizky was equally caustic with each one. There is no way in which the aspiring young student who hopes to become a virtuoso can go ahead faster than by playing a great deal for different people who are frank enough to speak out their minds and who are intelligent and experienced enough to give criticisms of value. In other words these beneficent critics by their constant pounding enable the student to get new angles of vision upon his own work.

CRITICS WHO HELP

No one is a better critic than the fellow pupil. Often he sees things which the teacher does not. I value the criticisms of my fellow artists very highly. In an assembly of pupils, however, where rivalry runs high and tongues are loosened by good-natured familiarity, criticisms of real worth are bound to be received. It is next to useless for the pianist to play before his so-called friends. The pupils' recital before smiling perfumed audiences of parents, aunts, brothers and admirers are usually misleading as far as their educational effect is concerned. They may have some value in accustoming the pupil to public appearance and exhibiting the teacher's work but they are likely to be wholly misleading to the pupil. The studios are filled with somewhat ghastly examples of young people who have been cajoled into believing that they have already made quite a respectable climb up Parnassus, when they have really not touched the foot hills. Flattery is the bomb that demolishes more honest effort than anything else.

Criticism that is well meant is easily detected from that which is merely empty praise or on the other hand stupid fault-finding. During all the time I was with Leschetizky, standing up under a bombardment of criticisms, I knew that he had only my good at heart. When he came to me as I was about to start upon my career as an artist he had

a box in his hand. In that box he had deposited
every coin I had paid him for my lessons. Not one
was missing. He knew that I had a struggle ahead
of me to get a start and he offered me back every
Heller I had ever given him. Such a man was
Leschetizky!

Sincerity

What is the virtuoso's most indispensable attribute? I should say "sincerity." If the artist is
not sincere he is nothing more than a showman.
Every time he goes to the platform he should go
with a message. If this spirit is cultivated during
the student days all the better. The public has a
right to expect sincerity from the artist. If the
artist falls before the blandishments of the public,
and plays merely to catch pennies, he will surely
suffer in the long run. The public now is too highly
educated not to distinguish clap-trap. The student
should be encouraged to approach every piece with
all possible sincerity and earnestness. Do not think
that anything that Beethoven, Mendelssohn, Schumann or Chopin has seen fit to write is too little to
deserve your very best. Be sincere in all you do
and your art will advance finely.

Taste in the Artist's Work

The artist should unceasingly strive to get down
to his own ideas—find out what he himself really

thinks. Someone has said that we continually think the thoughts of other people because we are too lazy to think our own. Of course the public has certain natural and human appetites which no virtuoso is foolish enough altogether to disregard, yet every program should be representative of the artist's individual character. This does not mean that he should emphasize his whims or exaggerate his personal prejudices but with all good sense he should strive to have every program he presents be himself in person and not some model after whom all others are foolishly copying.

Program-making is a distinctive art. It is conceivable that an artist who makes no effort to have his personal taste represented in his programs but who simply follows the conventions of another day may so stultify his work that progress would be impossible. In the olden days at the Leipsic Conservatory conventions were so strictly defined that Liszt and Chopin were practically debarred from many programs; and Liszt, to this day, from the Hochschule in Berlin! Conventions, then, should not be the main factor in making a good program. There are certain intellectual needs of a musical kind, as well as emotional demands, and these should be considered above all things. For instance, in considering variety the performer is often inclined to let it go with a variety of different names upon the program, whereas the main consideration is the variety which should come to the ear of the audience. Even leaving out of consideration those members of the audience who are ignorant of the significance of the names of great masters, there are still those musically trained people who are quite as human in their aural appetites and who will respond to a well ordered program and reject a poorly arranged program. Of course the virtuoso has to play a number of works which a certain portion of the musical public wants to hear. As a rule such works are those with which the public already has some familiarity or those by composers sufficiently discussed in print to have aroused a real curiosity to become acquainted with the compositions. After these considerations, the next would be variety in keys and modes, and then variety in forms. Who in the world would want to listen to three symphonies in G Major, one right after the other? Variety may be obtained from pieces in markedly different rhythms and metres. Certain pianists have, of course, given historical recitals, at which for instance have been performed a long series of Beethoven Sonatas. These have an educational value for the student and the professional, but with the general public six Beethoven Sonatas one right after the other would be like eating six big beefsteaks at one meal! The following would in many ways comply with the conditions which go to make a varied high-class program of the present day.

Note the constant change of key. It is neither the conventional "historical" program, nor is it eccentric.

SPECIAL PROGRAM

I

KEY			CHARACTER
F. Major	J. S. BACH	Italian Concerto	Representing the severely
	L. VAN BEETHOVEN	Sonata, Op. 106 or 111	classical style

II

C♯ Minor	F. CHOPIN	Scherzo	Romantic and Brilliant,
E Major		Etude (No. 10)	Slow Melodic
A Minor		Etude (No. 2)	Playful
C♯ Minor		Etude (No. 4)	Brilliant
F♯ Major		Prelude	Slow
B♮ Minor		Prelude	Rapid
A Minor		Mazurka	Reflective
F♯ Minor		Polonaise	Magnificent

III

E Major	M. RAVEL	Jeu d'Eaux	Atmospheric
E♭ Minor	CYRIL SCOTT	Lotos Land	Atmospheric
	M. MOSZKOWSKI	Venusberg music from *Tannhauser* arranged from Wagner.	Dramatic
	DEBUSSY	Suite	Characteristic

Of course this is only one of a great many different programs which would exhibit equal variety. There is so much to choose from that there is no need for monotony at any time. Of the new things of the above program, the Venusberg arrangement which Moszkowski has been good enough to dedicate to me is one of the most difficult pieces ever written for the piano. It is filled with the genius and fire of the original orchestral score and makes a fine number for the antepenult position on the program. Also it will be noticed that I finish the program with the Debussy suite. Time was when it seemed the custom to end the program with a kind of musical shock which consisted of bringing forward the player's most brilliant exhibition of bravura work, his *tour de force* as it were. This, however, is not altogether an artistic arrangement. In the good drama the climax is not reserved for the last curtain but usually comes at some previous moment. Consequently such a number as the Debussy after the gorgeous Moszkowski-Wagner number makes a better program. The artist who barters his art for easy ways to get applause must inevitably fall in the opinion of thinking people.

The Teacher's Opportunity

Those who have realized their hopes of becoming great virtuosos often find at the end of the journey that their goal was by no means what they had anticipated. The work is hard, unceasingly hard, and though the emoluments are frequently great, all human happiness is largely a matter of comparative degrees of satisfaction. The teacher who has not the fame and the income of the virtuoso also does not have the terrific strain, the disappointments, the gruelling criticism. Whether it is better to be the oak battling with the hurricane or the lovely rose in a pleasant shelterd garden must be decided by the individual starting out upon a career. To my mind it is far better to be one live, active, helpful teacher than two struggling, impotent, unsuccessful *virtuosi*. The teaching field is enormous. The virtuoso field is very small. Do not belittle the work of the teacher. It is upon the teacher's shoulders that civilization advances. If you are a teacher, be proud of it—rejoice in it, for there is no nobler occupation.

QUESTIONS IN STYLE, INTERPRETATION, EXPRESSION AND TECHNIC OF PIANOFORTE PLAYING

SERIES XXV

MARK HAMBOURG

1. What are the four channels through which musical training comes to the pupil?

2. What is the chief value of harmony to the piano student?

3. Through what may much time be saved in the study of a new piece?

4. State an indispensable attribute of the virtuoso.

5. What should be the main factor in making a good recital program?

6. State how variety may be obtained in a program.

7. Compare the teacher's career with that of the virtuoso.

PERCY GRAINGER

BIOGRAPHICAL

Mr. Grainger was born at Brighton, Melbourne, Australia, July 8, 1882. His mother was his first teacher. Thereafter he studied with Louis Pabst of Melbourne. He then set out to earn the means of travel to Germany and after several highly successful recitals and a large benefit concert, organized by Australia's greatest musician and composer, Professor Marshall Hall, had his wish gratified. In Germany he studied for six years with Professor James Kwast, and finally with the great Busoni. In 1900 he appeared in London as a virtuoso, and at once scored great successes. Thereafter he toured Great Britain, Australia, New Zealand, South Africa, and more recently Germany, Holland, Norway, Denmark, Finland, Russia, Bohemia and Switzerland. His fondness for things Scandinavian began as a child, and was beautifully rewarded by Grieg's admiration for the young Australian, about whom he wrote enthusiastically and prophetically in the European press, and whom he chose to play his Pianoforte Concerto at the great Leeds Musical Festival. After Grieg's death the widow of the Norwegian genius sent his watch and chain to Mr. Grainger as a souvenir of Grieg's affectionate friendship for him. Mr. Grainger's reverent admiration for Grieg's adaptations of Norwegian folk-music prompted him to explore the beauties of British folk-songs, as Grieg had done those of Norway. The result has been that Mr. Grainger has made vocal and pianoforte arrangements of many of these pieces—arrangements altogether unique in their charm and appropriateness. In 1914 Mr. Grainger came to this country, primarily for the purpose of completing some large orchestral and choral compositions already begun. But his great musical gifts were soon discovered, especially his talents as a piano virtuoso, and he found himself in great demand as a concert pianist, appearing with many of the Symphony Orchestras. At the same time, his compositions were more and more frequently placed on orchestral programs.

28

MODERNISM IN PIANOFORTE STUDY

PERCY GRAINGER

NEW EFFORTS WITH OLD MEANS

JUST at the moment when the musical pessimists were declaring that pianistic resources were coming to an end, we find ourselves on the doorstep of new forms of pianism, which, while they in no sense do away with the old means of interpretation, aid the pianist in bringing new effects even to the masterpieces of yesterday. It is interesting to think that with the advance of the art one's resources become more and more refined. Twenty years ago the whole aim of many pianoforte students seemed to be speed or the art of getting just as many notes as possible in a given space of time. With the coming of such composers as Debussy, Cyril Scott, Ravel and others, we find a grateful return of the delicate and refined in piano playing. There is a coming up again of the pianissimo. More and more artists are beginning to realize the potency of soft notes rightly shaded and delivered artistically.

The modern composer has a new reverence for the piano as an instrument. The great composers, such as Bach and Beethoven, thought of the piano as a medium for all-round expression; but perhaps they did not so often feel inspired by its specifically pianistic attributes as do several of the moderns. Many of the Beethoven Sonatas could be orchestrated and a symphonic effect produced. In other words, the magnificent thoughts of most of the great masters of the past were rarely peculiarly pianistic, though Scarlatti, Chopin, and Liszt in their day (just as Debussy, Albenez, Ravel and Cyril Scott today) divined the soul of the piano and made the instrument speak its own native tongue.

THE MODERN PIANO A PERCUSSION INSTRUMENT

Indeed the real nature of the modern piano as an instrument is in itself more or less of a modern discovery. No one would be altogether satisfied by trumpet passages played upon a violin, because the violin and the trumpet have characteristics which individualize them. In precisely the same fashion the piano has individual characteristics. The piano is distinctly an instrument of percussion—a beating of felt-covered hammers upon tightened wires. Once we realize this, a great deal may be learned. Debussy has retained in his pianistic vocabulary many of the beautiful kaleidoscopic effects a gifted child strumming upon the piano would produce, but which our overtrained ears might have rejected in the past. Thus his methods have implied a study of the problem of just how much dissonance can be artistically applied and yet keep his work within the bounds of the beautiful. It has been said that Debussy learned much from a Javanese instrument

called a Gamalan. This instrument is a kind of
orchestra of gongs. I have been told that when
the players from the far East performed at one
of the Paris expositions, Debussy was greatly attracted by their music, and lingered long near them
to note the enchanting effect of the harmonics from
the bells. There can be no doubt that he sought to
reproduce such an effect on that other instrument of
percussion, the piano, when he wrote his exquisite
Reflets dans l'eau, and the following significant
measures in *Pagodes:*

No. I.

In all gong effects we hear one note louder than the surrounding "aura" of ethereal harmonies. This suggests many new and delightful effects upon the piano, for all the past pianists have been accustomed to playing all the notes of a chord, for instance, with more or less the same degree of force. It seldom seemed to occur to the average piano student that it is possible to play chords in succession and at the same time bring out some inner voice so that the whole effect is delightfully altered.

Indeed, we are coming to a day when the pianist will more and more be expected to play melodies concealed in masses of chords. Busoni in his edition of the Bach Chorals (Breitkopf & Haertel, *Volksansgabe, No.* 1916) gives us a splendid instance of an inner voice carrying the melody in the *Nun freut euch, lieben Christen* (No. 4). The following measures serve to illustrate this. Any one who has heard Mr. Busoni play this will find it difficult to forget the clear sonority with which he

No. 2.

plays the melody and how delicate and exquisitely subdued is the lace-like embroidery which surrounds the melody.

In playing chords so that one note may stand out above the others we confront what many seem to think is a really difficult task, but as a matter of fact it is not. It is a habit easily acquired.

What is the need for ever making a note in a chord stand out above its fellows? In all good part-writing, whether for the piano or other instruments or for voices, each voice in a sequence of chords has some melodic value. Many voices have a distinctive melodic value. In the orchestra or in a quartet of strings or of human voices each part has a certain tone color which gives it individuality and distinguishes it from the other parts. But on the piano we have no such contrasting tone colors or tone qualities to work with. What in the orchestra, for instance, is accomplished largely by contrasts of *quality* we on the piano must accomplish by contrasts of *quantity,* or different sound strengths. Don't you see that the only recourse is to individualize the melody in an internal voice by making that melody louder, or by subduing the other notes in the chords? It is quite possible to play a chord in the following fashion:

No. 3.

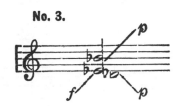

That is, the E flat is loud and the D flat and B flat are soft. Nothing is simpler. My own method is to hold my fingers rigidly; with the second finger, which would play the E flat, protruding downwards, while the thumb and fifth finger, which are to play the D flat and B flat, are kept high, so that the force of the blow descends on to the E flat key (which is pressed down as far as it will go), while the other two keys are only lightly struck (and pressed down only one-third or one-half of the tonal distance they could descend).

This opens up interesting vistas even yet not fully explored. It would be more profitable for many of our students to spend a little more time upon the quality of effects and a little less time in trying to clamber over an immense amount of technic work. Playing two such chords as the following in the manner indicated requires an amount of thought, hand control, far in excess of that demanded by many supposedly difficult technical exercises.

No. 4.

An Interesting Artistic Application

It is possible to show how this plan of bringing out the middle voice may be employed by quoting my pianistic setting of the lovely *Irish Tune from County Derry*. The melody is believed to be very old and was collected by Miss J. Ross, of Limavady, County Derry, and the melody was first published in the Petrie Collection of the Ancient Music of Ireland. It is a tune very susceptible to modern harmonic treatment, and if the student will play the first measures with the method of bringing out the melody notes in the inner part as we have described it, he will see that very rare effects may be produced.

No. 5. Slowish, but not dragged, and wayward in time.
M. M. ♪ = between 72 and 104.
Rubato il tempo, e non troppo lento.

New Effects With the Pedal

Modern pianism has brought into vogue certain pedal effects which were only employed by the most iconoclastic a few decades ago. A very striking effect of diminuendo, for instance, can be produced by what I call "half-pedaling." The problem is to melt from forte to pianissimo through the use of the pedal. By "half-pedaling" I mean repeatedly lifting up the damper pedal just so high that the dampers only partially arrest the vibrations of the strings, thereby accomplishing a gradual diminuendo. In the following three last measures of my *Colonial Song* for piano the notes marked with stars are gradually melted away by this process in the second bar of the example, though this is not the case with the other six notes, the keys of which are pressed down silently before the half-pedaling begins, so their dampers are not affected by the movements of the damper pedal. These six notes are thus heard vibrating on to the very end of the piece.

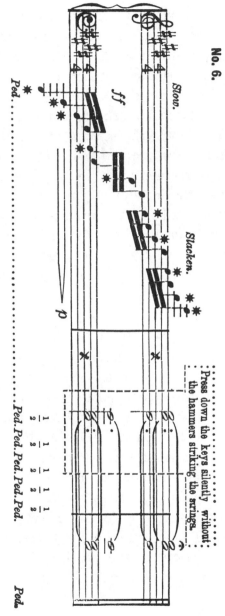

No. 6.

An illustration of a unique method of pedaling a passage requiring special treatment. It is only one of hundreds of possibilities of modern pedaling.

It seems to me that we live in an age in which
the piano has again come very much into its own.
The developments of the last fifteen or twenty years
seem to me enormous.   Again let me say that this
is a period in which the piano is not merely a practical and serviceable medium for expressing noble
and touching musical feelings of a nature not especially limited or adapted to the piano or any other
particular instrument, but in which the very soul
and body of the instrument, all its most individual
peculiarities and idiosyncracies, are especially
catered for, and in which the technical aspects of
the piano are developed to a degree and in a manner
so that they are able to play an emotional and highly
soulful role.

An Inspired Period

Composers such as Scarlatti, Couperin, Chopin
and Liszt at once leap to one's mind as creative
geniuses of this particularly high pianistic type.
They have not only written great music for the
piano, such as the giants Bach, Beethoven, Brahms,
but the greatness of their achievement lies in the
peculiarly pianistic note of their style and of the
elements contained in their works that prove unusually stimulating and developing to pianists playing them.   Though personally I feel perhaps the
deepest attraction in the works of men such as
Bach, Wagner, Grieg and Frederick Delius, in

whose creations the inventive germ and the inner musical idea and emotion comes always first, and the instrument or instruments employed are comparatively secondary considerations (men who compose much the same *kind* of music whether they write it for organ or chorus or piano); still I feel we can hardly ever value the refreshing stimulating incentive (especially for the executive artists performing such works) found in the work of men whose gifts lie to a great extent in the power to concentrate on the physical nature of the particular instrument employed and who are capable of quaffing technical and color resources to the very dregs as it were.

It seems to me we live in a period in which such technically inspired composers for the piano abound, and I think the results to pianists of all the new and fresh and lovely and startling piano creations that have appeared in print since, let us say, about 1900, have been extremely rich and their importance and benefit impossible to exaggerate. Pianistically speaking, it seems as if there never had existed a more prolific period than the present. What diversity! What contrasts between the work of Albeniz and Cyril Scott, Debussy, Ravel, Schönberg and Ornstein.

PIONEERS IN A NEW FIELD

At the risk of mentioning a very incomplete list,

I wish to specialize on those composers whose pianoforte works I have had the pleasure of being the
first to introduce into many different countries on
my tours in various parts of the world, as follows:
Debussy, Ravel, Cyril Scott, Frederick Delius, Albeniz. At various times I have had the joy of introducing these men for the first time to audiences
in England, Holland, Germany, Scandinavia, Australia, New Zealand, and I know no privilege more
enticing and no event connected with a performer's
career more satisfying and exciting and worth while
than being able to introduce the torch-bearing works
of new iconoclasts to broad-minded audiences all
over the world, hungry and eager for beautiful new
things.

The soulfully sensuous and wistfully tender and
pathetic creations of the modern French composers
have occasioned a reaction against "banging" and
over-energetic virtuoso playing in general for which
we can never be too thankful. They have reintro-
duced certain types of charmful pianism that had
been neglected since the days of Couperin and
Scarlatti. They have also opened our eyes to the
entrancing beauties of certain long pedal effects,
which are particularly convincing in Debussy's
Reflets dans l'eau, Pagodes, and in Ravel's *Jeux
d'eau* and *Oudines.* There are, after all, many very
purely percussive and bell-like and gong-like effects
peculiarly native to the nature of the metallic mod-

ern piano which lay dormant until so wonderfully developed by Ravel and Debussy, which no doubt they owe in part, if not chiefly, to their contact with Gamalans and other Eastern instruments and musics.

Cyril Scott's Unique Achievements

There are certain possibilities of the modern pianoforte that it seems to me only Cyril Scott has known how to utilize to their fullest extent. Modern musicians have long been profoundly attracted to irregular rhythms of every kind. As early as 1899 I was myself busy evolving a style of rhythmically irregular music in which every bar-length, every beat-length, could have a duration that had no regular relation whatever to those preceding or following it. If our present system can be described as "meter in music," then what I was attempting might be termed "prose in music." These experiments of mine led Cyril Scott to pursue highly original developments of his own.

It is one thing to write highly irregular rhythms for chorus or orchestra or chamber combinations; it is another thing to get such rhythms accurately performed, with complete unanimity between the different performers! Cyril Scott realized that the absolute solo nature of the piano offered unique opportunities. It is far easier for a single performer to reproduce complex rhythms than for

several musicians playing or singing together to do
so.   Therefore the most successful and revolution-
ary developments of irregular rhythms yet in print
can be studied in Cyril Scott's piano works, such
as his great *Sonata,* Op. 66, his *Suite,* Op. 75, and
such entrancing and highly original and significant
smaller numbers as the following from his *Poems*
for piano—*The Garden of Soul-sympathy, Bells,
The Twilight of the Year, Paradise Birds,* etc.

As a pianistic colorist he has exploited the metallic, bell-like, clanging upper octaves of the piano in
ways no other composer has, producing brittle iri-
descent cascades of chord-sounds that have a capti-
vating charm wholly their own.

Apart from all this, Cyril Scott's music most
soulfully expresses one of the most interesting,
noble and poetic artistic personalities of our age.

The Influence of Spanish Gipsy Music

It is highly interesting to trace the influence of
guitars, mandolins, etc., in such pieces as Debussy's
La Soirée dans Grenade and *Minstrels,* Ravel's
Alborada el Graziosa, and Albeniz's *Iberia.* Albeniz
developed the "two-hand" technic perhaps more
than anyone else.   His piano style might also be
nicknamed a "concertina" style, so much does it
consist of "right, left, right, left," devices.   Albeniz seems to me to give us a volume of sonority,
a dashing intensity and glowing brilliancy that have

been lacking in composers for the piano since Liszt and Balakirew, and without which we should be very much the poorer. At other times the vibrating gloom of his music suggests old Spanish pictures. But in all his phases he appears to me a real genius, occupying a wholly unique and precious niche amongst the greatest pianistic composers of all time.

A Notable Concerto

Frederick Delius's Pianoforte *Concerto in C Minor* is to my mind the most important, the most deeply musical and emotionally significant concerto produced for several decades. It is not merely a fine pianistic concerto, but apart from all that a glowing representative work by one of the greatest creators of all time. To many keen observers of modern compositional developments, the great Frederick Delius seems to tower above most or all of his contemporaries because of the irresistible emotional power, passion, and inner sincerity of his creations. A wizard in orchestration, a harmonist second to none, it is the human soul behind all his other marvelous qualities that marks him out as a genius among geniuses, and makes him so particularly touching and endearing, and accounts for the unique position among modern composers held by Delius in England, Germany, Holland and elsewhere, and the extraordinary international vogue of such complex creations as *Brigg Fair, Paris,*

Dance Rhapsody, Sea-drift, Appalachia, Mass of Life, On Hearing the First Cuckoo in Spring, etc.

His polyphony is marvelous and has an indefinable Bach-like quality that is no less noticeable in his emotional make-up and in the non-effect-seeking sincerity and depth of his whole being and utterance. His artistic soul is akin to great cosmic men such as Bach, Wagner, Goethe, Walt Whitman, Milton—he is most at home in great broad lines, and his work glows with a great lovingness, almost religious, in its all-embracing and cosmic breadth.

QUESTIONS IN STYLE, INTERPRETATION, EXPRESSION AND TECHNIC OF PIANOFORTE PLAYING

SERIES XXVI

PERCY GRAINGER

1. Give some of the chief differences between piano playing of twenty years ago and the piano playing of today.

2. Give the names of some composers whose compositions are peculiarly pianistic.

3. In what class of instruments does the piano properly belong?

4. From what oriental instrument did Debussey learn much?

5. Why is it desirable to emphasize certain notes in chords?

6. What have been some of the chief innovations of Cyril Scott?

7. Tell something of the pianistic accomplishments of Albeniz.

ALEXANDER LAMBERT

BIOGRAPHICAL

Alexander Lambert was born at Warsaw, November 1, 1863. His first teacher was his father, Henry Lambert. At the age of ten Alexander played for Rubinstein, who was much impressed with his talent, and gave the boy's father a letter to Julius Epstein at the Vienna Conservatory. At the conservatory he remained for four years, graduating with a medal shortly after he was sixteen years of age. When seventeen he moved to America, whither his parents had come. Here he developed his repertoire, through self-study, for three years. When twenty he returned to Europe, and toured Germany and Russia with the great Joachim. Moszkowski then took a great interest in the young pianist, and, in addition to dedicating a work to him, advised him to go to Weimar to study with Liszt. At Weimar he remained for many months, under the direct guidance of Liszt. Returning to America he appeared as a soloist with the orchestras of Seidl, Damrosch, Van der Stucken, and made highly successful appearances in recitals in New York, Boston, Chicago, and other cities. At the age of twenty-three, Lambert started in to teach, and soon found himself at the head of the highly successful New York College of Music, where he remained as director for eighteen years. Several of his pupils have appeared at important concerts here and abroad with notable success.

29

PROFITABLE PRACTICE
Versus
WASTED PRACTICE

ALEXANDER LAMBERT

WASTED PRACTICE AT THE OUTSTART

THE more experienced the teacher the more evident it is to him that no one can make a set of practice rules or a practice plan that would cover all cases. It is extremely difficult to get away from generalities, because each individual pupil is different from any and every other pupil and to make a hard-and-fast law for practice that would fit all would be like making one pair of spectacles and expect that pair to fit the eyes of many different people. The simile is an interesting one for if there can be so much difference in the focus of different eyes imagine what an immense difference there must be in the mental focus.

The first general rule for the teacher to observe in the practice of the beginner is to leave nothing undone to make the practice interesting and enthusiastic. The pupil should go to the keyboard alive with interest. It does not make much difference how the teacher accomplishes this so long as he really does it. You will find hundreds and hundreds of theories about how to teach, but they

are all worthless unless the teacher has the power
to grasp the essentials in connection with each case.

THROUGH THE EYES OF THE CHILD

The teacher must, of course, see the interesting
side of music himself. That is, he must see it
through the eyes of the child. The pupil comes
with a face that is a picture of unwillingness. He
should leave the studio with a face beaming with
the excitement of having learned something beautiful and profitable. Some people are able to do this
and some are not. Those who can create that kind
of enthusiasm which charges the pupil with the desire to work and work hard until the next lesson
are the successful teachers. They outstrip many
who may have better technical equipment and who
wonder why they do not succeed by parading the
fact that their training has been the most elaborate
of any of the teachers in town.

After all, the one great thing in all education is
simply *results*. If you want to know the greatest
secret of how to become a successful teacher, produce results, not ordinary, mediocre results, but results that are so artistic and so thorough that they
cannot fail to command respect and attention. My
friends used to say to me when I was director of
the New York College of Music, "Mr. Lambert,
you are very successful—you are a good business
man." It always made me laugh, as I never felt

that I was a good business man at all. I simply worked for results and saw that the practice of my pupils was resultful.

Before leaving the subject of enthusiasm, we might note that the pupil's attitude toward practice should have the serious attention of the teacher at all times. Most of the difficulties are easily remedied if the teacher is watchful. He should by no means glue his eyes on the keyboard alone. For instance, the face is a good barometer of the pupil's mental and nervous condition. Making faces indicates a nervous strain which, if not eradicated at once, will prevent one later on from acquiring an easy and graceful way of playing.

An Undisturbed Study Plan

The need for a good study plan or course is very important, and once the pupil has been advised that a certain course is best suited to his needs let him keep steadfastly on until he reaches some definite aim. Much time is wasted because the pupil is twisted one way and the other by people, who, however well meaning, are upsetting the teacher's plans and the pupil's work. Some pupils hold their ears open for all the foolish criticism imaginable.

"Why, my dear, you are practicing all wrong. The $XYZWX$ method would never permit you to practice in that way!"

The pupil thinks a moment and replies, "But

my teacher has been turning out successful pupils for years."

Then the "well-meaning" friend answers:

"That has nothing to do with it. Nobody thinks of studying by any other method than the $XYZWX$ method in these days."

The pupil runs off to the brand new and incomparable method. After a little while some other well-meaning friend comes along with another infallible method, and the pupil is again torn up from her regular practice, "by the roots" as it were, and planted in a new educational hot-box guaranteed to produce results finer than anything ever produced before. For this reason I have made it a practice not to criticize pupils of other teachers. All teachers have their own ideas and are entitled to think as their judgment prompts. It is most unjust to criticise the work of another teacher in good standing, as one may not perceive the purposes for which the other teacher is working. By criticising unfairly, all the pupil's confidence in his teacher (and therefore the confidence he should have in his practice periods) is distorted, and instead of an eager, positive, active pupil, we have a weak, listless wandering student who never reaches his goal."

REDUNDANCY IN PRACTICE

In the early stages of musical progress the pupil should be counseled to watch his own work so carefully that he may determine at home whether he works correctly or not—which passage needs repetition and which does not. And often even a simple little melody requires hard work. Good practice is intelligent repetition, but there is little intelligence in repeating anything without concentration of mind. Concentrate upon the difficult passages and work on them until they sound as fluent and simple as the ones that are now easy to you.

Indeed, one of the chief aims during practice is to develop the critical sense. Have you ever thought of it in that way? All the time you are working with your fingers at the keyboard you should be busy in your brain building up those faculties which discriminate very nicely indeed between what is artistic, effective, or beautiful, and that which is weak, banal or ugly. After all, the sum and substance of your musicianship apart from your actual keyboard work depends upon the mental balance or artistic right and artistic wrong which you should be building every moment during your practice.

Of course the advice of your teacher is in the first place of great value, in informing you upon those art principles which define beautiful playing and careless playing. There are certain laws of expression which have to do with form and design with which every teacher should acquaint his pupils, but the working out of these principles is done in the pupil's own mind and nowhere else. Practice that does not lead to this is certainly worthless.

If you were to listen to someone else playing you would be "all ears" for false notes, bad phrasing, poor pedaling. Listen to yourself in the same way, as though a stranger were playing—one might almost say as though a rival were playing. This makes for concentration and is always profitable.

Physical Conditions

The student should constantly realize how thoroughly practice is a matter of body building and brain building. There are times when practice is more injurious than beneficial. If the bodily health is bad the student should lessen his practice efforts or even stop entirely until better physical conditions are obtained. No teacher is smart enough to give a music lesson to a headache, a bad case of indigestion or la grippe. If any one of your pupils happen to be the victim of "legitimate," sickness let him stop until he recovers. You may lose a little in lesson fees, but why waste your time, your strength and your knowledge trying to teach when teaching is impossible?

The capacity of some students is limited. That is, they can take just so much at a time and do it well. It is much the same with the practice period. Practice as long at one time as you can practice well, and do not try to crowd one or two months'

work into one hour.   Do everything you do as
finely as you possibly can, even though you succeed
in learning no more than a few measures.   You
may be very fond of ice cream soda, but if you
attempt to devour five or six glasses of soda water,
one right after the other, the result will be painful.
Yet pupils are constantly doing much the same
thing in their practice periods.   I wonder whether
it is not the American spirit of restlessness?   We
find it hard to concentrate long upon one thing.

Too much work is worse than too little.   The
pupil who spends so many hours a day at the keyboard that he is obliged to put himself in the hands
of the doctor or the masseur loses all the time and
money he has spent upon his music and accomplishes nothing in the bargain.

Keeping the Right Mental Angle

It would hardly be an exaggeration to say that
years are wasted every minute through unintelligent practice.   This is by no means always the fault
of the teacher, as he cannot supply intelligence.   He
can merely strive to set up habits which will make
the student more exacting.

When the student starts to practice—that is,
practice in such a way that he will get something
out of his work, he should direct his mind as
definitely and as certainly as though he were taking
it to another room—a kind of chamber of practice.

While his mind is in that imaginary room there should be no intrusions from the outside, no looking out of the mental windows. This does not apply only to pieces and to studies alone, but to all modes of practice—everything.

For instance, my experience has shown me that scales are invaluable and I use them constantly with all pupils in all grades. The pupils are taught from the very first to concentrate upon the scales, just as though they were playing the most difficult piece. Their eyes never leave the fingers and the mind is constantly at work disciplining the fingers, insisting upon correct hand positions, controlling the touch, etc. Variety is to be had by practicing scales with special attention to any of the following matters, all equally important:

TOUCH
STRENGTH
SPEED
LIGHTNESS
SURETY
LOOSENESS, ETC.

Any one who has practiced scales right in these ways never professes to be bored with them. Many of the great pianists feel the necessity for a thorough and continual playing of the scales. The student who tries to do without them is making a very serious mistake indeed.

PRACTICE MUSICALLY

The worst kind of practice is perfunctory practice. The key board is a kind of treadmill for thousands of students. They play and play and play, and never consider the musical side of their work. In fact, there is very little difference between their work and that of an actor who might take Hamlet and recite it with the same sing-song that children use in saying the multiplication tables. In all your practice with pieces, every note, every motive, every phrase, every section you play, should be filled to the utmost with musical expression. That is, you should not leave a phrase pass under your fingers unless it has meant something to you. It should have passed through your consciousness and should carry a message to other ears, a message which is a part of you.

Do not do this in the hardest possible way. Take the natural, simple way—be yourself. Some unfortunate pupils imagine great effort, wrinkled foreheads and nervous anxiety will lead to results in practice. Quite the opposite is really true. Let your mind and your fingers do the work, not your face. If you wanted to walk gracefully you would not begin by putting your feet and legs in outrageous shapes and staggering along like a cripple. Learning to play is in some ways like learning to walk. Don't learn to stagger and stumble by permitting yourself repeatedly to stagger and stumble.

All work at the keyboard is for control. Control does not come about by forgiving little slips, getting stupidly excited or making blunders. Every pupil can get hold of himself and retain that hold so that mistakes become the exception instead of the rule.

REGULARITY IN PRACTICE

The great virtuoso who may never have given a lesson in his life and may have forgotten all about the conditions which existed during his student days, who may have been so talented that his case was no criterion by which the work of other less gifted pupils might be judged, often gives the following advice:

"Practice when you feel like it."

That is all very well for the virtuoso who has already acquired a giant technic, but over thirty years of experience with pupils in all grades, during which I have given personally thousands of lessons, has shown me that the only safe course for the average pupil is to

"Practice regularly or not at all."

Young pupils should report for their practice hours every day, just as they report for their school work. Pupils think that they can skip a day now and then without affecting their work so long as they "make up" by practicing three or four hours on one day.   Absurd!   This is like going without food for a week and then eating ten dinners one right after the other to catch up.

In fact, the main advantage in regular practice is that the mind goes to it after regular periods of rest.   The mind must be fresh and clear every moment.   Constant watch must be kept for unnecessary movements.   In these days of efficiency in manufacture we learn that all unnecessary movement is waste.   Any intelligent piano teacher could have told the so-called efficiency engineers that all good music pedagogs have been fighting to do away with unnecessary movements for years.   Indeed, it has gotten down to such a fine point now that the fingers are never raised higher than just enough to strike the notes effectively.   There was a day when the fingers were lifted to exaggerated heights, but then men began to think in this way—the high stepping horse is rarely the strong horse or the very fast horse.   Indeed, the race horse is almost never a high stepper when he is at his best.   If we wanted to learn to run we would not start by lifting our knees to our noses.

The amount of practice to be done each day is something which is wholly a matter of the teacher's discretion.   Each teacher has his ideas upon this subject, and does things in his own way, so I feel a little delicate about telling my own, but I never permitted any of my pupils to practice over four

hours.   My only advice to pupils upon assigning
work to be studied is to say, "Do as much as you
can learn perfectly."   If the pupil does only three
measures I am satisfied so long as those measures
are as nearly perfect as possible.   For the average
pupil of eighteen, in good health, three, or, at most,
four hours a day is ample.   More is likely to be injurious.   Some years ago I prepared a card giving
advice to students upon the subject of practice.
This is so nearly identical with what I am giving
today that it may be interesting to reprint this card.
It has gone into the hands of thousands.   Indeed, I
see nothing in my advice of two decades ago that
I would care to alter very radically today.

Advice to Students

Always practice systematically.

Seldom practice over four hours a day.   Don't
think that by practicing six or seven hours a day
you will become a greater artist than he who practices four hours a day.   Your fingers cannot stand
so long a strain, and if you persist, they will take
their revenge a few years later, when your fingers
will begin to lose their strength and surety.   A
student who cannot accomplish much in four hours,
will not in six.

Divide your hours for practicing thus: one hour
and a half in the morning; the same in the afternoon, and one hour in the evening.

In the morning devote half an hour to five-finger exercises and scales, half an hour to your études and half an hour to your sonata or piece. Do the same in the afternoon. The hour in the evening may be devoted to reviewing your last lesson.

Do not practice your whole lesson every day; divide it into equal parts. You can learn one page a day, where you could not learn two or three.

Always practice slowly and carefully. If you come across a difficult passage, practice it with each hand separately, repeating the passage first slowly and with strength, and then faster and more softly until you have mastered it.

Questions in Style, Interpretation, Expression and Technic of Pianoforte Playing

SERIES XXVII

ALEXANDER LAMBERT

1. What is the first general rule in all pianoforte practice?

2. How may a pupil's mental and nervous condition be readily detected?

3. What should be one of the chief aims during practice?

4. How should the pupil listen during practice?

5. How should physical health govern practice?

6. State six things which should be considered during scale practice.

7. Why should the pupil endeavor to discover the easiest form of practice?

8. What are the great advantages of regularity in practice?

9. How long should one practice daily?

10. How should difficult passages be conquered?

ALBERTO JONÁS

Biographical

Señor Jonás is known as a Spanish virtuoso, but in reality he is a cosmopolitan in every sense of the word. He has lived in nearly all the capitals of Europe, and also he resided for many years in America. His learning is wide and comprehensive in other lines than music. The fact that he speaks Spanish, French, German and English with equal facility has enabled him to make researches in many departments of science and literature in many countries. He has devoted much special attention to the nerves in pianoforte playing and has a thorough understanding of the physiological aspect of the subject. Señor Jonás was born at Madrid, June 8, 1868. After study in Spain he graduated at the Brussels Conservatory, winning the first prize in pianoforte playing and two first prizes in harmony. Later he studied with Anton Rubinstein in St. Petersburg, and made an international reputation as a pianist.

30

NERVOUSNESS IN PIANO PLAYING
ALBERTO JONÁS

NEURASTHENIA, THE AMERICAN DISEASE

MUSICIANS, notably music teachers, have the reputation of being nervous, and since America has been called by many "the country of nerves" it would seem that American music workers should be sufferers. This, however, is by no means an exclusively American disease nor are the only victims to be found among the American musicians. Pathologists, nevertheless, acknowledge that there is a great amount of nervousness in America and this is not said in the way of being a slur upon the country or its people. Inasmuch as an American physician, Dr. George M. Beard, as long ago as 1881 wrote a book entitled *American Nervousness, Its Causes and Consequences,* in which he dwells upon the fine organization of native Americans, their delicate skin, hair of soft texture and small bones, there can be no offense when American nervousness is discussed.

MUSICIANS USUALLY KNOW LITTLE OF CAUSE

Musicians who know little of other professional work than their own, naturally have only a very vague idea of the nature of nervousness or its causes. They do not realize that nervousness is in part the result of heredity, of environment, of personal habits and of mental attitude. With hereditary nervousness, the musician has little to do. He may guard his own habits of health to protect the nervous organization of his descendants, but it is only disconcerting to learn that he may himself have had an ancestry tending to predispose him towards nervousness. His environment, however, is a very different matter. That at least is partly open to his control, and moreover his habits may be regulated so that many "acquired" forms of nervousness may be avoided.

The musician should also know that the normal cure for nervous conditions is not to be found so much in medicine bottles as in work accomplished without hurry or flurry, but with care and a happy mind, plenty of rest, the right food and the right mental attitude (state of mind). The healthy, well-balanced person whose nerves begin to give way unconsciously seeks rest or finds a remedy. The musician, however, is kept up to a high tension by the enthusiasm for his work and his ambition to excel. He forgets his health and before one knows it there is a disastrous breakdown which enforces months of idleness. When he does discover that he is nervous, he promptly sets out to nurse his nervousness and ultimately makes it much like some grievance or some trouble for which he feels himself in no way responsible and for which he is ready to blame any person or any thing.

A SELF SUGGESTED COMPLAINT

Putting aside heredity and pathological conditions, nervousness comes under the head of self-suggested complaints. If one were to isolate the microbe of nervousness it would probably be found that it was nothing other than the magnification of self, although on the contrary in some cases it might be laid to the neglect of self.

Take the matter of food, for instance. Musicians eat at all hours, consume rich viands, often hurry through their meals and some unfortunately are addicted to the over use of alcohol. I do not refer now to those who indulge in wine or beer occasionally, but to those who consume the very strong drinks. As a matter of fact, there is less alcohol in a glass of well-brewed beer (German beer has 3½%) than in a poorly cooked potato. A raw potato contains 65% of alcohol. Nevertheless, the books by specialists on nervousness are filled with injunctions against the abuse of alcohol which is a most excellent fuel and motive power for machinery other than the human stomach.

I have seen American musicians rush back to work directly after a meal just like their brethren in the American business world. The German or the Frenchman rests after his meals, rests for perhaps half an hour and then returns refreshed with his digestion undisturbed by business cares. There can be no question that dyspepsia and nervousness are closely connected in many cases. Get the best book you can upon diet and eating, the right selection of foods, etc., and then use all of your will power to create habits of correct eating. This may show in your playing and study. Who knows, it may be just what you need most to get rid of nervousness.

The American Temperament and Nerves

America is a land of such amazing opportunity that the musician, like the business man, keeps himself constantly under a great strain to get ahead. No one can tell me that the Americans are not temperamental but many misconstrue the meaning of temperament and imagine it must be a form of nervous agitation. On the contrary it is a highly developed nervous organism under adequate control of the will. It is a lively exuberance and forceful expression of the feelings. In music it includes enthusiasm and the ardent desire to do justice to the beauties of a composition. The temperamental player will put more emphatic force in his strong utterances. He will give more passionate expression to phrases of love, sorrow, courage and despair. On the other hand, he is by the very nature of his art apt to step over the bounds. This exaggeration, which is ruinous to the interpretation of a great master work, is quite as apt to come from lack of the right artistic balance or judgment as it is from lack of a strong nervous system, but it probably comes more frequently from the latter.

Some Wonders of the Nervous System

In order that the musician may gain a better idea of the marvels of the nervous system and perhaps a higher respect for the wonderful piece of physiological machinery which we all have within us, I would suggest that he secure some good simple work upon the nerves and do a little close reading. In the first place, the number of nerve cells in the body is prodigious. Of course they have never been counted because it would be almost as easy to count the stars in the firmament. Estimates, however, place the number of nerve cells in the human body at hundreds of millions. Yet all these are connected in some mysterious and wonderful manner with the brain and the spinal cord. Sever certain nerves in your arm and you may apply a burning brand to your hand without feeling it. This illustrates how closely connected is the nervous system with the brain. Although you seem to feel pain in your finger when it is pricked with a pin, the sense of pain is after all in the brain. This is a very important fact for musicians to note. There are inferences which might be drawn therefrom which if properly understood would easily show how the pupil may be saved hours of labor by the right mental control.

Each nerve cell or neurone may be said to be independent, an anatomical physiological unit living by itself but at the same time connected with other nerve cells in a manner so marvelous that it is beyond the province of words to describe it. Nervous breakdown is usually caused by the slow disintegration of the nerve cells and nerve fibre. In some cases this disintegration has no serious outward signs. In other cases the hair commences to fall very rapidly, muscular action is less coordinate, at times even erratic, and the memory commences to weaken. Beware of these signs of nerve decay. It is time for you, Mr. Pianist, to investigate yourself and strive to build up your nervous organism.

Some Things the Pianist Should Know About Nerves

The pianist should know first of all that every effort requires nervous expenditure. That is, the something which caused the effort that was consumed in making it. It then becomes necessary for new nerve force to form. Just as a storage battery which has been used up needs to be charged again, the nerves must be re-charged with force for future endeavors. The storage battery gets its re-charge from the dynamo; but whence comes the force which re-charges the nerve cells no one really knows. The nutrition of the nerve cell is, however, in large measure dependent upon the blood supply and it may be assumed that anything which will improve the condition of the blood will at the same time make for better nerves. It may also be seen that the circulation of the blood must be kept in the very best possible condition.

There is no more stupid way in which the pianist or the piano student can waste his time than by long continued periods of practice without relaxation, general bodily exercise and plenty of deep breathing. A quick walk around the block, interspersed with good full breaths, often restores the nerve force and insures progress. For that reason short practice periods and many of them are better than one long period.

Are Pianists Especially Liable to Nervousness?

I do not think that pianists are more liable to nervousness than people in other professions as a result of the fact that the pianist is continually hitting with his highly sensitized finger tips all day long. As a matter of fact, the violinist exerts far more pressure upon the fingerboard of the violin. In other words, note for note the physical force demanded in the case of the violinist is greater than in the case of the pianist. Piano playing in itself does not promote nervousness. One has only to judge by the well-known performers. Most of the virtuosos I have known are exceptionally strong persons, with hearty appetites and good nerves. The great pianist must have fine nerves. He would never be able to stand the strain otherwise.

Nervousness comes to those who have not yet learned how to control themselves mentally and physically. The little teacher who worries and frets all the time—who tortures her life with imagining that awful things may occur and who takes every set-back as a calamity—she is the one who is the victim of neurasthenia. The teacher imagines that because success does not come at once she must be lacking in talent or is going behind. Real success in music study is at the end of a long journey. The piano student must learn to control his nerve-breaking eagerness to rush ahead.

Some Things the Parent Should Know

Nervousness at the practice hour is by no means unusual, and piano practice in itself may be made a source of nervousness if proper conditions are not observed. The pupil should always practice in a room alone. There is nothing which makes the pupil more nervous than petty disturbances such as people passing in and out of the room, annoying parental admonitions, other children playing in neighboring rooms. I insist upon the pupil having a comfortable chair during practice. There are certain positions in sitting and standing which are a great strain upon the nervous system. Ease at the keyboard can never be attained unless the pupil learns to sit easily and comfortably during practice, not on a revolving stool balanced like a performer in the circus, but upon a substantial comfortable chair.

Another matter which has to do with nerve strain is vision. See to it that the distribution of light in the practice room is right. The windows (and likewise the artificial light) should be behind or at the side of the performer, never in front of him. Eye strain may tire the pupil and lead to nervousness almost as quickly as in any other way. Many people are nervous and yet do not know that the cause could be removed by a good oculist. Another cause of nervousness which very few might suspect is the position of the music on the music rack. In the case of the grand piano the music is somewhat higher than in the case of the upright piano. Consequently when the music rack is too high the player's neck is held in a strained position. For this reason also (and for other reasons too), I discourage sitting too low at the piano. It forces the player to strain his neck, when reading music. All the great network of nerve ganglia located at the back of the neck is then strained.

THE NERVOUS PUPIL AT PRACTICE

When playing, the inexperienced pianist with tendencies toward nervousness seems for the most part afraid of missing notes or of forgetting some complicated passage. He does not seem concerned, however, over the equally important subject of whether his tone will be uniformly fine or whether his touch will be beautiful, whether the dynamic treatment will prove effective and within the canons of well-poised aesthetic judgment, whether the pedals are well employed, whether his playing will show a clear "distribution" or outline as regards the proper distinction of phrases, sections, periods, episodes, also of contrasts and climaxes. Yet were he to give serious, conscientious thought to all this while playing, he would in all probability not have time nor inclination to fret about accuracy or memory. Nervousness is often nothing more than self-consciousness unduly magnified over the real significance of the player's artistic message.

All this presupposes, of course, that the performer has completely mastered his piece. Mastery, that is a wonderful insurance against nervousness. I do not mean to say that anyone who has mastered a piece can not be nervous, but mastery brings a confidence hard to describe in any other way. When the pianist knows that he can play a work accurately and safely, and also beautifully, he should not fret.

If he does fret, he should look to the piece quite as much as to his own nerves.

But if one searches deeper, particularly into the psychological aspects of the subject, one will often find that underlying it all is a wrong, and let it be said frankly, not very noble attitude of mind. The performer is afraid because he consciously or unconsciously craves the applause and flattery of the listener. This should not be so and indeed is never the case with the true artist. He is, of course, glad if the audience understands him, he is also glad of the success and for all the good it may bring with it. But should the audience fail to respond and the apparent success not yet be his, then he should quietly investigate whether he has accomplished what he had set out to do, or whether the selections he had played were too deep, too abstract, or too new for the average audience to understand. There is certainly no real occasion for nervousness. The performer will honestly and sincerely criticize this performance with a view to future improvement and there will be no sterner nor fairer judge than he.

Therein lies the strength of the true artist with the view to future improvement. That thought will ever console him, for the artist lives in a world of ideals which he strives to reach, knowing full well that he will never quite attain them. Often an artist is greeted with great applause after the perform-

ance of a piece, but at the same time he realizes that
he has not done his best. The true artist will forget
the enthusiasm of the audience and set out to improve the defective passages even though the audience was mistaken.

Therefore whether the artist plays well or not
well he will always strive to improve his work,
either by keeping it up to the fine standard he
usually attains or by endeavoring to excel his own
past at future performances. The performer thus
becomes a constant student of his own playing—the
most absorbing subject he can possibly take up.
How can such a performer big or small entertain
the fear thought? He has far too much on his
mind to think of worry or nerves. He approaches
his task of playing for others without fear or trepi-
dation, but rather with the spirit of sincere investigation. Nervousness in public playing then becomes an impossibility because his aim and reward
lie higher than the immediate applause.

PRACTICAL TECHNICAL ADVICE ON NERVOUSNESS

Viewed from the practical, that is the physiological or technical standpoint, the nervousness of the
pianist occurs mostly in the changes of the hand
position at the keyboard. The more skips there are
in a composition, the greater is his fear of missing
notes. He has therefore to learn by painstaking
exercise to control himself more and more carefully

when changes of position occur. On the other hand "too much care will kill a cat," and he must acquire the necessary abandon and confidence in himself and attain the desired accuracy without seeming concerned about it.

How closely nervousness is connected with fear must be evident to anyone who has observed closely. *Every soldier* who goes into battle for the first time is *afraid*. If he manages to stick to his post while the bullets whiz past his head it is because disobedience or retreat would bring him death with equal certainty. It is only after repeated experiences that the soldier learns to keep cool while danger surrounds him on all sides. In the same manner it takes repeated experiences for the performer on the concert stage to master the courage which makes him oblivious of the audience.

Do not minimize that matter of courage. Were I to epitomize every conceivable requisite of good nerve control, whether intellectual, physical or moral I would choose that word *courage* as embodying them all. It takes courage at all times to make the nerves subservient to the will, courage to regulate one's life habits, courage to be oneself when in the presence of others, courage to entertain one's own artistic convictions—*courage,* COURAGE, *COURAGE.*

SENSIBLE REMEDIES FOR NERVOUSNESS

Let us consider for a few moments some of the sensible things which may be done to remedy some states of nervous trouble. Of course no one must suppose that there could be anything written in an article of this kind that would supply the assistance which only a trained physician can give in advanced cases of nervous breakdown. However, I am certain that there are a number of simple things which may be controlled and which will unquestionably help the musician, teacher, and student, if a little patience and persistence is employed to pursue these cures.

First of all the nervous musicians should remember, as we have previously said, that nervousness is often largely a matter of pose and self-consciousness. Like the child who cries only when some one is around, many people have nerves which are for exhibition purposes solely. Their manifestations of nervousness are really nothing more than appeals for sympathy. What is this but a mental angle, a wrong way of looking at things? Get out of it. Fight it. Be sincere and genuine, and you will realize that the world is not going to stand or fall because of the manner in which you play a certain piece. When a man looks for sympathy what he needs most of the time is a good kick. Those who deserve sympathy get it without begging for it.

It would be a splendid thing if some of the

nervous music teachers, or rather those who think they are nervous, should read Molière's delightful satirical comedy *Le Malade Imaginaire*. The imaginary sick man simply does not want to be cured, and it is not difficult to see how the tired teacher could take some very slight nervous disturbance and nurse it into a genuine case of neurasthenia.

RIGHT LIVING FOR MUSIC WORKERS

We are living in an age when there is a colossal appeal for higher and higher efficiency. The so-called efficiency expert places first of all good bodily health. Standards of musicianship constantly ascend so that one simply must possess good nerves to keep "in the swim." Here are a few of the essentials which in my opinion lead to good nerves.

1. Good healthy, simple food, cooked without unnecessary strong spices, eaten at leisure amid congenial surroundings and with an untroubled mind, not swallowed down in haste, with the mind worried by the care of the day. Food, of course, is assimilated in the stomach, but when one realizes how much the mind affects the circulation of the blood and the administration of the gastric juices in the stomach, one perceives how important the right mental condition during meals really is.

2. Abstinence from strong stimulants. If you have any doubt upon this subject, get almost any book on nerves, and you will find that the evidence

is uncompromisingly against the abuse of alcohol, or in fact any drug destined to affect the nerves. An exception might in some cases be made of well-brewed beer or good wine, partaken of in moderation.

3. Good moral habits. It need hardly be emphasized that immorality of any sort will in time undermine the strongest nervous system. It is the surest, quickest, deadliest, enemy of good nerves.

4. Plenty of work, physical and mental, *done with joy.*

5. Exercise in the open air, not occasionally but every day. *Deep breathing, when in the open air, done every day.*

6. In so far as possible, consistently early hours of retirement.

7. Sensible regulation of the day's work. Don't practice four hours one day and one-half an hour the next. If nerves are not helped by pose they are helped by poise. Think a little—is this the wise thing or is it a foolish thing? Your intellect was given you to guide you. Don't rush from a hurried lunch to a game of lawn tennis or a moving picture show. See that intervals of repose come between your intervals of energy. Attend to this for a few months and you will surely note a difference in your nervous condition.

8. Freedom from worry. Get rid of the idea or the habit of worrying, else all remedies for nerve

betterment will fail. Musicians, perhaps through too much confinement and long sedentary labor, are prone to worry about things of very little real consequence. Here again is the magnification of self. Just jot down somewhere the fact that you and all of your petty troubles will be out of the way only a very few years hence. This is a world of trouble or a world of joy pretty much as you choose to look at it. I do not mean with this to advocate callousness or indifference to the real issues of life. What I mean is that most of our worry is misplaced. As for real causes for grief, these will be dealt with according to our greater or lesser strength of mind and of purpose and to the stoutness and faith of our heart. No advice can be given here. Shakespeare has said it. Everyone can master a grief but he that has it.

9. Method and calm deliberation as to the distribution of your work and the disposing of the many things that have to be done daily: letter writing, telephone calls, visits, etc. If you find yourself confronted with a number of things to do, do not fret, but just take hold of the very first at hand and dispose of it calmly and with care.

10. Get *joy* out of your work.

The Habit of Nerve Control

I am of the opinion that by practice one can develop habits of nerve control that are in themselves

remedial. For years many musicians have retained
that absurd idea that fighting and fussing and
blustering was temperament and they have actually
cultivated it. No wonder they are nervous. Unless
they first of all cultivate the habit of repose they
will continue to be nervous for the rest of their
lives. They seem to develop a kind of artificial
eagerness to get things done before they can possibly
be done. If you are in a train, remember that you
will not get to your destination until the train gets
there. As a well known German author has said,
"Don't travel with your train, your auto, or the
street-car; let them carry you." Do not strive mentally or nervously to push the car forward with
every turn of the wheel. This impatience is the
juggernaut which grinds down more nervous systems than almost anything else excepting drugs.
Sit down at the keyboard with the spirit of impatience in your mind and everything you play will
be marked by nervous flurry.

Do you realize that nerves may be disciplined into
behavior almost as naughty children are disciplined?
If you set out to do something and forget what it
was that you wanted to do before you have accomplished it, if you drop or fumble everything you
take hold of, if you do not seem to be able to "hit
a right note" when playing, remember the trouble
is not in your hands or arms, but in your head, in
your mental poise. The median, radial, ulnar and

musculospiral nerves control the muscles of fingers, hands and arms. But the nucleus of all these nerves is situated in the cortex, in the head, whence are issued the orders that set these nerves in motion. Quiet your mental self, gain command of it, and watch the immediate change in the greater quiet and certainty of your motions. At one time I was exceedingly nervous and this in fact was what set me to work studying the condition. I went to a noted Berlin specialist and he enjoined me to hold out my hand with the palm downward. Of course there was a nervous trembling so characteristic and so annoying. "Now," he said, "hold the hand in front of the body, the arm not at full length but slightly bent, with the fingers not quite stretched out straight. Now continue gazing at your fingers and soothe by thought until the relaxed hand ceases to tremble." The thought indeed seemed to soothe the nerves and after a little time spent in gazing the condition was much bettered. After this he had me turn the palm downward and repeat the exercise. The simple turn of the hand resulted in producing the trembling again but with the treatment of fixing the eyes and concentrating the attention upon the hand I soon found that it became quite calm. I practiced this exercise several times each day for many weeks with the result that my nerve control was so much improved that my hand stopped shaking and trembling entirely. Since then my nerves have become exceedingly strong and quite subservient to my will. This is a form of cure with which very few people are familiar and I consider it extremely valuable. It is especially useful for pianists.

An equally ingenious test of nervousness is to procure a small vial like the old fashioned homeopathic pill bottle and put a little mercury or quicksilver in the bottom. Mercury can be secured at any good drug store. Clasp the vial with the tips of all five fingers and hold it with the top up. If you are in a state of poor nerve control the mercury will dance in the liveliest fashion. If your nerves are fairly well under control the mercury will be calm on the surface. It is extremely unusual ever to see the mercury absolutely calm even in the cases of people with very steady nerves.

A Very Vital Need

There is unquestionably a need for more consideration of the subject of nerves upon the part of American musicians. If I have given any advice in the foregoing which may prove advantageous to my American musical friends, it will give me great pleasure to know it. My attention has recently been called to a quotation from an article by Dr. Smith Ely Jelliffe, Editor of the *Journal of Nervous and Mental Diseases* which emphasizes my point. It reads, "Let it be remembered by the older generations and taught to the younger, that training and economizing of nerve force are vitally important to health and efficiency and that the great workers achieve their ends by that very quality of nervous energy, which if dissipated degenerates into nervousness."

QUESTIONS IN STYLE, INTERPRETATION, EXPRESSION AND TECHNIC OF PIANOFORTE PLAYING

SERIES XXVIII
ALBERTO JONÁS

1. To what is nervousness generally due?

2. In what is the normal cure for nervousness to be found?

3. What is temperament?

4. How do long-continued periods of practice injure the student's work?

5. Are pianists especially liable to nervousness?

6. Write out ten remedies for nervousness.

7. State how habits of nerve control may be cultivated.

A CATALOG OF SELECTED
DOVER BOOKS
IN ALL FIELDS OF INTEREST

A CATALOG OF SELECTED DOVER
BOOKS IN ALL FIELDS OF INTEREST

CONCERNING THE SPIRITUAL IN ART, Wassily Kandinsky. Pioneering work by father of abstract art. Thoughts on color theory, nature of art. Analysis of earlier masters. 12 illustrations. 80pp. of text. 5⅜ x 8½. 23411-8

ANIMALS: 1,419 Copyright-Free Illustrations of Mammals, Birds, Fish, Insects, etc., Jim Harter (ed.). Clear wood engravings present, in extremely lifelike poses, over 1,000 species of animals. One of the most extensive pictorial sourcebooks of its kind. Captions. Index. 284pp. 9 x 12. 23766-4

CELTIC ART: The Methods of Construction, George Bain. Simple geometric techniques for making Celtic interlacements, spirals, Kells-type initials, animals, humans, etc. Over 500 illustrations. 160pp. 9 x 12. (Available in U.S. only.) 22923-8

AN ATLAS OF ANATOMY FOR ARTISTS, Fritz Schider. Most thorough reference work on art anatomy in the world. Hundreds of illustrations, including selections from works by Vesalius, Leonardo, Goya, Ingres, Michelangelo, others. 593 illustrations. 192pp. 7⅛ x 10¼. 20241-0

CELTIC HAND STROKE-BY-STROKE (Irish Half-Uncial from "The Book of Kells"): An Arthur Baker Calligraphy Manual, Arthur Baker. Complete guide to creating each letter of the alphabet in distinctive Celtic manner. Covers hand position, strokes, pens, inks, paper, more. Illustrated. 48pp. 8¼ x 11. 24336-2

EASY ORIGAMI, John Montroll. Charming collection of 32 projects (hat, cup, pelican, piano, swan, many more) specially designed for the novice origami hobbyist. Clearly illustrated easy-to-follow instructions insure that even beginning papercrafters will achieve successful results. 48pp. 8¼ x 11. 27298-2

THE COMPLETE BOOK OF BIRDHOUSE CONSTRUCTION FOR WOOD-WORKERS, Scott D. Campbell. Detailed instructions, illustrations, tables. Also data on bird habitat and instinct patterns. Bibliography. 3 tables. 63 illustrations in 15 figures. 48pp. 5¼ x 8½. 24407-5

BLOOMINGDALE'S ILLUSTRATED 1886 CATALOG: Fashions, Dry Goods and Housewares, Bloomingdale Brothers. Famed merchants' extremely rare catalog depicting about 1,700 products: clothing, housewares, firearms, dry goods, jewelry, more. Invaluable for dating, identifying vintage items. Also, copyright-free graphics for artists, designers. Co-published with Henry Ford Museum & Greenfield Village. 160pp. 8¼ x 11. 25780-0

HISTORIC COSTUME IN PICTURES, Braun & Schneider. Over 1,450 costumed figures in clearly detailed engravings—from dawn of civilization to end of 19th century. Captions. Many folk costumes. 256pp. 8⅜ x 11¾. 23150-X

STICKLEY CRAFTSMAN FURNITURE CATALOGS, Gustav Stickley and L. & J. G. Stickley. Beautiful, functional furniture in two authentic catalogs from 1910. 594 illustrations, including 277 photos, show settles, rockers, armchairs, reclining chairs, bookcases, desks, tables. 183pp. 6½ x 9¼. 23838-5

AMERICAN LOCOMOTIVES IN HISTORIC PHOTOGRAPHS: 1858 to 1949, Ron Ziel (ed.). A rare collection of 126 meticulously detailed official photographs, called "builder portraits," of American locomotives that majestically chronicle the rise of steam locomotive power in America. Introduction. Detailed captions. xi+ 129pp. 9 x 12. 27393-8

AMERICA'S LIGHTHOUSES: An Illustrated History, Francis Ross Holland, Jr. Delightfully written, profusely illustrated fact-filled survey of over 200 American lighthouses since 1716. History, anecdotes, technological advances, more. 240pp. 8 x 10¾. 25576-X

TOWARDS A NEW ARCHITECTURE, Le Corbusier. Pioneering manifesto by founder of "International School." Technical and aesthetic theories, views of industry, economics, relation of form to function, "mass-production split" and much more. Profusely illustrated. 320pp. 6⅛ x 9¼. (Available in U.S. only.) 25023-7

HOW THE OTHER HALF LIVES, Jacob Riis. Famous journalistic record, exposing poverty and degradation of New York slums around 1900, by major social reformer. 100 striking and influential photographs. 233pp. 10 x 7⅞. 22012-5

FRUIT KEY AND TWIG KEY TO TREES AND SHRUBS, William M. Harlow. One of the handiest and most widely used identification aids. Fruit key covers 120 deciduous and evergreen species; twig key 160 deciduous species. Easily used. Over 300 photographs. 126pp. 5⅜ x 8½. 20511-8

COMMON BIRD SONGS, Dr. Donald J. Borror. Songs of 60 most common U.S. birds: robins, sparrows, cardinals, bluejays, finches, more–arranged in order of increasing complexity. Up to 9 variations of songs of each species.
Cassette and manual 99911-4

ORCHIDS AS HOUSE PLANTS, Rebecca Tyson Northen. Grow cattleyas and many other kinds of orchids–in a window, in a case, or under artificial light. 63 illustrations. 148pp. 5⅜ x 8½. 23261-1

MONSTER MAZES, Dave Phillips. Masterful mazes at four levels of difficulty. Avoid deadly perils and evil creatures to find magical treasures. Solutions for all 32 exciting illustrated puzzles. 48pp. 8¼ x 11. 26005-4

MOZART'S DON GIOVANNI (DOVER OPERA LIBRETTO SERIES), Wolfgang Amadeus Mozart. Introduced and translated by Ellen H. Bleiler. Standard Italian libretto, with complete English translation. Convenient and thoroughly portable–an ideal companion for reading along with a recording or the performance itself. Introduction. List of characters. Plot summary. 121pp. 5¼ x 8½. 24944-1

TECHNICAL MANUAL AND DICTIONARY OF CLASSICAL BALLET, Gail Grant. Defines, explains, comments on steps, movements, poses and concepts. 15-page pictorial section. Basic book for student, viewer. 127pp. 5⅜ x 8½. 21843-0

THE CLARINET AND CLARINET PLAYING, David Pino. Lively, comprehensive work features suggestions about technique, musicianship, and musical interpretation, as well as guidelines for teaching, making your own reeds, and preparing for public performance. Includes an intriguing look at clarinet history. "A godsend," *The Clarinet*, Journal of the International Clarinet Society. Appendixes. 7 illus. 320pp. 5⅜ x 8½. 40270-3

HOLLYWOOD GLAMOR PORTRAITS, John Kobal (ed.). 145 photos from 1926-49. Harlow, Gable, Bogart, Bacall; 94 stars in all. Full background on photographers, technical aspects. 160pp. 8⅜ x 11¼. 23352-9

THE ANNOTATED CASEY AT THE BAT: A Collection of Ballads about the Mighty Casey/Third, Revised Edition, Martin Gardner (ed.). Amusing sequels and parodies of one of America's best-loved poems: Casey's Revenge, Why Casey Whiffed, Casey's Sister at the Bat, others. 256pp. 5⅜ x 8½. 28598-7

THE RAVEN AND OTHER FAVORITE POEMS, Edgar Allan Poe. Over 40 of the author's most memorable poems: "The Bells," "Ulalume," "Israfel," "To Helen," "The Conqueror Worm," "Eldorado," "Annabel Lee," many more. Alphabetic lists of titles and first lines. 64pp. 5$\frac{3}{16}$ x 8¼. 26685-0

PERSONAL MEMOIRS OF U. S. GRANT, Ulysses Simpson Grant. Intelligent, deeply moving firsthand account of Civil War campaigns, considered by many the finest military memoirs ever written. Includes letters, historic photographs, maps and more. 528pp. 6⅛ x 9¼. 28587-1

ANCIENT EGYPTIAN MATERIALS AND INDUSTRIES, A. Lucas and J. Harris. Fascinating, comprehensive, thoroughly documented text describes this ancient civilization's vast resources and the processes that incorporated them in daily life, including the use of animal products, building materials, cosmetics, perfumes and incense, fibers, glazed ware, glass and its manufacture, materials used in the mummification process, and much more. 544pp. 6⅛ x 9¼. (Available in U.S. only.) 40446-3

RUSSIAN STORIES/RUSSKIE RASSKAZY: A Dual-Language Book, edited by Gleb Struve. Twelve tales by such masters as Chekhov, Tolstoy, Dostoevsky, Pushkin, others. Excellent word-for-word English translations on facing pages, plus teaching and study aids, Russian/English vocabulary, biographical/critical introductions, more. 416pp. 5⅜ x 8½. 26244-8

PHILADELPHIA THEN AND NOW: 60 Sites Photographed in the Past and Present, Kenneth Finkel and Susan Oyama. Rare photographs of City Hall, Logan Square, Independence Hall, Betsy Ross House, other landmarks juxtaposed with contemporary views. Captures changing face of historic city. Introduction. Captions. 128pp. 8¼ x 11. 25790-8

AIA ARCHITECTURAL GUIDE TO NASSAU AND SUFFOLK COUNTIES, LONG ISLAND, The American Institute of Architects, Long Island Chapter, and the Society for the Preservation of Long Island Antiquities. Comprehensive, well-researched and generously illustrated volume brings to life over three centuries of Long Island's great architectural heritage. More than 240 photographs with authoritative, extensively detailed captions. 176pp. 8¼ x 11. 26946-9

NORTH AMERICAN INDIAN LIFE: Customs and Traditions of 23 Tribes, Elsie Clews Parsons (ed.). 27 fictionalized essays by noted anthropologists examine religion, customs, government, additional facets of life among the Winnebago, Crow, Zuni, Eskimo, other tribes. 480pp. 6⅛ x 9¼. 27377-6

CATALOG OF DOVER BOOKS

FRANK LLOYD WRIGHT'S DANA HOUSE, Donald Hoffmann. Pictorial essay of residential masterpiece with over 160 interior and exterior photos, plans, elevations, sketches and studies. 128pp. 9¼ x 10¾. 29120-0

THE MALE AND FEMALE FIGURE IN MOTION: 60 Classic Photographic Sequences, Eadweard Muybridge. 60 true-action photographs of men and women walking, running, climbing, bending, turning, etc., reproduced from rare 19th-century masterpiece. vi + 121pp. 9 x 12. 24745-7

1001 QUESTIONS ANSWERED ABOUT THE SEASHORE, N. J. Berrill and Jacquelyn Berrill. Queries answered about dolphins, sea snails, sponges, starfish, fishes, shore birds, many others. Covers appearance, breeding, growth, feeding, much more. 305pp. 5¼ x 8¼. 23366-9

ATTRACTING BIRDS TO YOUR YARD, William J. Weber. Easy-to-follow guide offers advice on how to attract the greatest diversity of birds: birdhouses, feeders, water and waterers, much more. 96pp. 5³⁄₁₆ x 8¼. 28927-3

MEDICINAL AND OTHER USES OF NORTH AMERICAN PLANTS: A Historical Survey with Special Reference to the Eastern Indian Tribes, Charlotte Erichsen-Brown. Chronological historical citations document 500 years of usage of plants, trees, shrubs native to eastern Canada, northeastern U.S. Also complete identifying information. 343 illustrations. 544pp. 6½ x 9¼. 25951-X

STORYBOOK MAZES, Dave Phillips. 23 stories and mazes on two-page spreads: Wizard of Oz, Treasure Island, Robin Hood, etc. Solutions. 64pp. 8¼ x 11. 23628-5

AMERICAN NEGRO SONGS: 230 Folk Songs and Spirituals, Religious and Secular, John W. Work. This authoritative study traces the African influences of songs sung and played by black Americans at work, in church, and as entertainment. The author discusses the lyric significance of such songs as "Swing Low, Sweet Chariot," "John Henry," and others and offers the words and music for 230 songs. Bibliography. Index of Song Titles. 272pp. 6½ x 9¼. 40271-1

MOVIE-STAR PORTRAITS OF THE FORTIES, John Kobal (ed.). 163 glamor, studio photos of 106 stars of the 1940s: Rita Hayworth, Ava Gardner, Marlon Brando, Clark Gable, many more. 176pp. 8⅜ x 11¼. 23546-7

BENCHLEY LOST AND FOUND, Robert Benchley. Finest humor from early 30s, about pet peeves, child psychologists, post office and others. Mostly unavailable elsewhere. 73 illustrations by Peter Arno and others. 183pp. 5⅜ x 8½. 22410-4

YEKL and THE IMPORTED BRIDEGROOM AND OTHER STORIES OF YIDDISH NEW YORK, Abraham Cahan. Film Hester Street based on *Yekl* (1896). Novel, other stories among first about Jewish immigrants on N.Y.'s East Side. 240pp. 5⅜ x 8½. 22427-9

SELECTED POEMS, Walt Whitman. Generous sampling from *Leaves of Grass*. Twenty-four poems include "I Hear America Singing," "Song of the Open Road," "I Sing the Body Electric," "When Lilacs Last in the Dooryard Bloom'd," "O Captain! My Captain!"—all reprinted from an authoritative edition. Lists of titles and first lines. 128pp. 5³⁄₁₆ x 8¼. 26878-0

THE BEST TALES OF HOFFMANN, E. T. A. Hoffmann. 10 of Hoffmann's most important stories: "Nutcracker and the King of Mice," "The Golden Flowerpot," etc. 458pp. 5⅜ x 8½.   21793-0

FROM FETISH TO GOD IN ANCIENT EGYPT, E. A. Wallis Budge. Rich detailed survey of Egyptian conception of "God" and gods, magic, cult of animals, Osiris, more. Also, superb English translations of hymns and legends. 240 illustrations. 545pp. 5⅜ x 8½.   25803-3

FRENCH STORIES/CONTES FRANÇAIS: A Dual-Language Book, Wallace Fowlie. Ten stories by French masters, Voltaire to Camus: "Micromegas" by Voltaire; "The Atheist's Mass" by Balzac; "Minuet" by de Maupassant; "The Guest" by Camus, six more. Excellent English translations on facing pages. Also French-English vocabulary list, exercises, more. 352pp. 5⅜ x 8½.   26443-2

CHICAGO AT THE TURN OF THE CENTURY IN PHOTOGRAPHS: 122 Historic Views from the Collections of the Chicago Historical Society, Larry A. Viskochil. Rare large-format prints offer detailed views of City Hall, State Street, the Loop, Hull House, Union Station, many other landmarks, circa 1904-1913. Introduction. Captions. Maps. 144pp. 9⅜ x 12¼.   24656-6

OLD BROOKLYN IN EARLY PHOTOGRAPHS, 1865-1929, William Lee Younger. Luna Park, Gravesend race track, construction of Grand Army Plaza, moving of Hotel Brighton, etc. 157 previously unpublished photographs. 165pp. 8⅞ x 11¾.   23587-4

THE MYTHS OF THE NORTH AMERICAN INDIANS, Lewis Spence. Rich anthology of the myths and legends of the Algonquins, Iroquois, Pawnees and Sioux, prefaced by an extensive historical and ethnological commentary. 36 illustrations. 480pp. 5⅜ x 8½.   25967-6

AN ENCYCLOPEDIA OF BATTLES: Accounts of Over 1,560 Battles from 1479 B.C. to the Present, David Eggenberger. Essential details of every major battle in recorded history from the first battle of Megiddo in 1479 B.C. to Grenada in 1984. List of Battle Maps. New Appendix covering the years 1967-1984. Index. 99 illustrations. 544pp. 6½ x 9¼.   24913-1

SAILING ALONE AROUND THE WORLD, Captain Joshua Slocum. First man to sail around the world, alone, in small boat. One of great feats of seamanship told in delightful manner. 67 illustrations. 294pp. 5⅜ x 8½.   20326-3

ANARCHISM AND OTHER ESSAYS, Emma Goldman. Powerful, penetrating, prophetic essays on direct action, role of minorities, prison reform, puritan hypocrisy, violence, etc. 271pp. 5⅜ x 8½.   22484-8

MYTHS OF THE HINDUS AND BUDDHISTS, Ananda K. Coomaraswamy and Sister Nivedita. Great stories of the epics; deeds of Krishna, Shiva, taken from puranas, Vedas, folk tales; etc. 32 illustrations. 400pp. 5⅜ x 8½.   21759-0

THE TRAUMA OF BIRTH, Otto Rank. Rank's controversial thesis that anxiety neurosis is caused by profound psychological trauma which occurs at birth. 256pp. 5⅜ x 8½.   27974-X

A THEOLOGICO-POLITICAL TREATISE, Benedict Spinoza. Also contains unfinished Political Treatise. Great classic on religious liberty, theory of government on common consent. R. Elwes translation. Total of 421pp. 5⅜ x 8½.   20249-6

MY BONDAGE AND MY FREEDOM, Frederick Douglass. Born a slave, Douglass became outspoken force in antislavery movement. The best of Douglass' autobiographies. Graphic description of slave life. 464pp. 5⅜ x 8½. 22457-0

FOLLOWING THE EQUATOR: A Journey Around the World, Mark Twain. Fascinating humorous account of 1897 voyage to Hawaii, Australia, India, New Zealand, etc. Ironic, bemused reports on peoples, customs, climate, flora and fauna, politics, much more. 197 illustrations. 720pp. 5⅜ x 8½. 26113-1

THE PEOPLE CALLED SHAKERS, Edward D. Andrews. Definitive study of Shakers: origins, beliefs, practices, dances, social organization, furniture and crafts, etc. 33 illustrations. 351pp. 5⅜ x 8½. 21081-2

THE MYTHS OF GREECE AND ROME, H. A. Guerber. A classic of mythology, generously illustrated, long prized for its simple, graphic, accurate retelling of the principal myths of Greece and Rome, and for its commentary on their origins and significance. With 64 illustrations by Michelangelo, Raphael, Titian, Rubens, Canova, Bernini and others. 480pp. 5⅜ x 8½. 27584-1

PSYCHOLOGY OF MUSIC, Carl E. Seashore. Classic work discusses music as a medium from psychological viewpoint. Clear treatment of physical acoustics, auditory apparatus, sound perception, development of musical skills, nature of musical feeling, host of other topics. 88 figures. 408pp. 5⅜ x 8½. 21851-1

THE PHILOSOPHY OF HISTORY, Georg W. Hegel. Great classic of Western thought develops concept that history is not chance but rational process, the evolution of freedom. 457pp. 5⅜ x 8½. 20112-0

THE BOOK OF TEA, Kakuzo Okakura. Minor classic of the Orient: entertaining, charming explanation, interpretation of traditional Japanese culture in terms of tea ceremony. 94pp. 5⅜ x 8½. 20070-1

LIFE IN ANCIENT EGYPT, Adolf Erman. Fullest, most thorough, detailed older account with much not in more recent books, domestic life, religion, magic, medicine, commerce, much more. Many illustrations reproduce tomb paintings, carvings, hieroglyphs, etc. 597pp. 5⅜ x 8½. 22632-8

SUNDIALS, Their Theory and Construction, Albert Waugh. Far and away the best, most thorough coverage of ideas, mathematics concerned, types, construction, adjusting anywhere. Simple, nontechnical treatment allows even children to build several of these dials. Over 100 illustrations. 230pp. 5⅜ x 8½. 22947-5

THEORETICAL HYDRODYNAMICS, L. M. Milne-Thomson. Classic exposition of the mathematical theory of fluid motion, applicable to both hydrodynamics and aerodynamics. Over 600 exercises. 768pp. 6⅛ x 9¼. 68970-0

SONGS OF EXPERIENCE: Facsimile Reproduction with 26 Plates in Full Color, William Blake. 26 full-color plates from a rare 1826 edition. Includes "The Tyger," "London," "Holy Thursday," and other poems. Printed text of poems. 48pp. 5¼ x 7. 24636-1

OLD-TIME VIGNETTES IN FULL COLOR, Carol Belanger Grafton (ed.). Over 390 charming, often sentimental illustrations, selected from archives of Victorian graphics—pretty women posing, children playing, food, flowers, kittens and puppies, smiling cherubs, birds and butterflies, much more. All copyright-free. 48pp. 9¼ x 12¼. 27269-9

PERSPECTIVE FOR ARTISTS, Rex Vicat Cole. Depth, perspective of sky and sea, shadows, much more, not usually covered. 391 diagrams, 81 reproductions of drawings and paintings. 279pp. 5⅜ x 8½. 22487-2

DRAWING THE LIVING FIGURE, Joseph Sheppard. Innovative approach to artistic anatomy focuses on specifics of surface anatomy, rather than muscles and bones. Over 170 drawings of live models in front, back and side views, and in widely varying poses. Accompanying diagrams. 177 illustrations. Introduction. Index. 144pp. 8⅜ x11¼. 26723-7

GOTHIC AND OLD ENGLISH ALPHABETS: 100 Complete Fonts, Dan X. Solo. Add power, elegance to posters, signs, other graphics with 100 stunning copyright-free alphabets: Blackstone, Dolbey, Germania, 97 more–including many lower-case, numerals, punctuation marks. 104pp. 8⅛ x 11. 24695-7

HOW TO DO BEADWORK, Mary White. Fundamental book on craft from simple projects to five-bead chains and woven works. 106 illustrations. 142pp. 5⅜ x 8. 20697-1

THE BOOK OF WOOD CARVING, Charles Marshall Sayers. Finest book for beginners discusses fundamentals and offers 34 designs. "Absolutely first rate . . . well thought out and well executed."–E. J. Tangerman. 118pp. 7¾ x 10⅝. 23654-4

ILLUSTRATED CATALOG OF CIVIL WAR MILITARY GOODS: Union Army Weapons, Insignia, Uniform Accessories, and Other Equipment, Schuyler, Hartley, and Graham. Rare, profusely illustrated 1846 catalog includes Union Army uniform and dress regulations, arms and ammunition, coats, insignia, flags, swords, rifles, etc. 226 illustrations. 160pp. 9 x 12. 24939-5

WOMEN'S FASHIONS OF THE EARLY 1900s: An Unabridged Republication of "New York Fashions, 1909," National Cloak & Suit Co. Rare catalog of mail-order fashions documents women's and children's clothing styles shortly after the turn of the century. Captions offer full descriptions, prices. Invaluable resource for fashion, costume historians. Approximately 725 illustrations. 128pp. 8⅜ x 11¼. 27276-1

THE 1912 AND 1915 GUSTAV STICKLEY FURNITURE CATALOGS, Gustav Stickley. With over 200 detailed illustrations and descriptions, these two catalogs are essential reading and reference materials and identification guides for Stickley furniture. Captions cite materials, dimensions and prices. 112pp. 6½ x 9¼. 26676-1

EARLY AMERICAN LOCOMOTIVES, John H. White, Jr. Finest locomotive engravings from early 19th century: historical (1804–74), main-line (after 1870), special, foreign, etc. 147 plates. 142pp. 11⅜ x 8¼. 22772-3

THE TALL SHIPS OF TODAY IN PHOTOGRAPHS, Frank O. Braynard. Lavishly illustrated tribute to nearly 100 majestic contemporary sailing vessels: Amerigo Vespucci, Clearwater, Constitution, Eagle, Mayflower, Sea Cloud, Victory, many more. Authoritative captions provide statistics, background on each ship. 190 black-and-white photographs and illustrations. Introduction. 128pp. 8⅞ x 11¾. 27163-3

LITTLE BOOK OF EARLY AMERICAN CRAFTS AND TRADES, Peter Stockham (ed.). 1807 children's book explains crafts and trades: baker, hatter, cooper, potter, and many others. 23 copperplate illustrations. 140pp. 4⅝ x 6. 23336-7

VICTORIAN FASHIONS AND COSTUMES FROM HARPER'S BAZAR, 1867–1898, Stella Blum (ed.). Day costumes, evening wear, sports clothes, shoes, hats, other accessories in over 1,000 detailed engravings. 320pp. 9⅜ x 12¼. 22990-4

GUSTAV STICKLEY, THE CRAFTSMAN, Mary Ann Smith. Superb study surveys broad scope of Stickley's achievement, especially in architecture. Design philosophy, rise and fall of the Craftsman empire, descriptions and floor plans for many Craftsman houses, more. 86 black-and-white halftones. 31 line illustrations. Introduction 208pp. 6½ x 9¼. 27210-9

THE LONG ISLAND RAIL ROAD IN EARLY PHOTOGRAPHS, Ron Ziel. Over 220 rare photos, informative text document origin (1844) and development of rail service on Long Island. Vintage views of early trains, locomotives, stations, passengers, crews, much more. Captions. 8⅞ x 11¾. 26301-0

VOYAGE OF THE LIBERDADE, Joshua Slocum. Great 19th-century mariner's thrilling, first-hand account of the wreck of his ship off South America, the 35-foot boat he built from the wreckage, and its remarkable voyage home. 128pp. 5⅜ x 8½. 40022-0

TEN BOOKS ON ARCHITECTURE, Vitruvius. The most important book ever written on architecture. Early Roman aesthetics, technology, classical orders, site selection, all other aspects. Morgan translation. 331pp. 5⅜ x 8½. 20645-9

THE HUMAN FIGURE IN MOTION, Eadweard Muybridge. More than 4,500 stopped-action photos, in action series, showing undraped men, women, children jumping, lying down, throwing, sitting, wrestling, carrying, etc. 390pp. 7⅞ x 10⅝. 20204-6 Clothbd.

TREES OF THE EASTERN AND CENTRAL UNITED STATES AND CANADA, William M. Harlow. Best one-volume guide to 140 trees. Full descriptions, woodlore, range, etc. Over 600 illustrations. Handy size. 288pp. 4½ x 6⅜. 20395-6

SONGS OF WESTERN BIRDS, Dr. Donald J. Borror. Complete song and call repertoire of 60 western species, including flycatchers, juncoes, cactus wrens, many more–includes fully illustrated booklet. Cassette and manual 99913-0

GROWING AND USING HERBS AND SPICES, Milo Miloradovich. Versatile handbook provides all the information needed for cultivation and use of all the herbs and spices available in North America. 4 illustrations. Index. Glossary. 236pp. 5⅜ x 8½. 25058-X

BIG BOOK OF MAZES AND LABYRINTHS, Walter Shepherd. 50 mazes and labyrinths in all–classical, solid, ripple, and more–in one great volume. Perfect inexpensive puzzler for clever youngsters. Full solutions. 112pp. 8⅛ x 11. 22951-3

PIANO TUNING, J. Cree Fischer. Clearest, best book for beginner, amateur. Simple repairs, raising dropped notes, tuning by easy method of flattened fifths. No previous skills needed. 4 illustrations. 201pp. 5⅜ x 8½. 23267-0

HINTS TO SINGERS, Lillian Nordica. Selecting the right teacher, developing confidence, overcoming stage fright, and many other important skills receive thoughtful discussion in this indispensible guide, written by a world-famous diva of four decades' experience. 96pp. 5⅜ x 8½. 40094-8

THE COMPLETE NONSENSE OF EDWARD LEAR, Edward Lear. All nonsense limericks, zany alphabets, Owl and Pussycat, songs, nonsense botany, etc., illustrated by Lear. Total of 320pp. 5⅜ x 8½. (Available in U.S. only.) 20167-8

VICTORIAN PARLOUR POETRY: An Annotated Anthology, Michael R. Turner. 117 gems by Longfellow, Tennyson, Browning, many lesser-known poets. "The Village Blacksmith," "Curfew Must Not Ring Tonight," "Only a Baby Small," dozens more, often difficult to find elsewhere. Index of poets, titles, first lines. xxiii + 325pp. 5⅜ x 8¼. 27044-0

DUBLINERS, James Joyce. Fifteen stories offer vivid, tightly focused observations of the lives of Dublin's poorer classes. At least one, "The Dead," is considered a masterpiece. Reprinted complete and unabridged from standard edition. 160pp. 5$^3/_{16}$ x 8¼. 26870-5

GREAT WEIRD TALES: 14 Stories by Lovecraft, Blackwood, Machen and Others, S. T. Joshi (ed.). 14 spellbinding tales, including "The Sin Eater," by Fiona McLeod, "The Eye Above the Mantel," by Frank Belknap Long, as well as renowned works by R. H. Barlow, Lord Dunsany, Arthur Machen, W. C. Morrow and eight other masters of the genre. 256pp. 5⅜ x 8½. (Available in U.S. only.) 40436-6

THE BOOK OF THE SACRED MAGIC OF ABRAMELIN THE MAGE, translated by S. MacGregor Mathers. Medieval manuscript of ceremonial magic. Basic document in Aleister Crowley, Golden Dawn groups. 268pp. 5⅜ x 8½. 23211-5

NEW RUSSIAN-ENGLISH AND ENGLISH-RUSSIAN DICTIONARY, M. A. O'Brien. This is a remarkably handy Russian dictionary, containing a surprising amount of information, including over 70,000 entries. 366pp. 4½ x 6⅛. 20208-9

HISTORIC HOMES OF THE AMERICAN PRESIDENTS, Second, Revised Edition, Irvin Haas. A traveler's guide to American Presidential homes, most open to the public, depicting and describing homes occupied by every American President from George Washington to George Bush. With visiting hours, admission charges, travel routes. 175 photographs. Index. 160pp. 8¼ x 11. 26751-2

NEW YORK IN THE FORTIES, Andreas Feininger. 162 brilliant photographs by the well-known photographer, formerly with *Life* magazine. Commuters, shoppers, Times Square at night, much else from city at its peak. Captions by John von Hartz. 181pp. 9¼ x 10¾. 23585-8

INDIAN SIGN LANGUAGE, William Tomkins. Over 525 signs developed by Sioux and other tribes. Written instructions and diagrams. Also 290 pictographs. 111pp. 6⅛ x 9¼. 22029-X

ANATOMY: A Complete Guide for Artists, Joseph Sheppard. A master of figure drawing shows artists how to render human anatomy convincingly. Over 460 illustrations. 224pp. 8⅜ x 11¼. 27279-6

MEDIEVAL CALLIGRAPHY: Its History and Technique, Marc Drogin. Spirited history, comprehensive instruction manual covers 13 styles (ca. 4th century through 15th). Excellent photographs; directions for duplicating medieval techniques with modern tools. 224pp. 8⅜ x 11¼. 26142-5

DRIED FLOWERS: How to Prepare Them, Sarah Whitlock and Martha Rankin. Complete instructions on how to use silica gel, meal and borax, perlite aggregate, sand and borax, glycerine and water to create attractive permanent flower arrangements. 12 illustrations. 32pp. 5⅜ x 8½. 21802-3

EASY-TO-MAKE BIRD FEEDERS FOR WOODWORKERS, Scott D. Campbell. Detailed, simple-to-use guide for designing, constructing, caring for and using feeders. Text, illustrations for 12 classic and contemporary designs. 96pp. 5⅜ x 8½. 25847-5

SCOTTISH WONDER TALES FROM MYTH AND LEGEND, Donald A. Mackenzie. 16 lively tales tell of giants rumbling down mountainsides, of a magic wand that turns stone pillars into warriors, of gods and goddesses, evil hags, powerful forces and more. 240pp. 5⅜ x 8½. 29677-6

THE HISTORY OF UNDERCLOTHES, C. Willett Cunnington and Phyllis Cunnington. Fascinating, well-documented survey covering six centuries of English undergarments, enhanced with over 100 illustrations: 12th-century laced-up bodice, footed long drawers (1795), 19th-century bustles, 19th-century corsets for men, Victorian "bust improvers," much more. 272pp. 5⅜ x 8¼. 27124-2

ARTS AND CRAFTS FURNITURE: The Complete Brooks Catalog of 1912, Brooks Manufacturing Co. Photos and detailed descriptions of more than 150 now very collectible furniture designs from the Arts and Crafts movement depict davenports, settees, buffets, desks, tables, chairs, bedsteads, dressers and more, all built of solid, quarter-sawed oak. Invaluable for students and enthusiasts of antiques, Americana and the decorative arts. 80pp. 6½ x 9¼. 27471-3

WILBUR AND ORVILLE: A Biography of the Wright Brothers, Fred Howard. Definitive, crisply written study tells the full story of the brothers' lives and work. A vividly written biography, unparalleled in scope and color, that also captures the spirit of an extraordinary era. 560pp. 6⅛ x 9¼. 40297-5

THE ARTS OF THE SAILOR: Knotting, Splicing and Ropework, Hervey Garrett Smith. Indispensable shipboard reference covers tools, basic knots and useful hitches; handsewing and canvas work, more. Over 100 illustrations. Delightful reading for sea lovers. 256pp. 5⅜ x 8½. 26440-8

FRANK LLOYD WRIGHT'S FALLINGWATER: The House and Its History, Second, Revised Edition, Donald Hoffmann. A total revision–both in text and illustrations–of the standard document on Fallingwater, the boldest, most personal architectural statement of Wright's mature years, updated with valuable new material from the recently opened Frank Lloyd Wright Archives. "Fascinating"–*The New York Times*. 116 illustrations. 128pp. 9¼ x 10¾. 27430-6

PHOTOGRAPHIC SKETCHBOOK OF THE CIVIL WAR, Alexander Gardner. 100 photos taken on field during the Civil War. Famous shots of Manassas Harper's Ferry, Lincoln, Richmond, slave pens, etc. 244pp. 10⅝ x 8¼. 22731-6

FIVE ACRES AND INDEPENDENCE, Maurice G. Kains. Great back-to-the-land classic explains basics of self-sufficient farming. The one book to get. 95 illustrations. 397pp. 5⅜ x 8½. 20974-1

SONGS OF EASTERN BIRDS, Dr. Donald J. Borror. Songs and calls of 60 species most common to eastern U.S.: warblers, woodpeckers, flycatchers, thrushes, larks, many more in high-quality recording. Cassette and manual 99912-2

A MODERN HERBAL, Margaret Grieve. Much the fullest, most exact, most useful compilation of herbal material. Gigantic alphabetical encyclopedia, from aconite to zedoary, gives botanical information, medical properties, folklore, economic uses, much else. Indispensable to serious reader. 161 illustrations. 888pp. 6½ x 9¼. 2-vol. set. (Available in U.S. only.) Vol. I: 22798-7
Vol. II: 22799-5

HIDDEN TREASURE MAZE BOOK, Dave Phillips. Solve 34 challenging mazes accompanied by heroic tales of adventure. Evil dragons, people-eating plants, blood-thirsty giants, many more dangerous adversaries lurk at every twist and turn. 34 mazes, stories, solutions. 48pp. 8¼ x 11. 24566-7

LETTERS OF W. A. MOZART, Wolfgang A. Mozart. Remarkable letters show bawdy wit, humor, imagination, musical insights, contemporary musical world; includes some letters from Leopold Mozart. 276pp. 5⅜ x 8½. 22859-2

BASIC PRINCIPLES OF CLASSICAL BALLET, Agrippina Vaganova. Great Russian theoretician, teacher explains methods for teaching classical ballet. 118 illustrations. 175pp. 5⅜ x 8½. 22036-2

THE JUMPING FROG, Mark Twain. Revenge edition. The original story of The Celebrated Jumping Frog of Calaveras County, a hapless French translation, and Twain's hilarious "retranslation" from the French. 12 illustrations. 66pp. 5⅜ x 8½. 22686-7

BEST REMEMBERED POEMS, Martin Gardner (ed.). The 126 poems in this superb collection of 19th- and 20th-century British and American verse range from Shelley's "To a Skylark" to the impassioned "Renascence" of Edna St. Vincent Millay and to Edward Lear's whimsical "The Owl and the Pussycat." 224pp. 5⅜ x 8½. 27165-X

COMPLETE SONNETS, William Shakespeare. Over 150 exquisite poems deal with love, friendship, the tyranny of time, beauty's evanescence, death and other themes in language of remarkable power, precision and beauty. Glossary of archaic terms. 80pp. 5$\frac{3}{16}$ x 8¼. 26686-9

THE BATTLES THAT CHANGED HISTORY, Fletcher Pratt. Eminent historian profiles 16 crucial conflicts, ancient to modern, that changed the course of civilization. 352pp. 5⅜ x 8½. 41129-X

THE WIT AND HUMOR OF OSCAR WILDE, Alvin Redman (ed.). More than 1,000 ripostes, paradoxes, wisecracks: Work is the curse of the drinking classes; I can resist everything except temptation; etc. 258pp. 5⅜ x 8½. 20602-5

SHAKESPEARE LEXICON AND QUOTATION DICTIONARY, Alexander Schmidt. Full definitions, locations, shades of meaning in every word in plays and poems. More than 50,000 exact quotations. 1,485pp. 6½ x 9¼. 2-vol. set.
Vol. 1: 22726-X
Vol. 2: 22727-8

SELECTED POEMS, Emily Dickinson. Over 100 best-known, best-loved poems by one of America's foremost poets, reprinted from authoritative early editions. No comparable edition at this price. Index of first lines. 64pp. 5³⁄₁₆ x 8¼. 26466-1

THE INSIDIOUS DR. FU-MANCHU, Sax Rohmer. The first of the popular mystery series introduces a pair of English detectives to their archnemesis, the diabolical Dr. Fu-Manchu. Flavorful atmosphere, fast-paced action, and colorful characters enliven this classic of the genre. 208pp. 5³⁄₁₆ x 8¼. 29898-1

THE MALLEUS MALEFICARUM OF KRAMER AND SPRENGER, translated by Montague Summers. Full text of most important witchhunter's "bible," used by both Catholics and Protestants. 278pp. 6⅝ x 10. 22802-9

SPANISH STORIES/CUENTOS ESPAÑOLES: A Dual-Language Book, Angel Flores (ed.). Unique format offers 13 great stories in Spanish by Cervantes, Borges, others. Faithful English translations on facing pages. 352pp. 5⅜ x 8½. 25399-6

GARDEN CITY, LONG ISLAND, IN EARLY PHOTOGRAPHS, 1869–1919, Mildred H. Smith. Handsome treasury of 118 vintage pictures, accompanied by carefully researched captions, document the Garden City Hotel fire (1899), the Vanderbilt Cup Race (1908), the first airmail flight departing from the Nassau Boulevard Aerodrome (1911), and much more. 96pp. 8⅞ x 11¾. 40669-5

OLD QUEENS, N.Y., IN EARLY PHOTOGRAPHS, Vincent F. Seyfried and William Asadorian. Over 160 rare photographs of Maspeth, Jamaica, Jackson Heights, and other areas. Vintage views of DeWitt Clinton mansion, 1939 World's Fair and more. Captions. 192pp. 8⅞ x 11. 26358-4

CAPTURED BY THE INDIANS: 15 Firsthand Accounts, 1750-1870, Frederick Drimmer. Astounding true historical accounts of grisly torture, bloody conflicts, relentless pursuits, miraculous escapes and more, by people who lived to tell the tale. 384pp. 5⅜ x 8½. 24901-8

THE WORLD'S GREAT SPEECHES (Fourth Enlarged Edition), Lewis Copeland, Lawrence W. Lamm, and Stephen J. McKenna. Nearly 300 speeches provide public speakers with a wealth of updated quotes and inspiration–from Pericles' funeral oration and William Jennings Bryan's "Cross of Gold Speech" to Malcolm X's powerful words on the Black Revolution and Earl of Spenser's tribute to his sister, Diana, Princess of Wales. 944pp. 5⅜ x 8⅜. 40903-1

THE BOOK OF THE SWORD, Sir Richard F. Burton. Great Victorian scholar/adventurer's eloquent, erudite history of the "queen of weapons"–from prehistory to early Roman Empire. Evolution and development of early swords, variations (sabre, broadsword, cutlass, scimitar, etc.), much more. 336pp. 6⅛ x 9¼.
25434-8

CATALOG OF DOVER BOOKS

AUTOBIOGRAPHY: The Story of My Experiments with Truth, Mohandas K. Gandhi. Boyhood, legal studies, purification, the growth of the Satyagraha (nonviolent protest) movement. Critical, inspiring work of the man responsible for the freedom of India. 480pp. 5⅜ x 8½. (Available in U.S. only.) 24593-4

CELTIC MYTHS AND LEGENDS, T. W. Rolleston. Masterful retelling of Irish and Welsh stories and tales. Cuchulain, King Arthur, Deirdre, the Grail, many more. First paperback edition. 58 full-page illustrations. 512pp. 5⅜ x 8½. 26507-2

THE PRINCIPLES OF PSYCHOLOGY, William James. Famous long course complete, unabridged. Stream of thought, time perception, memory, experimental methods; great work decades ahead of its time. 94 figures. 1,391pp. 5⅜ x 8½. 2-vol. set.
Vol. I: 20381-6   Vol. II: 20382-4

THE WORLD AS WILL AND REPRESENTATION, Arthur Schopenhauer. Definitive English translation of Schopenhauer's life work, correcting more than 1,000 errors, omissions in earlier translations. Translated by E. F. J. Payne. Total of 1,269pp. 5⅜ x 8½. 2-vol. set.
Vol. 1: 21761-2   Vol. 2: 21762-0

MAGIC AND MYSTERY IN TIBET, Madame Alexandra David-Neel. Experiences among lamas, magicians, sages, sorcerers, Bonpa wizards. A true psychic discovery. 32 illustrations. 321pp. 5⅜ x 8½. (Available in U.S. only.) 22682-4

THE EGYPTIAN BOOK OF THE DEAD, E. A. Wallis Budge. Complete reproduction of Ani's papyrus, finest ever found. Full hieroglyphic text, interlinear transliteration, word-for-word translation, smooth translation. 533pp. 6½ x 9¼. 21866-X

MATHEMATICS FOR THE NONMATHEMATICIAN, Morris Kline. Detailed, college-level treatment of mathematics in cultural and historical context, with numerous exercises. Recommended Reading Lists. Tables. Numerous figures. 641pp. 5⅜ x 8½. 24823-2

PROBABILISTIC METHODS IN THE THEORY OF STRUCTURES, Isaac Elishakoff. Well-written introduction covers the elements of the theory of probability from two or more random variables, the reliability of such multivariable structures, the theory of random function, Monte Carlo methods of treating problems incapable of exact solution, and more. Examples. 502pp. 5⅜ x 8½. 40691-1

THE RIME OF THE ANCIENT MARINER, Gustave Doré, S. T. Coleridge. Doré's finest work; 34 plates capture moods, subtleties of poem. Flawless full-size reproductions printed on facing pages with authoritative text of poem. "Beautiful. Simply beautiful."–*Publisher's Weekly.* 77pp. 9¼ x 12. 22305-1

NORTH AMERICAN INDIAN DESIGNS FOR ARTISTS AND CRAFTSPEOPLE, Eva Wilson. Over 360 authentic copyright-free designs adapted from Navajo blankets, Hopi pottery, Sioux buffalo hides, more. Geometrics, symbolic figures, plant and animal motifs, etc. 128pp. 8⅜ x 11. (Not for sale in the United Kingdom.) 25341-4

SCULPTURE: Principles and Practice, Louis Slobodkin. Step-by-step approach to clay, plaster, metals, stone; classical and modern. 253 drawings, photos. 255pp. 8⅛ x 11. 22960-2

THE INFLUENCE OF SEA POWER UPON HISTORY, 1660–1783, A. T. Mahan. Influential classic of naval history and tactics still used as text in war colleges. First paperback edition. 4 maps. 24 battle plans. 640pp. 5⅜ x 8½. 25509-3

CATALOG OF DOVER BOOKS

THE STORY OF THE TITANIC AS TOLD BY ITS SURVIVORS, Jack Winocour (ed.). What it was really like. Panic, despair, shocking inefficiency, and a little heroism. More thrilling than any fictional account. 26 illustrations. 320pp. 5⅜ x 8½.
20610-6

FAIRY AND FOLK TALES OF THE IRISH PEASANTRY, William Butler Yeats (ed.). Treasury of 64 tales from the twilight world of Celtic myth and legend: "The Soul Cages," "The Kildare Pooka," "King O'Toole and his Goose," many more. Introduction and Notes by W. B. Yeats. 352pp. 5⅜ x 8½.
26941-8

BUDDHIST MAHAYANA TEXTS, E. B. Cowell and others (eds.). Superb, accurate translations of basic documents in Mahayana Buddhism, highly important in history of religions. The Buddha-karita of Asvaghosha, Larger Sukhavativyuha, more. 448pp. 5⅜ x 8½.
25552-2

ONE TWO THREE . . . INFINITY: Facts and Speculations of Science, George Gamow. Great physicist's fascinating, readable overview of contemporary science: number theory, relativity, fourth dimension, entropy, genes, atomic structure, much more. 128 illustrations. Index. 352pp. 5⅜ x 8½.
25664-2

EXPERIMENTATION AND MEASUREMENT, W. J. Youden. Introductory manual explains laws of measurement in simple terms and offers tips for achieving accuracy and minimizing errors. Mathematics of measurement, use of instruments, experimenting with machines. 1994 edition. Foreword. Preface. Introduction. Epilogue. Selected Readings. Glossary. Index. Tables and figures. 128pp. 5⅜ x 8½.   40451-X

DALÍ ON MODERN ART: The Cuckolds of Antiquated Modern Art, Salvador Dalí. Influential painter skewers modern art and its practitioners. Outrageous evaluations of Picasso, Cézanne, Turner, more. 15 renderings of paintings discussed. 44 calligraphic decorations by Dalí. 96pp. 5⅜ x 8½. (Available in U.S. only.)   29220-7

ANTIQUE PLAYING CARDS: A Pictorial History, Henry René D'Allemagne. Over 900 elaborate, decorative images from rare playing cards (14th–20th centuries): Bacchus, death, dancing dogs, hunting scenes, royal coats of arms, players cheating, much more. 96pp. 9¼ x 12¼.   29265-7

MAKING FURNITURE MASTERPIECES: 30 Projects with Measured Drawings, Franklin H. Gottshall. Step-by-step instructions, illustrations for constructing handsome, useful pieces, among them a Sheraton desk, Chippendale chair, Spanish desk, Queen Anne table and a William and Mary dressing mirror. 224pp. 8⅛ x 11¼.
29338-6

THE FOSSIL BOOK: A Record of Prehistoric Life, Patricia V. Rich et al. Profusely illustrated definitive guide covers everything from single-celled organisms and dinosaurs to birds and mammals and the interplay between climate and man. Over 1,500 illustrations. 760pp. 7½ x 10⅛.   29371-8